GCSE OCR Gateway
Chemistry
Higher Revision Guide

This book is for anyone doing **GCSE OCR Gateway Chemistry** at higher level.

GCSE Science is all about **understanding how science works**.
And not only that — understanding it well enough to be able to **question** what you hear on TV and read in the papers.

But you can't do that without a fair chunk of **background knowledge**. Hmm, tricky.

Happily this CGP book includes all the **science facts** you need to learn, and shows you how they work in the **real world**. And in true CGP style, we've explained it all as **clearly and concisely** as possible.

It's also got some daft bits in to try and make the whole experience at least vaguely entertaining for you.

What CGP is all about

Our sole aim here at CGP is to produce the highest quality books — carefully written, immaculately presented and dangerously close to being funny.

Then we work our socks off to get them out to you — at the cheapest possible prices.

Contents

Chemical Concepts

Module C1 — Carbon Chemistry

Module C2 — Rocks and Metals

Module C3 — The Periodic Table

Module C4 — Chemical Economics

Module C5 — How Much?

Module C6 — Chemistry Out There

Exam Skills

Published by Coordination Group Publications Ltd.

From original material by Richard Parsons.

Editors:
Ellen Bowness, Gemma Hallam, Sarah Hilton, Sharon Keeley, Andy Park, Kate Redmond, Ami Snelling, Claire Thompson, Julie Wakeling.

Contributors:
Mike Bossart, Sandy Gardner, Lucy Muncaster, Mike Thompson.

ISBN: 978 1 84146 570 8

With thanks to Barrie Crowther, John Moseley and Glenn Rogers for the proofreading.
With thanks to Laura Phillips for the copyright research.

Groovy website: www.cgpbooks.co.uk

Printed by Elanders Hindson Ltd, Newcastle upon Tyne.
Jolly bits of clipart from CorelDRAW®

Chemical Formulas

There's no getting away from formulas in Chemistry. You could hide them at the back of your wardrobe or under your pillow for a bit, but eventually you'll need to take them out and LEARN them. They're in every module in Chemistry — and that's why they are here, right at the beginning of the book.

You Need to Know About Displayed and Molecular Formulas...

Here we go then... atoms are the building blocks that everything is made from. Atoms can form bonds with other atoms to make molecules. Molecules containing different types of atoms are called compounds.

Chemists often use formulas to show molecules and compounds. It's often quicker, and they tell us more information about the substance — like how many atoms of each type there are.

This is called a molecular formula. It shows the number and type of atoms in a molecule.

This is called a displayed formula. It shows the atoms and the covalent bonds (see p.46) in a molecule as a picture.

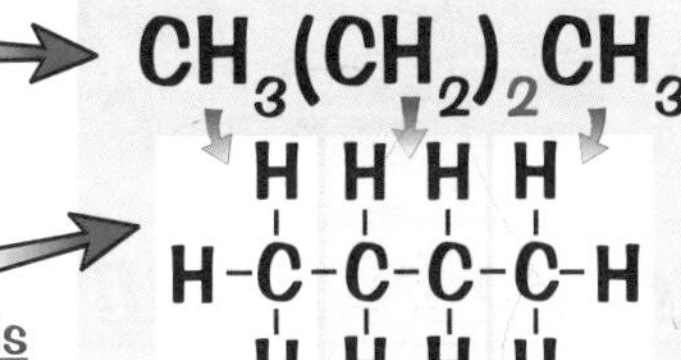

The 2 after the bracket means that there are 2 lots of CH_2. So altogether there are 4 carbon atoms and 10 hydrogen atoms.

In the exam they might give you a displayed formula and ask you to write down the molecular formula. Easy — just count up the number of each type of atom and write it as above. What's even better, you can write $CH_3(CH_2)_2CH_3$ as C_4H_{10}. It just doesn't get any easier. Not in Chemistry.

...And How to Work Out Chemical Formulas

There are some formulas you should know without even having to think about them, like oxygen (O_2), carbon dioxide (CO_2) and water (H_2O). Others are more difficult to remember — so you need to be able to work them out. That means you have to learn the stuff in the table on the inside front cover and how to use it. The main thing to remember is that in compounds the total charge must always add up to zero.

Here's a sample from the table:

Positive Ions		Negative Ions	
Zinc	Zn^{2+}	Oxide	O^{2-}
Aluminium	Al^{3+}	Carbonate	CO_3^{2-}
Iron(II)	Fe^{2+}		
Iron(III)	Fe^{3+}		

Some metals (like iron, copper and tin) can form ions with different charges. The number in brackets after the name tells you the size of the positive charge on the ion — and luckily for us, this makes the charge really easy to remember. E.g. an iron(II) ion has a charge of 2+, so it's Fe^{2+}.

EXAMPLE: Find the formula for zinc carbonate.

Find the charges on a zinc ion and a carbonate ion.
A zinc ion is Zn^{2+} and a carbonate ion is CO_3^{2-}.
To balance the total charge you need one zinc ion to every one carbonate ion. So the formula of zinc carbonate must be:

$$ZnCO_3$$

EXAMPLE: Find the formula for aluminium oxide.

Find the charges on an aluminium ion and an oxide ion.
An aluminium ion is Al^{3+} and an oxide ion is O^{2-}.
To balance the total charge you need two aluminium ions to every three oxide ions. So the formula of aluminium oxide must be:

$$Al_2O_3$$

Some chemicals have slightly more interesting names...

With so many chemicals around, you'd think there might be some interesting names... And there are. There's windowpane (C_9H_{12}). And angelic acid ($CH_3CHC(CH_3)COOH$). There's the mineral named after mineralogist Wilfred Welsh, which goes by the name of welshite ($Ca_2SbMg_4FeBe_2Si_4O_2O$). And if diethyl azodicarboxylate is a bit much, you can just call it DEAD. Better than boring names like 'ethene'.

Chemical Equations

If you're going to get anywhere in Chemistry you need to know about chemical equations...

Chemical Changes are Shown Using Chemical Equations

One way to show a chemical reaction is to write a word equation — these are dead easy.

Another way is a kind of shorthand — using a symbol equation. These are a little more complicated, but they're quick to write and tell you more information, like the chemical formulas and the number of each type of atom on both sides of the equation.

Here's an example — you're told that magnesium burns in oxygen, giving magnesium oxide.

So here's the word equation: Magnesium + oxygen → magnesium oxide

And here's the symbol equation: $2Mg + O_2 \rightarrow 2MgO$

Symbol Equations Need to be Balanced

1) There must always be the same number of atoms on both sides — they can't just disappear.
2) You balance the equation by putting numbers in front of the formulas where needed. Take this equation for reacting sulfuric acid with sodium hydroxide:

$$H_2SO_4 + NaOH \rightarrow Na_2SO_4 + H_2O$$

The formulas are all correct but the numbers of some atoms don't match up on both sides. You can't change formulas like H_2SO_4 to H_2SO_5. You can only put numbers in front of them:

Method: Balance Just One Type of Atom at a Time

The more you practise, the quicker you get, but all you do is this:

1) Find an element that doesn't balance and pencil in a number to try and sort it out.
2) See where it gets you. It may create another imbalance, but if so, pencil in another number and see where that gets you.
3) Carry on chasing unbalanced elements and it'll sort itself out pretty quickly.

I'll show you: In the equation above you'll notice we're short of H atoms on the RHS (Right-Hand Side).

1) The only thing you can do about that is make it $2H_2O$ instead of just H_2O:

$$H_2SO_4 + NaOH \rightarrow Na_2SO_4 + 2H_2O$$

2) But that now gives too many H atoms and O atoms on the RHS, so to balance that up you could try putting 2NaOH on the LHS (Left-Hand Side):

$$H_2SO_4 + 2NaOH \rightarrow Na_2SO_4 + 2H_2O$$

3) And suddenly there it is! Everything balances. And you'll notice the Na just sorted itself out.

They can ask you in the exam to balance symbol equations using formulas that have bits in brackets — like $CH_3(CH_2)_2CH_3$ on the last page. Don't worry about that, just make sure you're clear before you start how many of each type of atom there are — in this case it's 4 carbons and 10 hydrogens.

It's all about getting the balance right...

Balancing equations isn't as scary as it looks — you just plug numbers in till it works itself out. Get some practice in — you'll see. You can balance equations with displayed formulas in exactly the same way. Just make sure there are the same number of each type of atom on both sides — dead easy.

Food Additives

All sorts of natural and synthetic additives get put in food, generally to improve quality or shelf life.

Additives Make Food Last Longer and Look and Taste Better

1) Food colours (should) make food look more appetising. They're often used in sweets and soft drinks. A place you might not expect to find food colouring is mushy peas, which contain a green dye. Chocolate cake mixes often contain a brown food colouring (which you don't need in a proper homemade cake if you use enough cocoa powder).
2) Flavour enhancers bring out the taste and smell of food without adding a taste of their own (they're not flavourings as such). They're often added to packet soups, sausages and ready meals.
3) Antioxidants help to preserve food — see below.
4) Emulsifiers help oil and water blend together in foods like salad cream and ice cream — see below.

Additives with E numbers have passed a safety test and can be used in the European Union.
Food colourings have E numbers between 100 and 181, e.g. E127 is erythrosine (a red dye) and E150's caramel.
Antioxidants are E300-E340, e.g. E330 is citric acid.
Flavour enhancers are E620-E640, e.g. E621 is monosodium glutamate.
You don't have to remember these for the exam, but it gives you some idea about how they're organised.

Antioxidants Stop Foods Reacting with Oxygen

1) When some foods react with oxygen, they go off. Oxygen can turn the fat in food into nasty-smelling and nasty-tasting substances — e.g. butter goes rancid when it's exposed to the air. Oxygen can discolour food — apples and bananas go brown when they're cut up and left in the open air.
2) Antioxidants are added to foods that contain fat or oil to stop them reacting with oxygen — e.g. sausages. Bakery products, jam and instant soup also contain antioxidants. So now you know.

Emulsifiers Help Oil and Water Mix

1) You can mix an oil with water to make an emulsion. Emulsions are made up of lots of droplets of one liquid suspended in another liquid.
2) Oil and water naturally separate into two layers with the oil floating on top of the water — they don't "want" to mix. Emulsifiers help to stop the two liquids in an emulsion from separating out.
3) Mayonnaise, low-fat spread and ice cream are foods which contain emulsifiers.
4) Emulsifiers are molecules with one part that's attracted to water and another part that's attracted to oil or fat. The bit that's attracted to water is called hydrophilic, and the bit that's attracted to oil is called hydrophobic.

emulsifier molecule

hydrophilic (likes water, hates oil)

hydrophobic (likes oil, hates water)

5) The hydrophilic end of each emulsifier molecule latches onto water molecules.
6) The hydrophobic end of each emulsifier molecule cosies up to oil molecules.
7) When you shake oil and water together with a bit of emulsifier, the oil forms droplets, surrounded by a coating of emulsifier... with the hydrophilic bit facing outwards. Other oil droplets are repelled by the hydrophilic bit of the emulsifier, while water molecules latch on. So the emulsion won't separate out. Clever.

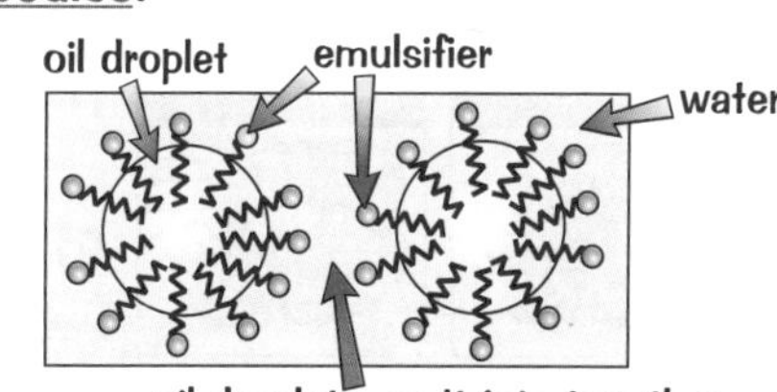

Add me to food and it'll disappear...

The long-term effects of some additives aren't known. A lot of food manufacturers now make additive-free products for people who don't want to take the risk. There is, as yet, no additive-free exam though. So you'll need to learn this page — antioxidants, emulsifiers, hydrophilic bits and all.

Food Packaging

Here's a page about food packaging. (Surprisingly, it's not nearly as dull as you might think.)

Food "Goes Off" If It's Stored for a Long Time

1) Food "going off" is usually down to the action of bacteria or moulds, which grow in or on the food and begin to break it down. They produce waste products that smell and taste nasty and cause food poisoning, so all you can do is to chuck the food in the bin.
2) There's a lot of demand nowadays for food that keeps for longer. It's easier (and cheaper) to transport to shops. Also, our shopping habits have changed — most people now do one big weekly shop in a supermarket, instead of popping out to their local grocers every day as most people did 50 years ago. It's a lot more convenient, but it does mean that food is kept lying around the house for longer.
3) Additives can help food last longer (see last page) and so can modern packaging.

Active and Intelligent Packaging Does More Than Wrap Food

The food industry uses new technology to create "active packaging" to help food last for longer.

1) Active packaging and intelligent packaging don't only form a barrier between the food and the outside world. They can control, and even react to what's happening inside the package.
2) Active packaging is packaging which changes something inside the package.

> Example: "Widgets" in beer cans release gas when the can's opened, to give the beer a foamy "head".

3) Intelligent packaging can monitor the food and tell the customer whether the food is still okay or if it's gone off.

> Example: Special dyes which change colour faster the warmer they get can be used to tell if a food's been warm for long enough for microbes to grow.

Ink gets darker faster when it's warm.

- Very fresh
- Still fresh
- Still fresh, eat now.
- Not fresh if centre is darker than ring.

Example — Self-heating and Self-cooling Cans

1) Self-heating cans use an exothermic reaction (see p.17) to produce heat and warm up the contents of the can.
2) Self-cooling cans use evaporation to cool down their contents.
3) Some of these cans also use thermochromic pigments (see p.21) which change colour when the contents are at the correct temperature.

Self-heating can

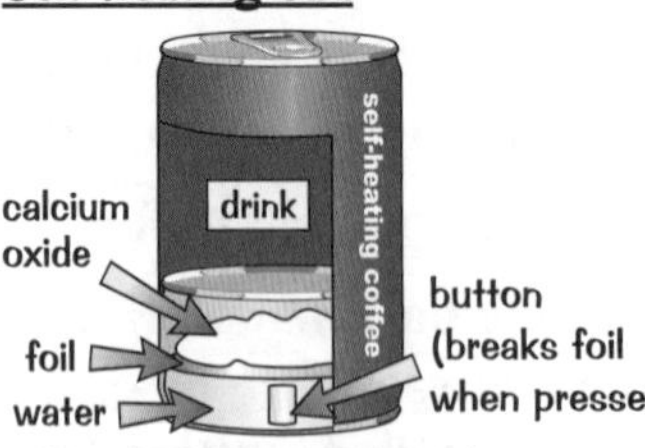

When the button's pressed, water and calcium oxide mix, react, and produce heat.

Self-cooling can

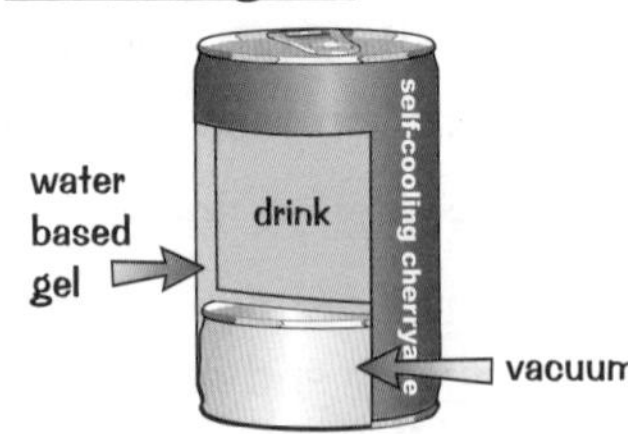

When can's opened, water in the gel evaporates into the vacuum. This cools the drink by about 15 °C.

Example — Removal of Water from Inside a Packet

mould (yuk)

no mould

1) Fresh food sometimes produces moisture inside the packaging. This can cause bacteria or mould to grow.
2) Chemicals such as silica gel are desiccants and absorb water. Manufacturers put sachets of silica into some food packets to absorb excess water, which makes it more difficult for bacteria and mould to grow.

Intelligent packaging... clever tin cans...

Imagine a hot summer's day — you twist the base of your drinks can, wait for the coloured dot on the can to change colour, then sup your ice-cold drink. Neato. Don't panic if you don't "get" how it works — in the exam you'll be given the data you need, you'll just have to interpret it.

Cooking and Chemical Change

This is a page about irreversible chemical changes. When you cook things, the chemical structure of the substance changes, and it can't change back. (In my case, cooking and burning are similar processes.)

Some Foods Have to be Cooked

There are loads of different ways to cook food — e.g. boiling, steaming, grilling, frying and cooking in an oven or a microwave.

1) Many foods have a better taste and texture when cooked.
2) Some foods are easier to digest once they're cooked (e.g. potatoes, flour). See below for why.
3) The high temperatures involved in cooking also kill off those nasty little microbes that cause disease — this is very important with meat.
4) Some foods are poisonous when raw, and must be cooked to make 'em edible — e.g. red kidney beans contain a poison that's only destroyed by at least 10 minutes boiling (and 2 hours cooking in total).

Cooking Causes Chemical Changes

Cooking food produces new substances. That means a chemical change has taken place. Once cooked, you can't change it back. The cooking process is irreversible.

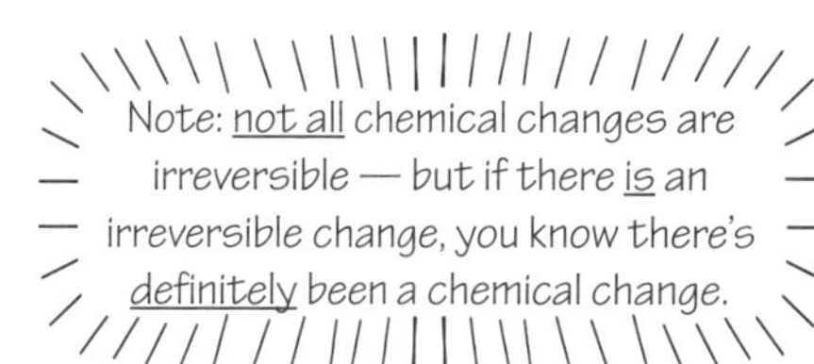

e.g. Eggs and Meat

Eggs and meat are good sources of protein. Protein molecules change shape when you heat them. The energy from cooking breaks some of the chemical bonds in the protein and this allows the molecule to take a different shape. This gives the food a more edible texture. The change is irreversible. It's called denaturing.

e.g. Potatoes

Potatoes are a good source of carbohydrates. Obviously, potatoes are plants, so each potato cell is surrounded by a cellulose cell wall. Humans can't digest cellulose, so this makes it difficult to get to the contents of the cells. Cooking the potato breaks down the cell wall, making it a lot easier to digest.

Baking Powder Undergoes a Chemical Change When Heated

1) When you heat baking powder, it undergoes thermal decomposition.
2) Thermal decomposition is when a substance breaks down into simpler substances when heated. Many thermal decompositions are helped along by a catalyst. (Thermal decomposition is different from a lot of reactions you'll come across, since there's only one substance to start with.)
3) Baking powder contains the chemical sodium hydrogencarbonate. You need to know the word and symbol equations for its thermal decomposition:

The word equation is: sodium hydrogencarbonate → sodium carbonate + carbon dioxide + water

The symbol equation is: $2NaHCO_3 \rightarrow Na_2CO_3 + CO_2 + H_2O$

4) Baking powder is used in baking cakes — the carbon dioxide produced makes the cake rise.
5) You can check that it is actually carbon dioxide that has been formed by using a chemical test —

Carbon dioxide can be detected using limewater — CO_2 turns limewater cloudy when it's bubbled through.

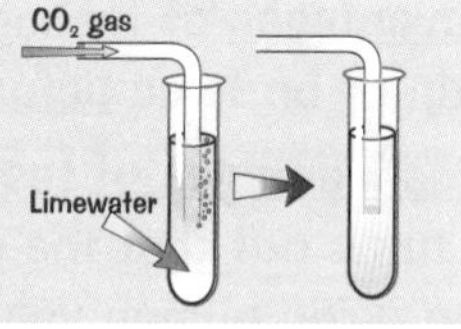

You'll need to learn this page for your eggsam...

Cooking is a kind of chemistry — when you cook something, you're bringing about chemical change. The changes are irreversible, as you'll know if you've ever tried to unscramble an egg.

Perfumes

Some things smell nice, some don't... it's all down to the chemicals a substance contains.

Perfumes Can be Natural or Artificial

1) Chemicals that smell nice are used as perfumes and air fresheners. Esters are often used as perfumes as they usually smell quite pleasant.
2) Esters are pretty common in nature. Loads of common food smells (plus those in products like perfumes) contain natural esters.
3) Esters are also manufactured synthetically to enhance food flavours or aromas, e.g. there are esters (or combinations of esters) that smell of rum, apple, orange, pineapple, and so on. And esters are responsible for the distinctive smell of pear drops.

Esters are Made by Esterification

A carboxylic acid is an acid built around one or more carbon atoms.

1) Esters can be made by heating a carboxylic acid with an alcohol. (This is an example of esterification.)
2) An acid catalyst is usually used (e.g. concentrated sulfuric acid).

Acid + Alcohol → Ester + Water

Learn this equation.

Method: Mix 10 cm³ of a carboxylic acid such as ethanoic acid with 10 cm³ of an alcohol such as ethanol. Add 1 cm³ of concentrated sulfuric acid to this mixture and warm gently for about 5 minutes. Tip the mixture into 150 cm³ of sodium carbonate solution (to neutralise the acids) and smell carefully (by wafting the smell towards your nose). The fruity-smelling product is the ester.

Perfumes Need Certain Properties

You can't use any old chemical with a smell as a perfume. You need a substance with certain properties:

1) Easily evaporates — or else the perfume particles won't reach your nose and you won't be able to smell it... bit useless really.
2) Non-toxic — it mustn't seep through your skin and poison you.
3) Doesn't react with water — or else it would react with the water in sweat.
4) Doesn't irritate the skin — or else you couldn't apply it directly to your neck or wrists. If you splash on any old substance you risk burning your skin.
5) Insoluble in water — if it was soluble in water it would wash off every time you got wet.

Don't forget that even if a substance has all these properties, it still might smell pretty bad and so be unsuitable for a perfume.

New Perfumes and Cosmetics Have to be Tested

Companies are always developing new cosmetic products to sell to us. Before they're released to the shops, they need to be tested thoroughly to make sure they're safe to use. They should be non-toxic and shouldn't irritate the eyes or skin. Pretty obvious, I'm sure you'll agree. But some tests are carried out using animals, which is a bit more controversial.

Advantages of testing new cosmetics on animals: We get an idea of whether they're likely to irritate the skin or be toxic before humans use them (though an animal test won't necessarily apply to humans).

Disadvantages of testing on animals: The tests could cause pain and suffering to the animals (especially if it turns out that the cosmetic is toxic). And animals can't choose whether or not to take part in the tests (so using human volunteers instead could be a possibility in certain circumstances).

My dog's got no nose — how does he smell? (Answer below)

Perfume needs to smell nice, but not everyone agrees on what smells nice. Perfume also needs to be safe, but not everyone agrees on the best way to test for this. That's life for you.

Like I said, he's got no nose so he can't smell.

Kinetic Theory & Forces Between Particles

You can explain a lot of things (including perfumes) if you get your head round this lot.

States of Matter — Depend on the Forces Between Particles

All stuff is made of particles (molecules, ions or atoms) that are constantly moving, and the forces between these particles can be weak or strong, depending on whether it's a solid, liquid or a gas.

1) There are strong forces of attraction between particles, which holds them in fixed positions in a very regular lattice arrangement.
2) The particles don't move from their positions, so all solids keep a definite shape and volume, and don't flow like liquids.
3) The particles vibrate about their positions — the hotter the solid becomes, the more they vibrate (causing solids to expand slightly when heated).

If you heat the solid (give the particles more energy), eventually the solid will melt and become liquid.

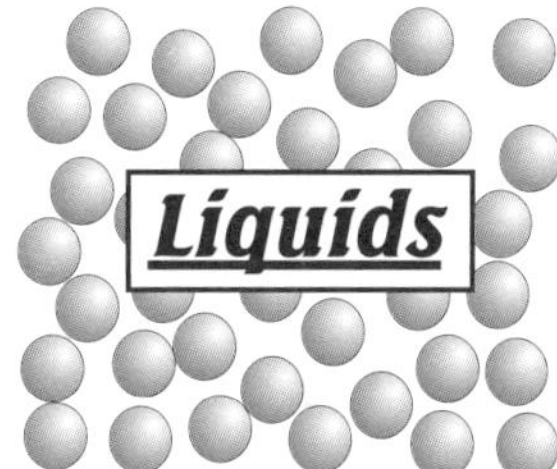

1) There is some force of attraction between the particles. They're free to move past each other, but they do tend to stick together.
2) Liquids don't keep a definite shape and will flow to fill the bottom of a container. But they do keep the same volume.
3) The particles are constantly moving with random motion. The hotter the liquid gets, the faster they move. This causes liquids to expand slightly when heated.

If you now heat the liquid, eventually it will boil and become gas.

1) There's next to no force of attraction between the particles — they're free to move. They travel in straight lines and only interact when they collide.
2) Gases don't keep a definite shape or volume and will always fill any container. When particles bounce off the walls of a container they exert a pressure on the walls.
3) The particles move constantly with random motion. The hotter the gas gets, the faster they move. Gases either expand when heated, or their pressure increases.

How We Smell Stuff — Volatility's the Key

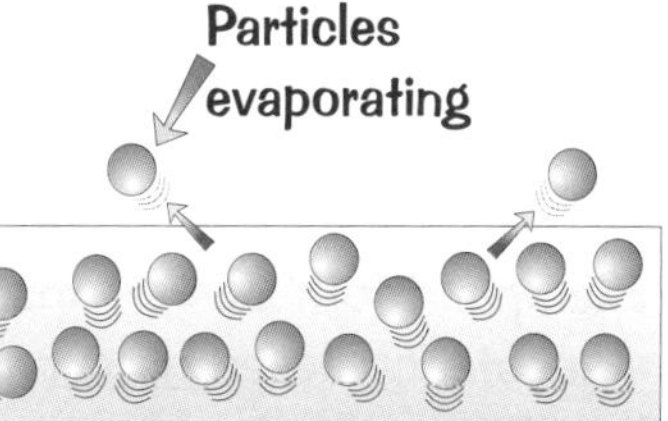

1) When a liquid is heated, the heat energy goes to the particles, which makes them move faster.
2) Some particles move faster than others.
3) Fast-moving particles at the surface will overcome the forces of attraction from the other particles and escape. This is evaporation.
4) How easily a liquid evaporates is called its volatility.

So... the evaporated particles are now drifting about in the air, the smell receptors in your nose pick up the chemical — and hey presto — you smell it.

Perfumes need to be quite volatile so they evaporate enough for you to smell them.

Eau de sweaty sock — thankfully not very volatile...

Take another smelly chemical — petrol. The molecules in petrol are held together (otherwise it wouldn't be a liquid), but they must be constantly escaping (evaporating) in order for you to smell it. That's why you shouldn't have naked flames at a petrol station... the vapour from the pumps could catch fire.

Solutions

Solutions are all around you — e.g. sea water, bath salts... And inside you even — e.g. instant coffee...

A Solution is a Mixture of Solvent and Solute

When you add a solid (the solute) to a liquid (the solvent) the bonds holding the solute molecules together sometimes break and the molecules then mix with the molecules in the liquid — forming a solution. This is called dissolving. Whether the bonds break depends on how strong the attractions are between the molecules within each substance and how strong the attractions are between the two substances.

Here's some definitions you need to know:

1) Solute – is the substance being dissolved.
2) Solvent – is the liquid it's dissolving into.
3) Solution – is the mixture of the solute plus the solvent.
4) Soluble – means it will dissolve.
5) Insoluble – means it will NOT dissolve.
6) Solubility – a measure of how much will dissolve.

E.g. brine is a solution of salt and water — if you evaporated off the solvent (the water), you'd see the solute (the salt) again.

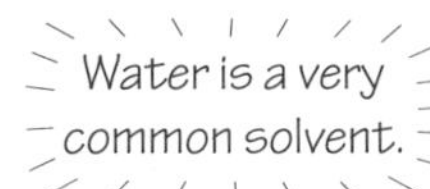

Nail Varnish is Insoluble in Water...

Nail varnish doesn't dissolve in water. This is for two reasons:

1) The molecules of nail varnish are strongly attracted to each other. This attraction is stronger than the attraction between the nail varnish molecules and the water molecules.
2) The molecules of water are strongly attracted to each other. This attraction is stronger than the attraction between the water molecules and the nail varnish molecules.

Because the two substances are more attracted to themselves than each other, they don't form a solution.

...but Soluble in Acetone

Nail varnish dissolves in acetone — more commonly known as nail varnish remover. This is because the attraction between acetone molecules and nail varnish molecules is stronger than the attractions holding the two substances together.

So the solubility of a substance depends on the solvent used.

Lots of Things are Solvents

Alcohols and esters can be used as solvents, and so can lots of other weird and wacky organic molecules. Ability to dissolve a solute isn't the only consideration though... some solvents are horribly poisonous.

Example: Mothballs are made of a substance called naphthalene. Imagine you've trodden a mothball into your carpet. Choose one of the solvents from the table to clean it up.

solvent	solubility of naphthalene	boiling point	other properties
water	0 g/100 g	100 °C	safe
methanol	9.7 g/100 g	65 °C	flammable
ethyl acetate	18.5 g/100 g	77 °C	flammable
dichloromethane	25.0 g/100 g	40 °C	Extremely toxic

Looking at the data, water wouldn't be a good choice because it doesn't dissolve the naphthalene. Dichloromethane would dissolve it easily, but it's very toxic. Of the two solvents left, ethyl acetate dissolves more naphthalene (so you won't need as much). Ethyl acetate is best (just don't set light to it).

Learn this page, it's the only solution...

If you ever spill bright pink nail varnish (or any other colour for that matter) on your carpet, go easy with the nail varnish remover. If you use too much, the nail varnish dissolves in the remover, forming a solution which can go everywhere — and you end up with an enormous bright pink stain... aaagh.

Polymers

Plastics are made up of lots of molecules joined together. They're like long chains.

Plastics are Long-Chain Molecules Called Polymers

1) Plastics are formed when lots of small molecules called monomers join together to give a polymer.
2) They're usually carbon based (and the monomers are very often alkenes — see p.11).

Addition Polymers are Made Under High Pressure

The monomers that make up addition polymers have a double covalent bond. Molecules with at least one double covalent bond between carbon atoms are called unsaturated compounds. Molecules with no double bond between carbon atoms are saturated compounds.

Under high pressure and with a catalyst (see p.34) to help them along, many unsaturated small molecules open up those double bonds and "join hands" (polymerise) to form long saturated chains called polymers.

Ethene becoming polyethene or "polythene", is the easiest example:

Many single ethenes $n(C=C)$ → (Pressure and Catalyst) → Polyethene $(-C-C-)_n$

The 'n' just means there can be any number of monomers.

You'll need to be able to construct the displayed formula of an addition polymer, given the displayed formula of its monomer. Dead easy — the carbons just all join together in a row with no double bonds between them.

The name of the plastic comes from the type of monomer it's made from — you just stick the word "poly" in front of it:

Propene can form polypropene: Propene $n(CH_2=CHCH_3)$ → Polypropene $(-CH_2-CH(CH_3)-)_n$

A molecule called styrene will polymerise into polystyrene: Styrene → Polystyrene; ⬡ $= C_6H_5$

Forces Between Molecules Determine the Properties of Plastics

Strong covalent bonds hold the atoms together in long chains. But it's the bonds between the different molecule chains that determine the properties of the plastic.

Weak Forces:

Long chains held together by weak forces are free to slide over each other. This means the plastic can be stretched easily, and will have a low melting point.

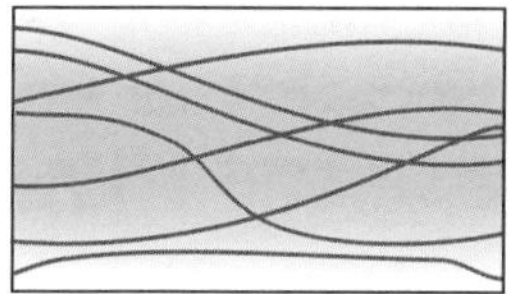

Strong Forces:

Plastics with stronger bonds between the polymer chains have higher melting points and can't be stretched, as the crosslinks hold the chains firmly together.

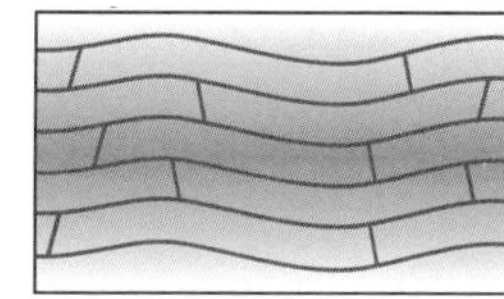

Revision — it's all about stringing lots of facts together...

Which monomer a polymer is made from affects the properties of the plastic, which also affects what the plastic can be used for (more about the uses of plastics on p.10, by the way). For this page, you need to be completely sure about what a monomer is, and how polymers are made.

Polymers and Their Uses

Plastics are fantastically useful. You can make novelty football pencil sharpeners and all sorts.

Polymers' Properties Decide What They're Used For

Different polymers have different physical properties — some are stronger, some are stretchier, some are more easily moulded, and so on. These different physical properties make them suited for different uses.

- Strong, rigid polymers such as high density polyethene are used to make plastic milk bottles.
- Light, stretchable polymers such as low density polyethene are used for plastic bags and squeezy bottles. Low density polyethene has a low melting point, so it's no good for anything that'll get very hot.

- PVC is strong and durable, and it can be made either rigid or stretchy. The rigid kind is used to make window frames and piping. The stretchy kind is used to make synthetic leather.
- Polystyrene foam is used in packaging to protect breakable things, and it's used to make disposable coffee cups (the trapped air in the foam makes it a brilliant thermal insulator).
- Heat-resistant polymers such as melamine resin and polypropene are used to make plastic kettles.

Polymers are Often Used to Make Clothes

1) Nylon is a synthetic polymer often used to make clothes. Fabrics made from nylon are not waterproof on their own, but can be coated with polyurethane to make tough, hard-wearing and waterproof outdoor clothing which also keeps UV light out.
2) One big problem is that the polyurethane coating doesn't let water vapour pass through it. So if you get a bit hot (or do a bit of exercise), sweat condenses on the inside. This makes skin and clothes get wet and uncomfortable — the material isn't breathable.
3) Some fabrics, e.g. GORE-TEX® products, have all the useful properties of nylon/polyurethane ones, but they're also breathable — if you sweat the water vapour can escape, so there's no condensation.

1) GORE-TEX® fabrics are made by laminating a thin film of a plastic called expanded PTFE onto a layer of another fabric, such as polyester or nylon — this makes the PTFE sturdier.
2) The PTFE film has tiny holes which let water vapour pass through — so it's breathable. But it's waterproof, since the holes aren't big enough to let big water droplets through and the PTFE repels liquid water.
3) This material is great for outdoorsy types — they can hike without getting rained on or soaked in sweat.

water molecules pass through the tiny holes
nylon / polyester
PTFE film
raindrop too big to get through holes
sweat evaporating from skin (as water vapour)

Non-biodegradable Plastics Cause Disposal Problems

1) Most polymers aren't "biodegradable" — they're not broken down by micro-organisms, so they don't rot. This property is actually kind of useful until it's time to get rid of your plastic.
2) It's difficult to get rid of plastics — if you bury them in a landfill site, they'll still be there years later. Landfill sites fill up quickly, and they're a waste of land. And a waste of plastic.
3) When plastics are burnt, some of them release gases such as acidic sulfur dioxide and poisonous hydrogen chloride and hydrogen cyanide. So burning's out, really. Plus it's a waste of plastic.
4) The best thing is to reuse plastics as many times as possible and then recycle them if you can. Sorting out lots of different plastics for recycling is difficult and expensive, though.
5) Chemists are working on a variety of ideas to produce biodegradable polymers.

Disposal problems — you should go and see a doctor...

If you're making a product, you need to pick your plastic carefully. It's no good trying to make a kettle out of a plastic that melts at 50 °C — you'll end up with a messy kitchen, a burnt hand and no cuppa. You'd also have a bit of difficulty trying to wear clothes made of brittle, un-bendy plastic.

Alkanes and Alkenes

Hydrocarbons are basically fuels such as petrol and diesel. They're made of just carbon and hydrogen atoms. So $C_{10}H_{22}$ is a hydrocarbon, but $CH_3COOC_3H_7$ (an ester) is not — it's got oxygen atoms in it.

Alkanes Have All C–C Single Bonds

1) Alkanes are made up of chains of carbon atoms with single covalent bonds between them.
2) They're called saturated hydrocarbons because they have no spare bonds left (i.e. no double bonds that can open up and have things join onto them).
3) You can tell the difference between an alkane and an alkene (see below) by adding the substance to bromine water. An alkane won't decolourise the bromine water. This is because it has no spare bonds, so it can't react with the bromine.
4) Alkanes won't form polymers — same reason again, no spare bonds.
5) The first four alkanes are methane (natural gas), ethane, propane and butane.
6) They burn cleanly, producing carbon dioxide and water.

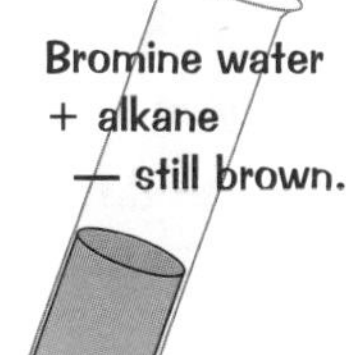

1) Methane: CH_4 (natural gas)

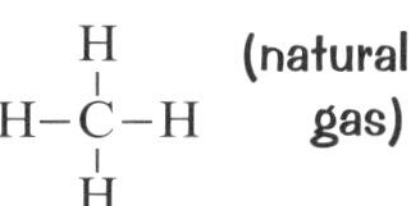

2) Ethane: C_2H_6

3) Propane: C_3H_8

4) Butane: C_4H_{10}

All alkanes have the formula: C_nH_{2n+2}

Alkenes Have a C=C Double Bond

1) Alkenes are chains of carbon atoms with one or more double covalent bonds.
2) They're called unsaturated hydrocarbons because double bonds can open up and let things join on.
3) This is why they will decolourise bromine water. They form bonds with the bromine.
4) Alkenes are more reactive due to the double bond all poised and ready to just pop open. They form polymers by opening up their double bonds to 'hold hands' in a long chain.

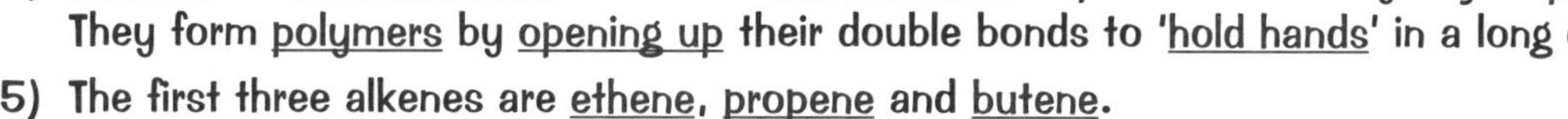

5) The first three alkenes are ethene, propene and butene.
6) They tend to burn with a smoky flame, producing soot (carbon).

Bromine water + alkene — decolourised

1) Ethene: C_2H_4

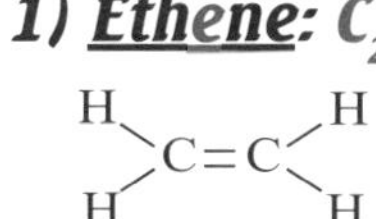

2) Propene: C_3H_6

3) Butene: C_4H_8

All alkenes containing one double bond have the formula: C_nH_{2n}

Covalent Bonds Hold Atoms in a Molecule Together

1) All the atoms in hydrocarbon molecules are held together by covalent bonds. These covalent bonds are very strong. They form when atoms 'share' electrons.
2) This way both atoms get a full outer shell — which is an atom's main aim in life.
3) Each covalent bond provides one extra shared electron for each atom. And each atom involved has to make enough covalent bonds to fill up its outer shell. So carbon atoms always want to make a total of 4 bonds, while hydrogen atoms only want to make 1. Double bonds involve sharing 2 pairs.

A hydrogen atom needs 2 electrons in its outer shell.

A carbon atom needs 8 electrons in its outer shell.

Alkane anybody who doesn't learn this lot properly...

Covalent bonds are so sweet — the little atoms sharing their electrons. Heartwarming.

Fractional Distillation of Crude Oil

Fossil fuels like coal, oil and gas are called non-renewable fuels as they take so long to make that they're being used up much faster than they're being formed. They're finite resources — one day they'll run out.

Crude Oil is Separated into Different Hydrocarbon Fractions

1) Crude oil is formed from the buried remains of plants and animals — it's a fossil fuel. Over millions of years, with high temperature and pressure, the remains turn to crude oil, which can be drilled up.
2) Crude oil is a mixture of lots of different hydrocarbons. Remember that hydrocarbons are chains of carbon atoms (e.g. alkanes and alkenes) of various lengths.
3) The different compounds in crude oil are separated using a fractionating column. The oil is heated until most of it has turned into gas. The gases enter the fractionating column (and the liquid bit, bitumen, is drained off at the bottom). In the column there's a temperature gradient (i.e. it's hot at the bottom and gets gradually cooler as you go up).
4) Fractional distillation works because the shorter hydrocarbons have lower boiling points. They turn back into liquid and drain out of the column later on, when they're further up. You end up with the crude oil mixture separated out into different fractions containing molecules with similar boiling points.

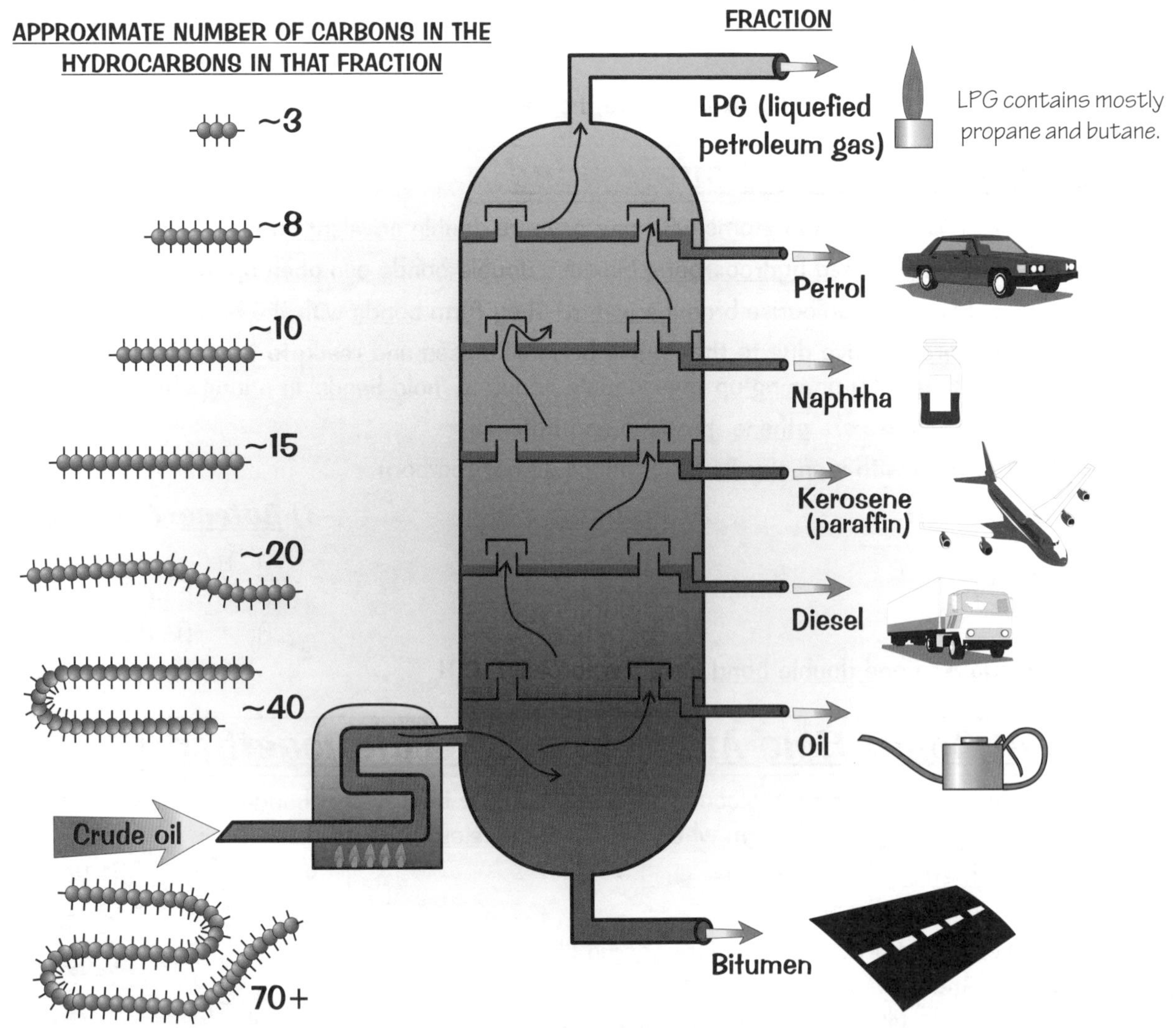

How much petrol is in crude oil — just a fraction...

In the exam, you could be given a diagram of the distillation column, and asked to add labels, or say where on the column petrol would be drained off, or diesel. This means you need to learn the diagram on the page — don't just glance at it and assume you know it. Cover up the page and test yourself.

Hydrocarbon Properties — Bonds

The examiners seem quite keen that you know why long hydrocarbon chains boil at a higher temperature than short hydrocarbon chains. If that's what they want, then you'd best give it to them...

Hydrocarbon Properties Change as the Chain Gets Longer

As the size of the hydrocarbon molecule increases:

1) The boiling point increases.
2) It gets less flammable (doesn't set on fire so easily).
3) It gets more viscous (doesn't flow so easily).
4) It gets less volatile (i.e. doesn't evaporate so easily).

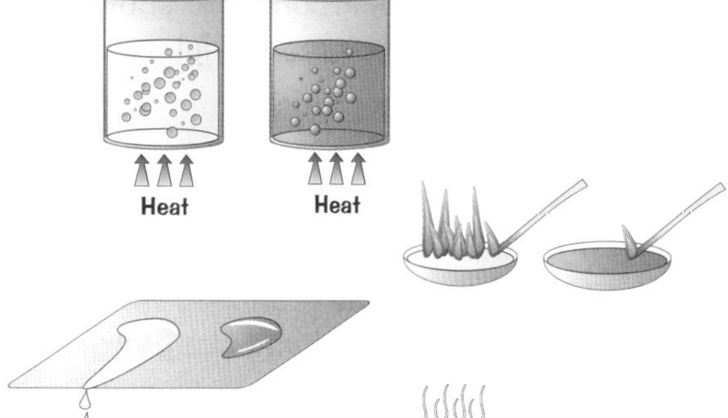

That's how fractional distillation works — you can separate out the random mixture of all kinds of hydrocarbons into groups (fractions) that have similar chain lengths and so similar properties. Then you can use them for various useful things like powering vehicles, heating homes and making roads. It works because one of those properties that each group has in common is the boiling point.

But you don't get off that easily — how come similar lengths of chain have similar boiling points anyway? Curious little fellas these examiner types, you know, expecting you to explain things. Read on for the whys and wherefores...

It's All Down to the Bonds In and Between Hydrocarbons

1) There are two important types of bond in crude oil:
   a) The strong covalent bonds between the carbons and hydrogens within each hydrocarbon molecule.
   b) The intermolecular forces of attraction between different hydrocarbon molecules in the mixture.
2) When the crude oil mixture is heated, the molecules are supplied with extra energy.
3) This makes the molecules move about more. Eventually a molecule might have enough energy to overcome the intermolecular forces that keep it with the other molecules.
4) It can now go whizzing off as a gas.
5) The covalent bonds holding each molecule together are much stronger than the intermolecular forces, so they don't break. That's why you don't end up with lots of little molecules.
6) The intermolecular bonds break a lot more easily in small molecules than they do in bigger molecules. That's because the intermolecular forces of attraction are much stronger between big molecules than they are between small molecules.
7) It makes sense if you think about it — even if a big molecule can overcome the forces attracting it to another molecule at a few points along its length, it's still got lots of other places where the force is still strong enough to hold it in place.
8) That's why big molecules have higher boiling points than small molecules do.

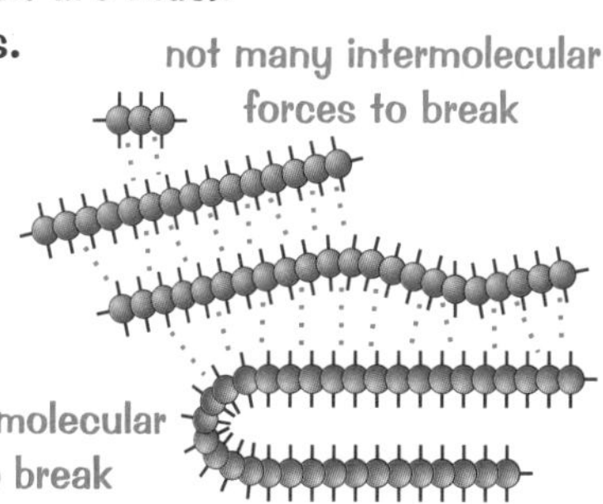

Positively boiling over with chemistry fun...

One minute it's all petrol and kerosene, the next it's all molecules and forces and covalent bonds. That's the way with chemistry. If you can scribble down a reasonable version of the stuff about intermolecular bonds and boiling point, you'll get the marks. Which is what it's all about.

Cracking

Crude oil fractions from fractional distillation are split into smaller molecules — this is called cracking. It's dead important — otherwise we might not have enough fuel for cars and planes and things.

Cracking is Splitting Up Long-Chain Hydrocarbons

1) Cracking turns long hydrocarbons into shorter molecules which are much more useful.
2) It's a form of thermal decomposition, which is just breaking molecules down into simpler molecules by heating them. This means breaking strong covalent bonds, so you need lots of heat and a catalyst.

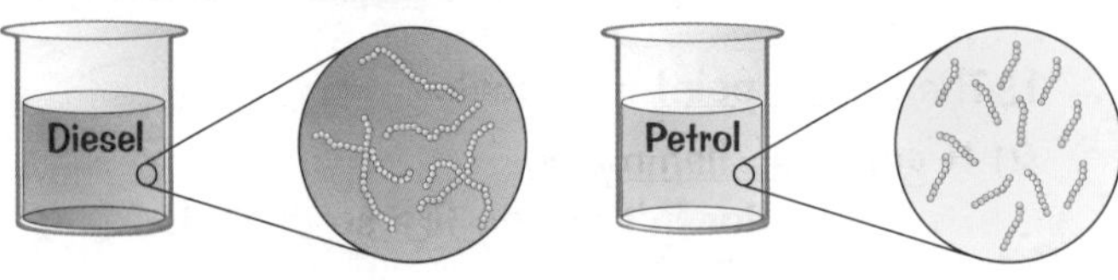

3) A lot of the longer molecules produced from fractional distillation are cracked into smaller ones because there's more demand for products like petrol and kerosene (jet fuel) than for diesel or lubricating oil.
4) Cracking also produces extra alkenes, which are needed for making plastics.

Conditions Needed for Cracking: Hot, Plus a Catalyst

1) Vaporised hydrocarbons are passed over powdered catalyst at about 400 °C – 700 °C.
2) Aluminium oxide is the catalyst used. The long-chain molecules split apart or "crack" on the surface of the bits of catalyst.

See p.34 for more about catalysts.

Long-chain hydrocarbon molecule → Shorter alkane molecule + Alkene

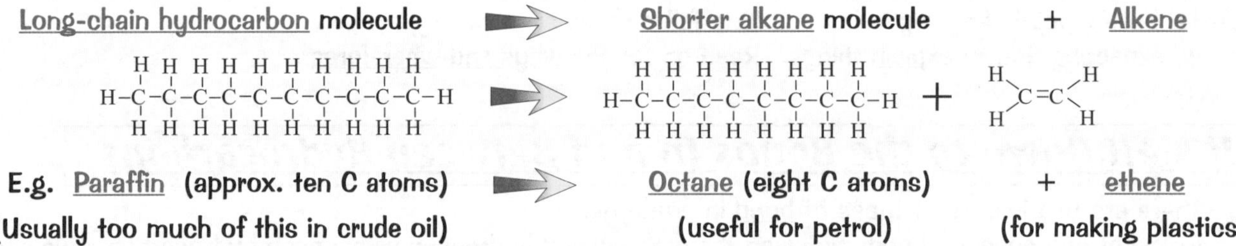

E.g. Paraffin (approx. ten C atoms) → Octane (eight C atoms) + ethene

(Usually too much of this in crude oil) (useful for petrol) (for making plastics)

3) You can use the apparatus shown below to crack liquid paraffin in the lab:

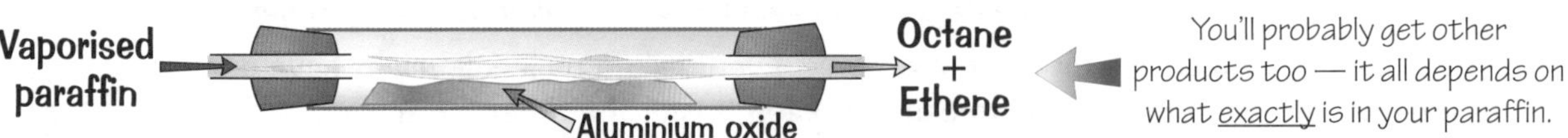

You'll probably get other products too — it all depends on what exactly is in your paraffin.

Cracking Helps Match Supply and Demand

The examiner might give you a table like the one below to show the supply and demand for various fractions obtained from crude oil. You could be asked which fraction is more likely to be cracked to provide us with petrol and diesel (demand for petrol and diesel is greater than the amount in crude oil).

Fraction	Approx % in crude oil	Approx % demand
LPG	2	4
Petrol and naphtha	16	27
Kerosene	13	8
Diesel	19	23
Oil and bitumen	50	38

OK, you could use the kerosene fraction to supply the extra petrol and the oil and bitumen fraction to supply the extra diesel. Or you could crack the oil and bitumen to supply both the extra petrol and the extra diesel. This might be cleverer, as there's a lot more oil/bitumen.

Don't crack up, it's not that bad...

Cracking helps an oil refinery match its supply of useful products (e.g. petrol) with the demand for them. Remember, you can crack any long hydrocarbon chain into smaller chains, but you can't make longer chains from shorter ones by cracking (duh...). Learn the temperature and catalyst and the lab diagram.

Fuels from Crude Oil

Crude oil is found in the Earth's crust. There's a massive oil industry, with scientists working to find oil reserves, pump the oil out of the ground, and turn it into useful products.

Oil is Very Useful Stuff, but It Can Cause Big Problems Too

Most of the problems with crude oil happen when it's being transported from one place to another.

1) It's carried in massive tanker ships. Occasionally these ships crash on coastal rocks, letting crude oil escape. Oil floats on water and the action of waves and tides spreads it out into big oil slicks.
2) Oil covers sea birds' feathers, and stops them being waterproof. Water then soaks the downy feathers that usually keep birds warm, so the birds die of cold. Birds swallow the oil as they try to clean it off their feathers, and get poisoned. Also, birds can't fly when their feathers are matted with oil.
3) Seals and other sea mammals can be poisoned by swallowing oil.
4) When the slick comes ashore, beaches get covered in a thick, smelly coating of oil. Not the best place for a bit of sun-bathing. Cleaning up a beach after an oil spill is expensive and can take a long time.

We're Using More Fossil Fuels All the Time

1) Crude oil provides the energy needed to do lots of pretty vital things — like manufacture all kinds of products, generate electricity, heat homes, cook...
2) Oil provides the fuel for most modern transport — cars, trains, planes, the lot.
3) It also provides the raw materials needed to make various chemicals, including plastics.
4) As the Earth's population increases and as more countries become more developed, more and more fossil fuels are burned to provide them with electricity, manufactured goods, etc. etc.
5) But crude oil resources are limited and non-renewable. As they get used up, the price of crude oil will rise, so plastics and fuels will get more expensive. And maybe one day there won't be enough oil to make all the fuel and plastics we'd like to.
6) Our dependence on crude oil is bad in other ways too. Burning fuels from crude oil produces greenhouse gases which cause climate change.

There's Lots to Consider When Choosing the Best Fuel

1) Energy value (i.e. amount of energy) — funnily enough, this isn't always as important as it may seem.
2) Availability — there's not much point in choosing a fuel you can't get hold of easily.
3) Storage — some fuels take up a lot of space, and some produce flammable gases.
4) Cost — some fuels are expensive, but still good value in terms of energy content etc.
5) Toxicity — poisonous fumes are a problem. You might avoid fuels which are toxic if eaten or drunk.
6) Ease of use — whether it lights easily, whether you can move it safely.
7) Pollution — e.g. will you be adding to acid rain and the greenhouse effect... There are also small-scale things to consider like smoke.

Example: You're at home and there's a power cut. You want a cup of tea. The only fuels you have in the house are candles or meths (in a spirit burner). Which one would you use to boil the water?

Fuel	Energy per gram	Rate of energy produced	Flame
Meths	28 kJ	15 kJ per minute	Clean
Candle	50 kJ	8 kJ per minute	Smoky

Even though a candle has more energy per gram, you'd probably choose meths because it's quicker and cleaner.

Oil not be impressed if you don't bother learning this...

We use loads of oil. Loads. At the moment, we're dependent on oil for many different things. That'd be all very well if we had lots of it, but we don't. So we have to make sure we can get hold of oil from countries that do. Which is where the politics begins... and therefore arguments. Ho hum.

Burning Fuels

A fuel is a substance that reacts with oxygen to release useful energy. Remember that definition.

Complete Combustion Happens When There's Plenty of Oxygen

The complete combustion of any hydrocarbon in oxygen will produce only carbon dioxide and water as waste products, which are both quite clean and non-poisonous.

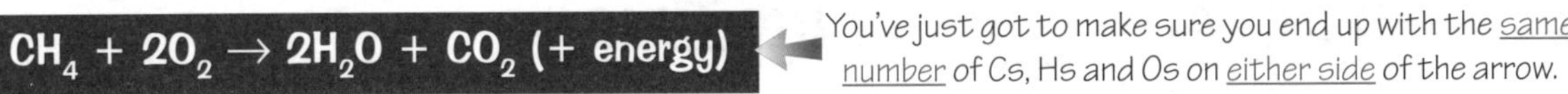

(+ energy)

1) Many gas heaters release these waste gases into the room, which is perfectly OK. As long as the gas heater is working properly and the room is well ventilated there's no problem.
2) This reaction, when there's plenty of oxygen, is known as complete combustion. It releases lots of energy and only produces those two harmless waste products. When there's plenty of oxygen and combustion is complete, the gas burns with a clean blue flame.
3) You need to be able to give a balanced symbol equation for the complete combustion of a simple hydrocarbon fuel when you're given its molecular formula. It's pretty easy — here's an example:

Lots of CO_2 isn't ideal, but the alternatives are worse (see below).

$CH_4 + 2O_2 \rightarrow 2H_2O + CO_2$ (+ energy)

You've just got to make sure you end up with the same number of Cs, Hs and Os on either side of the arrow.

You can show a fuel burns to give CO_2 and H_2O...

The water pump draws gases from the burning hexane through the apparatus. Water collects inside the cooled U-tube and you can show that it's water by checking its boiling point. The limewater turns milky, showing that carbon dioxide is present.

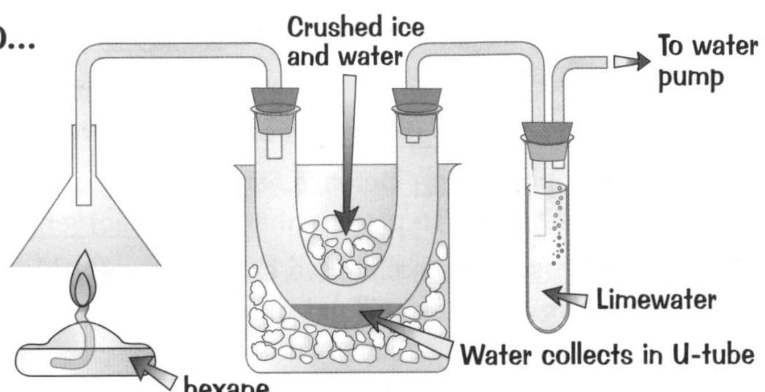

Incomplete Combustion of Hydrocarbons is NOT Safe

1) If there isn't enough oxygen the combustion will be incomplete. This gives carbon monoxide and carbon as waste products, and produces a smoky yellow flame. Incomplete combustion produces less energy than complete combustion does.

(+ energy)

2) The carbon monoxide is a colourless, odourless and poisonous gas and it's very dangerous. Every year people are killed while they sleep due to faulty gas fires and boilers filling the room with deadly carbon monoxide (CO) and nobody realising — this is why it's important to regularly service gas appliances. The black carbon given off produces sooty marks — a clue that the fuel is not burning fully.
3) So basically, you want lots of oxygen when you're burning fuel — you get more energy given out, and you don't get any messy soot or poisonous gases.

You need to be able to write a balanced symbol equation for incomplete combustion too, e.g.

$4CH_4 + 6O_2 \rightarrow C + 2CO + CO_2 + 8H_2O$ (+ energy)

This is just one possibility. The products depend on the quantity of the reactants present...

... E.g. you could also have: $2CH_4 + 3O_2 \rightarrow 2CO + 4H_2O$ — the important thing is that the equation is balanced.

Blue flame good, orange flame bad...

This is why people should get their gas appliances serviced every year, and get carbon monoxide detectors fitted. Carbon monoxide really can kill people in their sleep — scary stuff. Don't let that scare you off from learning everything that's on this page — any of it could come up in the exam.

Energy Transfer in Reactions

Chemical reactions can either release heat energy, or take in heat energy.

Combustion is an Exothermic Reaction — Heat's Given Out

An EXOTHERMIC REACTION is one which GIVES OUT ENERGY to the surroundings, usually in the form of HEAT, which is shown by a RISE IN TEMPERATURE.

The best example of an exothermic reaction is burning fuels.
This obviously gives out a lot of heat — it's very exothermic.

In an Endothermic Reaction, Heat is Taken In

An ENDOTHERMIC REACTION is one which TAKES IN ENERGY from the surroundings, usually in the form of HEAT, which is shown by a FALL IN TEMPERATURE.

Endothermic reactions are less common and less easy to spot. One example is thermal decomposition. Heat must be supplied to cause the compound to decompose, e.g. cracking (see p.14).

Temperature Changes Help Decide If a Reaction's Exo or Endo

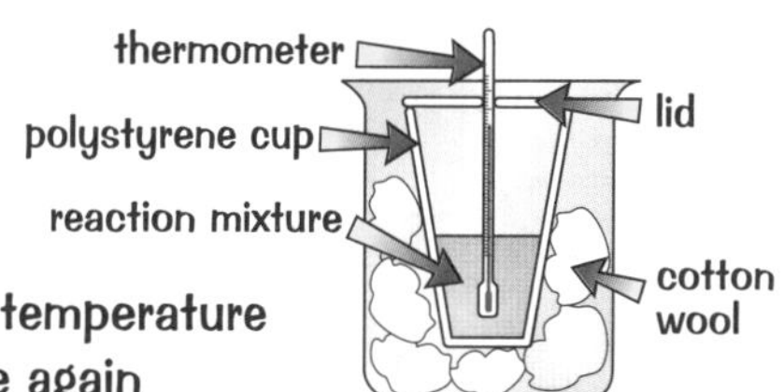

1) You can measure the amount of energy produced by a chemical reaction (in solution) by taking the temperature of the reactants, mixing them in a polystyrene cup and measuring the temperature of the solution at the end of the reaction. Easy.
2) Adding an acid to an alkali is an exothermic reaction. Measure the temperature of the alkali before you add the acid, then measure the temperature again after adding the acid and mixing — you'll see an increase in temperature.
3) Dissolving ammonium nitrate in water is an endothermic reaction. Adding a couple of spatulas of ammonium nitrate to a polystyrene cup of water results in a drop in temperature.

Energy Must Always be Supplied to Break Bonds... ...and Energy is Always Released When Bonds Form

1) During a chemical reaction, old bonds are broken and new bonds are formed.
2) Energy must be supplied to break existing bonds — so bond breaking is an endothermic process.
3) Energy is released when new bonds are formed — so bond formation is an exothermic process.

BOND BREAKING - ENDOTHERMIC

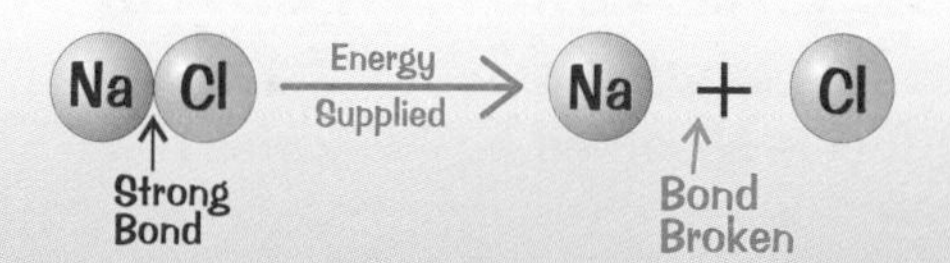

BOND FORMING - EXOTHERMIC

4) In an exothermic reaction, the energy released in bond formation is greater than the energy used in breaking old bonds.
5) In an endothermic reaction, the energy required to break old bonds is greater than the energy released when new bonds are formed.

Chemistry in "real-world application" shocker...

When you see Stevie Gerrard hobble off the pitch and press a bag to his leg, he's using an endothermic reaction. The cold pack contains an inner bag full of water and an outer one full of ammonium nitrate. When he presses the pack the inner bag breaks and they mix together. The ammonium nitrate dissolves in the water and, as this is an endothermic reaction, it draws in heat from Stevie's injured leg.

Measuring the Energy Content of Fuels

Different fuels give out different amounts of energy when they burn. One way to measure the energy content of fuels is by using a none-too-fancy copper cup (or a "calorimeter", to give it its proper name).

Use Specific Heat Capacity to Calculate Energy Transferred

1) This "calorimetric" experiment involves heating water by burning a liquid fuel.
2) If you measure (i) how much fuel you've burned and (ii) the temperature change of the water, you can work out how much energy is supplied by each gram of fuel.
3) You also need to know water's specific heat capacity — this is the amount of energy needed to raise the temperature of 1 gram of water by 1 °C. The specific heat capacity of water is 4.2 J/g/°C — so it takes 4.2 joules of energy to raise the temperature of 1 g of water by 1 °C.
4) If you do the same experiment with different fuels, you can compare their energy transferred per gram. If a fuel has a higher energy content per gram, you need less fuel to cause the same temperature rise.

Calorimetric Method — Reduce Heat Loss as Much as Possible

1) It's dead important to make as much heat as possible go into heating up the water. Reducing draughts is the key here — use a screen to act as a draught excluder (and don't do it next to an open window).

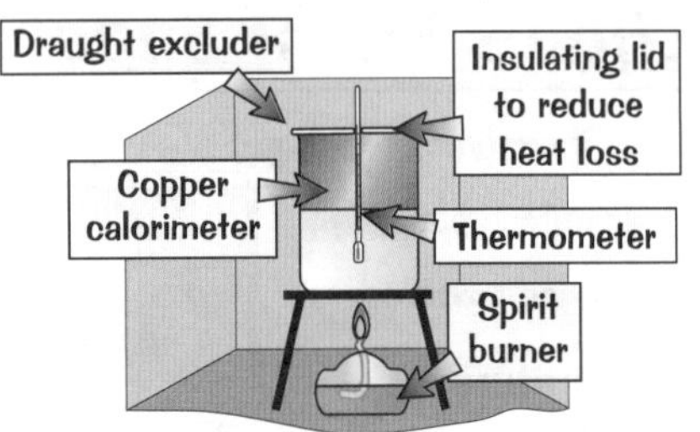

2) Put some fuel into a spirit burner (or use a bottled gas burner if the fuel is a gas) and weigh the burner full of fuel.
3) Measure out, say, 200 cm^3 of water into a copper calorimeter.
4) Take the initial temperature of the water — then put the burner under the calorimeter and light the wick.
5) While the water's heating up, stir it every now and then to distribute the heat evenly.
6) When the heat from the burner has made the water temperature rise by 20-30 °C, blow out the spirit burner and make a note of the highest temperature the water reaches.
7) Reweigh the burner and fuel.
8) If you're comparing two fuels, repeat the procedure with the second fuel.

Three Calculations to Find the Energy Output Per Gram of Fuel

1) You find the mass of fuel burned by subtracting the final mass of fuel and burner from the initial mass of fuel and burner. Simple.
2) The amount of energy transferred to the water is given by:

$$\text{ENERGY TRANSFERRED (in J)} = \text{MASS OF WATER (in g)} \times \text{SPECIFIC HEAT CAPACITY OF WATER (= 4.2)} \times \text{TEMPERATURE CHANGE (in °C)}$$

3) Then the energy given out per gram of fuel is given by:

$$\text{ENERGY GIVEN OUT PER GRAM (in J/g)} = \frac{\text{ENERGY TRANSFERRED (in J)}}{\text{MASS OF FUEL BURNED (in g)}}$$

(This is assuming that all the energy given out by the burning fuel is absorbed by the water.)

Make It a Fair Comparison by Keeping Conditions the Same

1) To compare the energy content of different fuels you need to do the same experiment several times, but using a different fuel in the burner each time.
2) For the comparison to be fair, everything (except the fuel used) should be the same.
3) This means that: (i) you should use the same apparatus, (ii) you should use the same amount of water each time, (iii) the water should start and finish at the same temperature each time.

Hope you've got the energy to revise all this...

In the exam they might give you data from simple calorimetric experiments involving the combustion of fuel to compare, and you'll have to use it to say which fuel releases the most energy. Pretty easy.

Revision Summary for Module C1

Okay, if you were just about to turn the page without doing these revision summary questions, then stop. What kind of an attitude is that... Is that really the way you want to live your life... running, playing and having fun... Of course not. That's right. Do the questions. It's for the best all round.

1)* A molecule has the molecular formula $CH_3(CH_2)_4CH_3$. How many H and C atoms does it contain?
2)* Write down the displayed formula for a molecule with the molecular formula C_3H_8.
3) Write down the symbol equation for magnesium reacting with oxygen.
4)* Balance this equation which shows sodium reacting with water: $Na + H_2O \rightarrow NaOH + H_2$.
5) Why are antioxidants added to food? Give an example of a food containing added antioxidants.
6) What is an emulsifier? Briefly explain how an emulsifier does its job.
7) Give an example of how active packaging can improve food quality.
8) Silica gel sachets are placed into some chilled food packets. Explain how this improves food safety.
9) Explain why we don't eat uncooked potatoes.
10) Give the word equation for the thermal decomposition of baking powder (sodium hydrogencarbonate).
11) Esterification produces an ester and water — what are the reactants?
12) Give three properties that a substance must have in order to make a good perfume.
13) A substance keeps the same volume, but changes its shape according to the container it's held in. Is it a solid, a liquid or a gas? How strong are the forces of attraction between its particles?
14) What does it mean if a liquid is said to be very volatile?
15) In salt water, what is: a) the solute, b) the solution?
16) Explain why nail varnish doesn't dissolve in water.
17) Give three things that polythene is commonly used for.
18) Give one disadvantage of burning plastics and one disadvantage of burying them.
19) Name the monomer that's used to make polythene.
20) Plastic bags stretch and melt easily. Are the forces between the polymer chains weak or strong?
21) Describe a test you can do to tell whether a particular hydrocarbon is an alkane or an alkene.
22) Give the general formula for an alkene containing one double bond.
23) How many covalent bonds are there in a molecule of methane?
24) True or false: in a fractionating column the shortest hydrocarbons leave the column at the bottom.
25) Give three ways that the properties of hydrocarbons change as they increase in size.
26) Why can small hydrocarbon molecules change state from liquid to gas more easily than big ones?
27) What is cracking used for?
28) What two conditions are needed for cracking to happen, and why?
29) Describe two ways in which oil slicks affect wildlife.
30) Give two reasons why the amount of fossil fuel being used is increasing all the time.
31) Give four factors which affect the choice of fuel for a job.
32) Give three advantages of complete combustion over incomplete combustion.
33)* Write down a balanced symbol equation for the incomplete combustion of ethane (C_2H_6).
34) Give an example of: a) an endothermic reaction, b) an exothermic reaction.
35) Is bond breaking an exothermic or an endothermic reaction?
36) Give the formula that you would use to find the amount of energy transferred to the water in a calorimetric experiment.
37) Give three things you should do in order to make sure a calorimetric experiment is as accurate as possible.

* Answers on p.108.

Paints and Pigments

It's not immediately obvious why a section on rocks and metals would start off with a page on paints. But... different minerals in the Earth are different colours, and these minerals have been used as pigments for thousands of years. Put it like that, and it begins to make a bit of sense.

Pigments Give Paints Their Colours

1) Paint usually contains the following bits: solvent, binding medium and pigment.
2) The pigment gives the paint its colour.
3) The binding medium is a liquid that carries the pigment bits and holds them together. When the binding medium turns to solid, it sticks the pigments to the surface you've painted.
4) The solvent is the stuff that keeps the binding medium and pigment runny — as a liquid when it's in the tin or as a paste when it is still in the tube.

Paints are Colloids

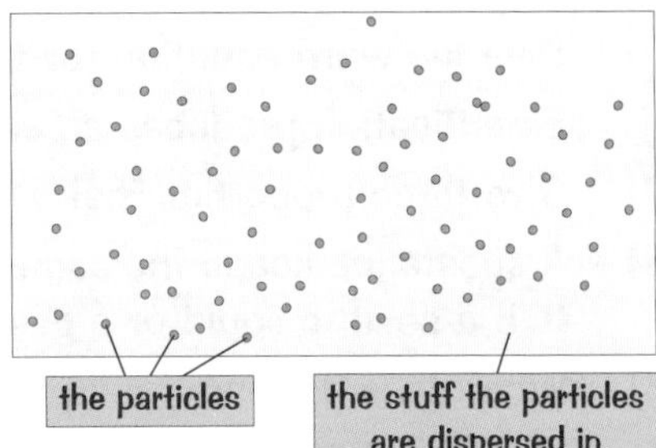

1) A colloid consists of really tiny particles of one kind of stuff dispersed in (mixed in with) another kind of stuff. They're mixed in, but not dissolved.
2) The particles can be bits of solid, droplets of liquid or bubbles of gas.
3) Colloids don't separate out because the particles are so small. They don't settle out at the bottom.
4) In an oil paint, the pigment is in really tiny bits dispersed in the oil. And then the solvent (if there is one — there isn't always) dissolves the oil to keep it all runny.

Some Paints are Water-based and Some are Oil-based

1) Emulsion paints are water-based. The solvent in the paint is water, and the binding medium is usually a polymer such as polyurethane, acrylic or latex.
2) Traditional gloss paint and artists' oil paints are oil-based. This time, the binding material is oil, and the solvent in the paint is an organic compound that'll dissolve oil. Turpentine is used as a solvent for artists' oil paints. Some solvents in oil-based paints produce fumes which can be harmful — it's best to make sure there's plenty of ventilation when using oil-based gloss.
3) Whether you're creating a masterpiece in oils or painting your bedroom wall, you normally brush on the paint as a thin layer. The paint dries as the solvent evaporates. (A thin layer dries a heck of a lot quicker than a thick layer.)
4) With a water-based emulsion, the solvent evaporates, leaving behind the binder and pigment as a thin solid film. A thin layer of emulsion paint dries quite quickly.
5) Oil-based paints take rather longer to dry because the oil has to be oxidised by oxygen in the air before it turns solid.

Some modern gloss paints are water-based.

In the exam, you might be asked to choose the best kind of paint for a job, given some info about paints.

For example, to paint the outside part of a door you'd want a waterproof, hard-wearing paint. Oil-based paints are more hard-wearing than water-based paints, so you'd probably go for an oil-based gloss.

To paint bedroom walls you'd want a paint that goes on easily, dries quickly, and doesn't produce harmful fumes. Water-based emulsion fits the bill here.

The world was black and white before the 1950s — I saw it on TV...

There's heaps of different types of paint — and some are more suitable for certain jobs than others. Like if you're repainting your car, watercolours are definitely not the way to go. And likewise if you painted your little sister's face with gloss paint, your mum would probably ground you for a year.

Dyes and Special Pigments

Dyes dissolve, pigments don't — that's the basic difference between a dye and a pigment.

Dyes are Used to Colour Fabrics

1) Dyes have been used to add colour to fabric for thousands of years. Originally, people made dyes from plants by grinding the plant with water or another solvent and draining off the liquid.
2) Over the past hundred years or so, people have invented heaps of new synthetic dyes.

For example, indigo dye comes from a plant.

The use of these synthetic dyes has increased the number of colours available to colour fabrics. For example, before the 1860s the only really purple dye in the world was made from very rare purple sea snails (sounds bonkers, but it's true), so it was incredibly expensive. Purple clothes were pretty much limited to royalty until synthetic purple dyes were invented in 1856.

Thermochromic Pigments Change Colour When Heated

1) Thermochromic pigments change colour or become transparent when heated or cooled.
2) Different pigments change colour at different temperatures, so a mixture of different pigments can be used to make a colour-coded temperature scale. These are used to make basic thermometers that you stick on your forehead to take your temperature.
3) Thermochromic pigments are used in fancy electric kettles that change colour as the water boils.
4) They're used on drinks mugs to warn when the drink is too hot.
5) They're also used on drinks cans and bottles to indicate when the contents are cold enough to drink.
6) Thermochromic dyes can be used to colour fabrics, which is useful if you want a T-shirt which changes colour when the fabric gets hot.

1) Thermochromic pigments can be mixed with acrylic paint, giving a wide range of colour changes. For example, mixing a blue thermochromic pigment that loses its colour above 27 °C with a yellow acrylic paint would give a paint that's green below 27 °C and yellow above 27 °C.

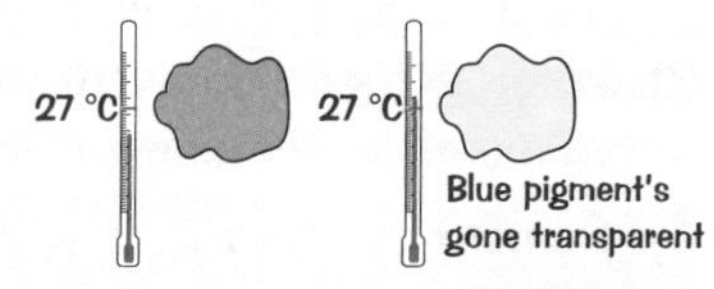

2) These paints are used on novelty mugs. For example, some mugs have a design that changes colour when a hot drink's poured into them.
   Other mugs use a thermochromic pigment that becomes transparent when heated. A picture underneath the paint is only visible when a hot drink is poured in.

Phosphorescent Pigments Glow in the Dark

1) Phosphorescent pigments absorb natural or artificial light and store the energy in their molecules. This energy is released as light over a period of time — from a few seconds to a couple of hours.
2) An obvious use is a watch or clock with glow-in-the-dark hands.
3) Other uses include traffic signs, emergency exit signs, toys and novelty decorations.
4) Glow-in-the-dark watches used to be made with radioactive paints. These paints would glow for years without needing to be "charged up" by putting 'em in the light. Unfortunately, a lot of them weren't very safe, and could give quite a dose of atomic radiation. Phosphorescent pigments were developed as a much safer alternative.

Thermochromic pigments — the truth behind mood rings...

For a brief spell in the early 1990s colour-changing T-shirts were reeeeally cool. Although I was never quite sure why you'd want to show the world just how hot and sweaty your armpits were. Glow-in-the-dark erasers too... I mean... when do you *ever* need to rub out mistakes in the dark?

Construction Materials

Loads of different construction materials are made from stuff found on or just under the Earth's surface. For example, there are metals like aluminium and iron, rocks such as granite, limestone and marble, and then there are man-made materials like bricks, cement, concrete and glass.

Aluminium and Iron are Extracted from Ores in Rocks

Rocks are usually a mixture of minerals. Ores are minerals we can get useful materials from. Aluminium and iron are construction materials that can be extracted from their ores.

Glass is Made by Melting Limestone, Sand and Soda

1) Just heat up limestone (calcium carbonate) with sand (silicon dioxide) and soda (sodium carbonate) until it melts.
2) When the mixture cools it comes out as glass. It's as easy as that. Eat your heart out Mr Pilkington.

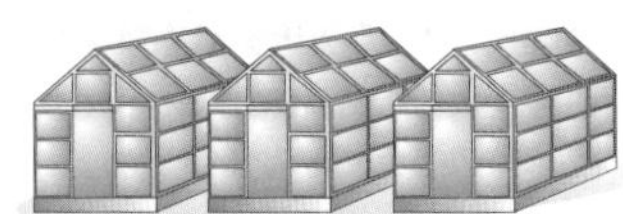

Bricks are Made from Clay

1) Clay is a mineral formed from weathered and decomposed rock. It's soft when it's dug up out of the ground, which makes it easy to mould into bricks.
2) But it can be hardened by firing at very high temperatures. This makes it ideal as a building material — bricks can withstand the weight of lots more bricks on top of them.

Limestone and Clay are Heated to Make Cement

1) Clay contains aluminium and silicates.
2) Powdered clay and powdered limestone are roasted in a rotating kiln to produce a complex mixture of calcium and aluminium silicates, called cement.
3) When cement is mixed with water a slow chemical reaction takes place. This causes the cement to gradually set hard.
4) Cement can be mixed with sand, gravel and water to make concrete.
5) Concrete is a very quick and cheap way of constructing buildings — and it shows... — concrete has got to be the most hideously unattractive building material ever known.
6) Reinforced concrete is a "composite material" — it's a combination of concrete and steel rods. It's a better construction material than ordinary concrete because it combines the hardness of concrete with the strength of steel, but it isn't any prettier than plain old concrete.

Extracting Rocks Can Cause Environmental Damage

1) Quarrying uses up land and destroys habitats. It costs money to make quarry sites look pretty again.
2) Transporting rock can cause noise and pollution.
3) The quarrying process itself produces dust and makes a lot of noise — they often use dynamite to blast the rock out of the ground.
4) The waste materials from mines and quarries produce unsightly tips.
5) Disused sites can be dangerous. Every year people drown in former quarries that have been turned into (very very deep) lakes. Disused mines have been known to collapse — this can cause subsidence (including huge holes appearing and buildings cracking, railway lines twisting etc.).

Bricks are like eggs — they both have to be laid...

If red houses are made of red bricks and blue houses are made of blue bricks, then what colour bricks are greenhouses made of? If you said green, then you're not properly awake and most likely you need to go back and read the page again. If you correctly identified that a greenhouse is made of glass rather than green bricks, then continue to the next page. Once you've learnt all the above, obviously.

Extracting Pure Copper

Copper is often dug out of the ground as an ore called malachite. In theory, the copper could be extracted by reducing it with carbon (unreactive metals can often be extracted from ores by a process called reduction). The problem is that the copper produced by reduction isn't pure enough for use in electrical conductors. And the purer it is, the better it conducts. So another method is usually used...

Electrolysis is Used to Obtain Very Pure Copper

1) Electrolysis means "splitting up with electricity".
2) It requires a liquid (called the electrolyte) which will conduct electricity. Electrolytes are usually free ions dissolved in water. Copper(II) sulfate solution is the electrolyte used in purifying copper — it contains Cu^{2+} ions.
3) The electrical supply acts like an electron pump:

> 1) It pulls electrons off copper atoms at the anode, causing them to go into solution as Cu^{2+} ions.
> 2) It then offers electrons at the cathode to nearby Cu^{2+} ions to turn them back into copper atoms.
> 3) The impurities are dropped at the anode as a sludge, whilst pure copper atoms bond to the cathode.
> 4) The electrolysis can go on for weeks and the cathode is often twenty times bigger at the end of it.

The cathode is the negative electrode. It starts as a thin piece of pure copper and more pure copper adds to it.

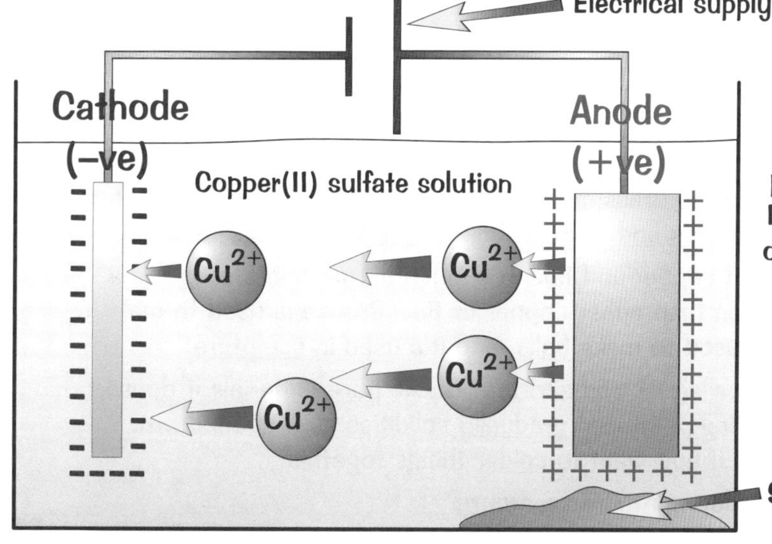

The anode is the positive electrode. It's just a big lump of impure (boulder) copper, which will dissolve.

Pure copper is deposited on the pure cathode (–ve)

The reaction at the cathode is:

$$Cu^{2+}_{(aq)} + 2e^- \rightarrow Cu_{(s)}$$

Copper dissolves from the impure anode (+ve)

The reaction at the anode is:

$$Cu_{(s)} \rightarrow Cu^{2+}_{(aq)} + 2e^-$$

Recycling Copper Saves Money and Resources

1) It's cheaper to recycle copper than it is to mine and extract new copper.
2) Recycling copper uses only 15% of the energy that'd be used to mine and extract the same amount. So recycling copper helps to conserve the world's supply of fossil fuels, and reduces carbon dioxide emissions. Hurrah.

Revision and Electrolysis — they can both go on for weeks...

Electrolysis ain't cheap — it takes a lot of electricity, which costs money. It's the only way of getting pure enough copper for electrical wires though, so it's worth it. This isn't such a bad page to learn — try writing a mini-essay about it. Don't forget to have a go at drawing the diagram from memory too.

Alloys

Different metals have different properties, but by combining them with other elements you can create a new material that keeps some of the properties of the original materials, and has some extra properties too.

An Alloy is a Mixture of a Metal and Other Elements

1) Alloys can be a mixture of two or more different metals (like brass or bronze).
2) They can also be a mixture of a metal and a non-metal (like steel).
3) Alloys often have properties that are different from the metals they are made from — and these new properties often make the alloy more useful than the pure metal.

Steel is an Alloy of Iron and Carbon

1) Steel is harder than iron.
2) Steel is also stronger than iron, as long as the amount of carbon does not get larger than about 1%.
3) Iron on its own will rust fairly quickly, but steel is much less likely to rust. A small amount of carbon makes a big difference.
4) A lot of things are made from steel — girders, bridges, engine parts, cutlery, washing machines, saucepans, ships, drill bits, cars etc. There's more about steel in car manufacture on the next page.

Brass, Bronze, Solder and Amalgam are also Alloys

1) Brass is an alloy of copper and zinc. Most of the properties of brass are just a mixture of those of the copper and zinc, although brass is harder than either of them. Brass is used for making brass musical instruments (trumpets, trombones, French horns etc.). It's also used for fixtures and fittings such as screws, springs, doorknobs etc.
2) Bronze is an alloy of copper and tin. It's much harder and stronger than tin, and it's more resistant to corrosion than either copper or tin. Bronze is used to make springs and motor bearings. It's also used to make bells, and it's used in sculpture.
3) Solder is usually an alloy of lead and tin. Unlike pure materials it doesn't have a definite melting point, but gradually solidifies as it cools down. This is pretty useful if you want to solder things together.
4) An amalgam is an alloy containing mercury. A large-scale use of one kind of amalgam is in dentistry, for filling teeth.

   Modern fillings tend to be made from tooth-coloured resin instead. This is partly because amalgam fillings are dark silvery in colour and therefore rather obvious in your mouth, and partly because some people worry that the mercury in the amalgam could cause health problems (although there's not much evidence for this).

Some Alloys are Smart

1) Nitinol is the name given to a family of alloys of nickel and titanium that have shape memory.
2) This means they "remember" their original shape, and go back to it even after being bent and twisted.
3) This has increased the number of uses for alloys. You can get specs with Nitinol frames — these can be bent and even sat on and they still go back into their original shape.

I eat bits of metal all day — it's my staple diet...

You need metals or alloys with different properties for different uses. For example, to make an engine part that's going to get very hot, you need to use something with a high melting point. And if you're building an aircraft you're going to need something that's strong and light. If you get a question in the exam about what alloy is best for a particular job, just use a bit of common sense and you'll be fine.

Building Cars

There are loads of different materials in your average car — different materials have different properties and so have different uses. Makes sense.

Iron and Steel Corrode Much More than Aluminium

Iron corrodes easily. In other words, it rusts. The word "rust" is only used for the corrosion of iron, not other metals.

Rusting only happens when the iron's in contact with both oxygen (from the air) and water.

The chemical reaction that takes place when iron corrodes is an oxidation reaction. The iron gains oxygen to form iron(III) oxide. Water then becomes loosely bonded to the iron(III) oxide and the result is hydrated iron(III) oxide — which we call rust.

Learn the word equation for the reaction: **Iron + oxygen + water → hydrated iron(III) oxide**

Unfortunately, rust is a soft crumbly solid that soon flakes off to leave more iron available to rust again.

And if the water's salty or acidic, rusting will take place a lot quicker. Cars in coastal places rust a lot because they get covered in salty sea-spray. Cars in dry deserty places hardly rust at all.

Aluminium doesn't corrode when it's wet. This is a bit odd because aluminium is more reactive than iron. What happens is that the aluminium reacts very quickly with oxygen in the air to form aluminium oxide. A nice protective layer of aluminium oxide sticks firmly to the aluminium below and stops any further reaction taking place (the oxide isn't crumbly and flaky like rust, so it won't fall off).

Car Bodies: Aluminium or Steel?

Aluminium has two big advantages over steel:

1) It has a much lower density, so the car body of an aluminium car will be lighter than the same car made of steel. This gives the aluminium car much better fuel economy, which saves fuel resources.
2) A car body made with aluminium corrodes less and so it'll have a longer lifetime.

But aluminium has a massive disadvantage. It costs an awful lot more than steel. This is why car manufacturers build cars out of steel — comes down to money.

Also, you can't weld two bits of aluminium together, you have to use fiddly little rivets. Steel welds easily.

You Need Various Materials to Build Different Bits of a Car

1) Steel is strong and it can be hammered into sheets and welded together — good for the bodywork.
2) Copper's a good electrical conductor and can be pulled into wires — it's used for the electrical wiring.
3) Aluminium's strong and has a low density — it's used for parts of the engine, to reduce weight.
4) Glass is transparent — cars need windscreens and windows.
5) Plastics are light and hardwearing, so they're used as internal coverings for doors, dashboards etc. They're also electrical insulators, used for covering electrical wires.
6) Fibres (natural and synthetic) are hard-wearing, so they're used to cover the seats and floor.

Unless you can afford leather seats, that is.

Recycling Cars is Important

1) As with all recycling, the idea is to save natural resources, save money and reduce landfill use.
2) At the moment a lot of the metal from a scrap car is recycled, though most of the other materials (e.g. plastics, rubber etc.) go into landfill. But European laws are now in place saying that 85% of the materials in a car (rising to 95% of a car by 2015) must be recyclable.
3) The biggest problem with recycling all the non-metal bits of a car is that they have to be separated before they can be recycled. Sorting out different types of plastic is a pain in the neck.

My Mini wants to be a Porsche in its next life...

When manufacturers choose materials for cars, they have to weigh up alternatives — they balance safety, environmental impact, and cost. In the exam, you could be asked to do the same. Sounds fun.

The Three Different Types of Rock

You can use rocks (or stuff in them) to make all sorts of things, but not all rocks are the same. Scientists classify rocks according to how they're formed. The three different types are: sedimentary, metamorphic and igneous. Sedimentary rocks are generally pretty soft, while igneous rocks are well hard.

There are Three Steps in the Formation of Sedimentary Rock

1) Sedimentary rocks are formed from layers of sediment laid down in lakes or seas.
2) Over millions of years the layers get buried under more layers and the weight pressing down squeezes out the water.
3) Fluids flowing through the pores deposit natural mineral cement.

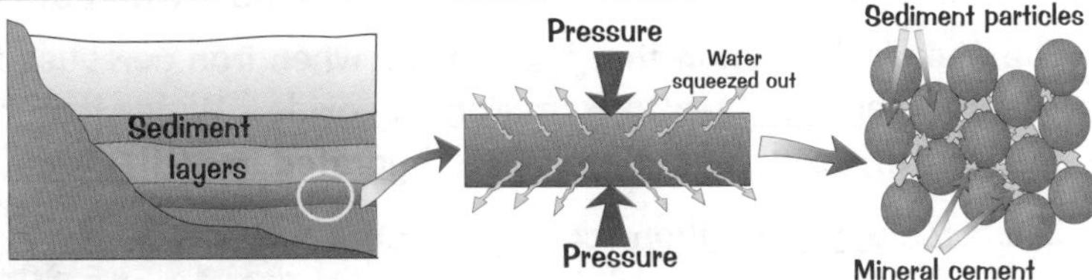

Limestone is a Sedimentary Rock Formed from Seashells

1) Limestone is mostly formed from seashells. It's mostly calcium carbonate and grey/white in colour. The original shells are mostly crushed, but there can still be quite a few fossilised shells remaining.
2) When limestone is heated it thermally decomposes to make calcium oxide and carbon dioxide:

Calcium carbonate → calcium oxide + carbon dioxide

$$CaCO_3(s) \rightarrow CaO(s) + CO_2(g)$$

Thermal decomposition is when one substance chemically breaks down into at least two new substances when it's heated.

Metamorphic Rocks are Formed from Other Rocks

1) Metamorphic rocks are formed by the action of heat and pressure on sedimentary (or even igneous) rocks over long periods of time.
2) The mineral structure and texture may be different, but the chemical composition is often the same.
3) So long as the rocks don't actually melt they're classed as metamorphic. If they melt and turn to magma, they're gone (though they may eventually resurface as igneous rocks — see below).

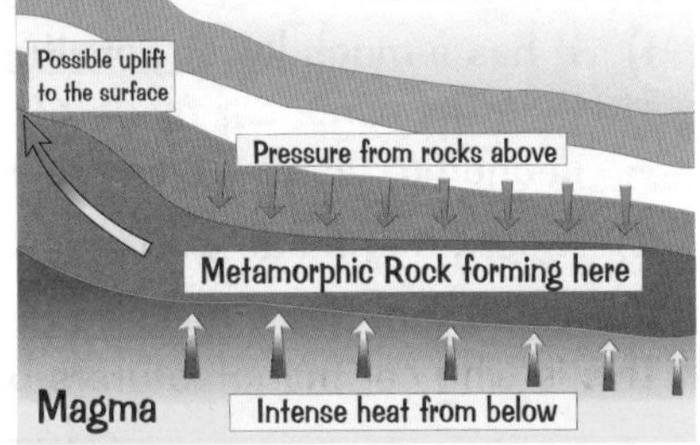

Marble is a Metamorphic Rock Formed from Limestone

Marble is another form of calcium carbonate. Very high temperatures break down the limestone and it reforms as small crystals. This gives marble a more even texture and makes it much harder.

Igneous Rocks are Formed from Fresh Magma

1) Igneous rocks form when molten magma pushes up into the crust (or right through it) before cooling and solidifying. They contain various different minerals in randomly arranged interlocking crystals.
2) There are two types of igneous rocks, extrusive and intrusive:

EXTRUSIVE igneous rocks cool QUICKLY ABOVE GROUND, forming SMALL crystals, e.g. basalt and rhyolite.

INTRUSIVE igneous rocks cool SLOWLY UNDERGROUND, forming BIG crystals, e.g. granite and gabbro.

Extrusive igneous — cools above ground

Intrusive igneous — cools underground and eventually gets exposed by erosion

Molten magma rises up

Granite is very hard (even harder than marble). It's ideal for steps and buildings.

Igneous rocks are real cool — or they're magma...

The extrusive igneous rock basalt is made of the same minerals as the intrusive rock gabbro — they both contain lots of iron. But gabbro is coarser than basalt because it cools slower, giving it bigger crystals. Rhyolite and its coarser brother granite are made of the same stuff too — they both contain lots of silicon.

The Earth's Structure

It's tricky to study the structure of the Earth — you can't just dig down to the Earth's centre. But after studying the evidence, this is what scientists think is down there...

Crust, Mantle, Outer and Inner Core

1) The crust is Earth's thin outer layer of solid rock (its average depth is about 20 km). There are two types of crust — continental crust (forming the land), and oceanic crust (under oceans).
2) The lithosphere includes the crust and upper part of the mantle below, and is made up of a jigsaw of 'plates'. The lithosphere is relatively cold and rigid, and is over 100 km thick in places.
3) The mantle extends from the crust almost halfway to the centre of the Earth. It's got all the properties of a solid but it can flow very slowly. As you go deeper into the mantle the temperature increases and it becomes less rigid.
4) The core is just over half the Earth's radius. It's mostly iron and nickel, and is where the Earth's magnetic field originates.
5) The inner core is solid, while the outer core is liquid.
6) Radioactive decay creates a lot of the heat inside the Earth.
7) This heat causes convection currents, which cause the plates of the lithosphere to move (which is bad news for some people — see below).

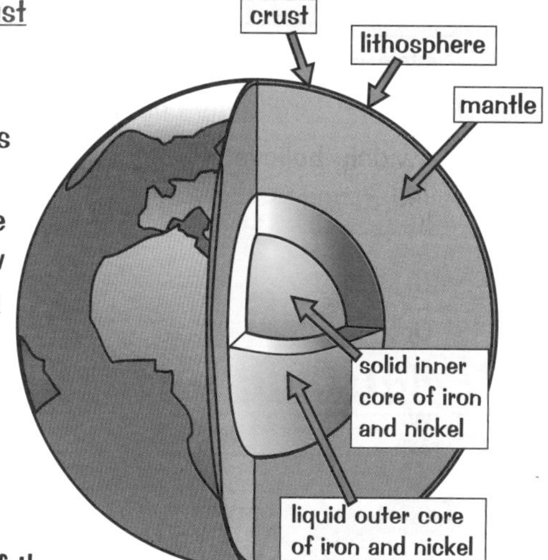

The Earth's Surface is Made Up of Large Plates of Rock

1) These so-called tectonic plates are like big rafts that float on the mantle (they're less dense than the mantle).
2) This map shows the edges of these plates. As they move, the continents move too.
3) Most of the plates are moving at a speed of about 1 cm or 2 cm per year.
4) Volcanoes and earthquakes often occur where the plates meet (see p.29). It's the movement of the plates that causes them. The locations of some major earthquakes and volcanoes are shown below.

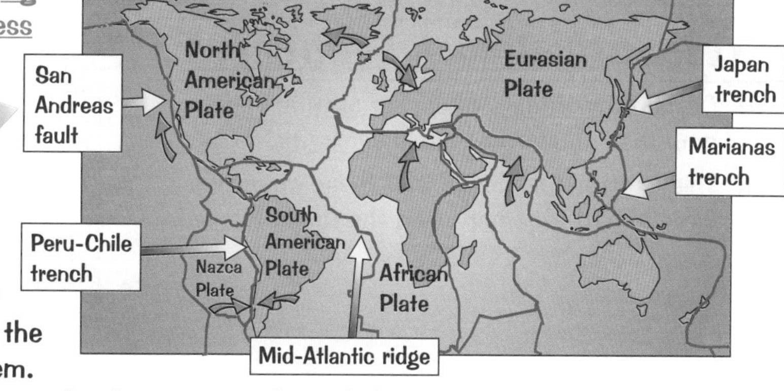

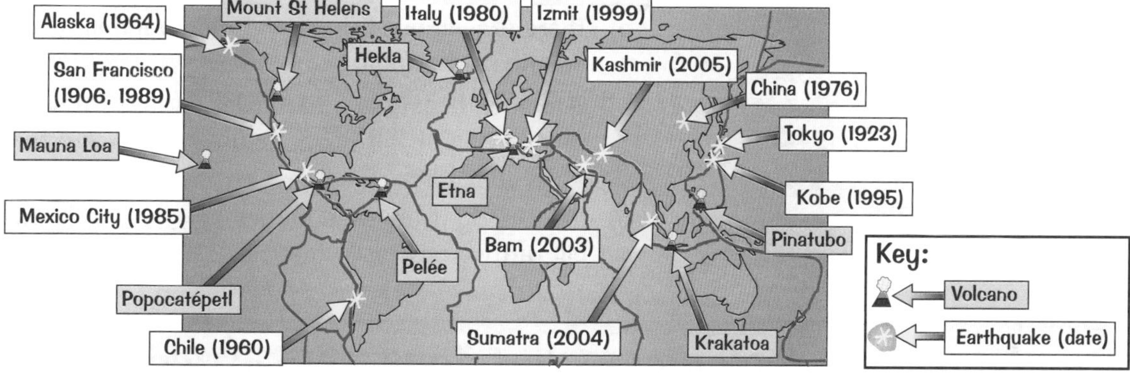

1 or 2 cm a year — that's as fast as your fingernails grow...

The lithosphere of our little blue and green planet is pretty active, and is responsible for a fair amount of trouble. Make sure you know all about plate tectonics (the theory of the large rocky rafts and what causes them to move around) — there's lots more coming up...

Evidence for Plate Tectonics

A bloke called Alfred Wegener put forward his theory about the Earth's continents slowly drifting along in 1915, but not many people believed it. This was partly because he didn't have a good explanation for why it happened, partly because he wasn't a qualified geologist, and partly because the theory was so weird. But the truth will out, as they say — and the evidence now suggests the 'rocky raft' idea is correct.

1) Jigsaw Fit — the Supercontinent 'Pangaea'

a) There's a very obvious jigsaw fit between Africa and South America.
b) The other continents can also be fitted in without too much trouble.
c) It's widely believed that they once all formed a single land mass, now called Pangaea.

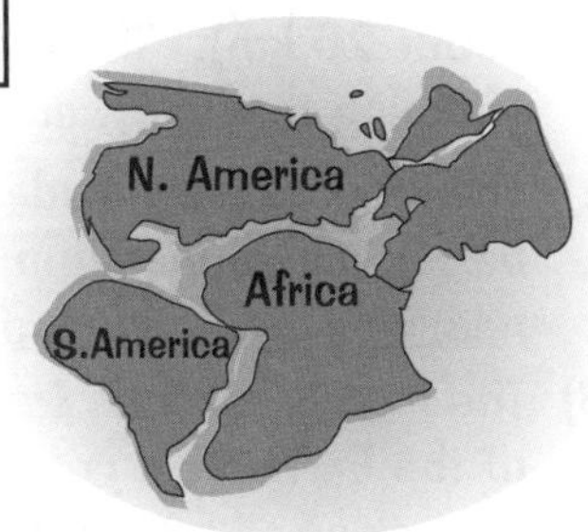

2) Matching Fossils in Africa and South America

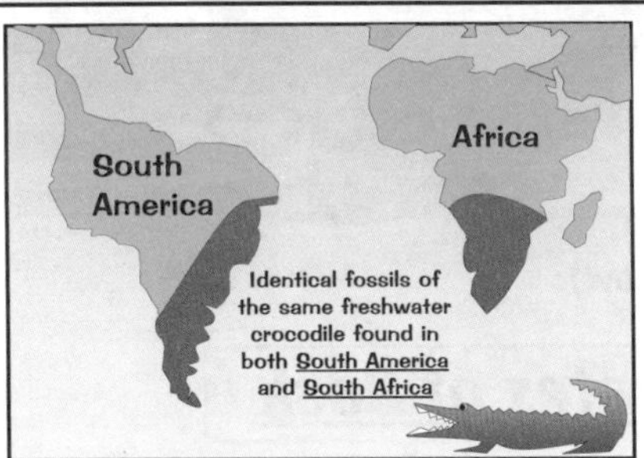

a) Identical plant fossils of the same age have been found in rocks in South Africa, Australia, Antarctica, India and South America, which strongly suggests they were all joined once upon a time.
b) Animal fossils support the theory too. There are identical fossils of a freshwater crocodile found in both Brazil and South Africa. It certainly didn't swim across.

3) Identical Rock Sequences

a) Certain rock layers of similar ages in various countries show remarkable similarity.
b) This is strong evidence that these countries were joined together when the rocks formed.

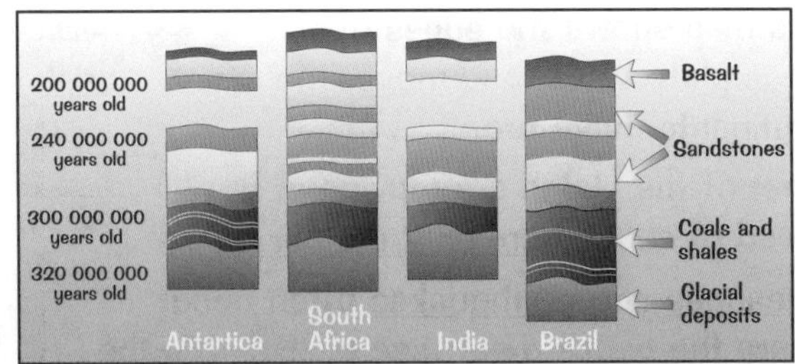

4) Living Creatures: The Earthworm

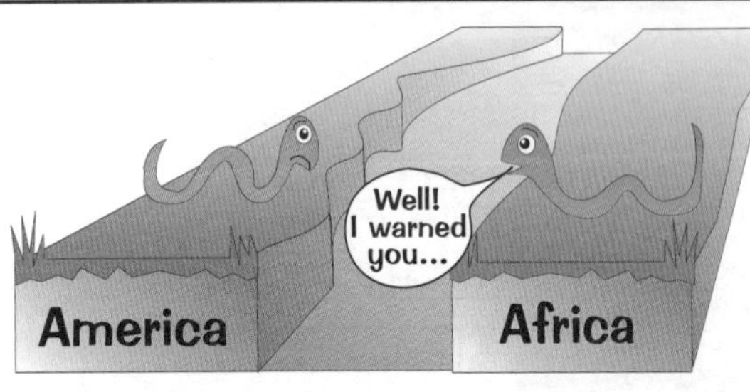

a) There are various living creatures found in both America and Africa.
b) One such beasty is a particular earthworm which is found living at the tip of South America and the tip of South Africa.
c) Most likely it travelled across ever so slowly on the big raft we now call America.

Learn about plate tectonics — but don't get carried away...

So there you go. Alfred Wegener's ideas were originally thought to be bonkers (the fact that he'd used some inaccurate data didn't help — one scientist claimed that the forces Wegener's theory needed would have stopped the Earth rotating). But as technology improved and more evidence was gathered (including from the bottom of the ocean), it turned out that Wegener's ideas were pretty convincing after all. But it took a while — it was only in the 1960s that scientists really accepted the theory.

Volcanic Eruptions

The theory of plate tectonics not only explains why the continents move, it also makes sense of natural hazards such as volcanoes and earthquakes.

Volcanoes are Formed by Molten Rock

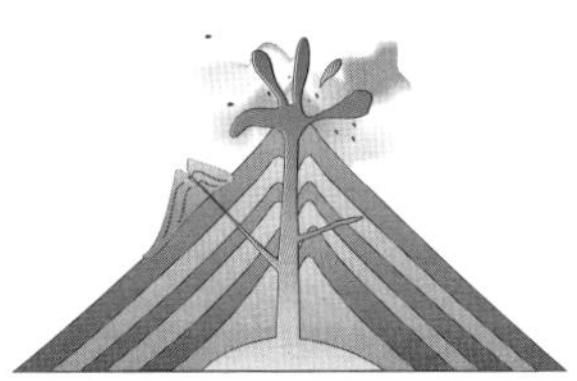

1) Volcanoes occur when molten rock from the mantle emerges through the Earth's crust.
2) Magma less dense than the crust rises up (through the crust) and 'boils over' where it can — sometimes quite violently if the pressure is released suddenly. (When the molten rock is below the surface of the Earth it's called magma — but when it erupts from a volcano it's called lava.)

Oceanic and Continental Crust Colliding Causes Volcanoes

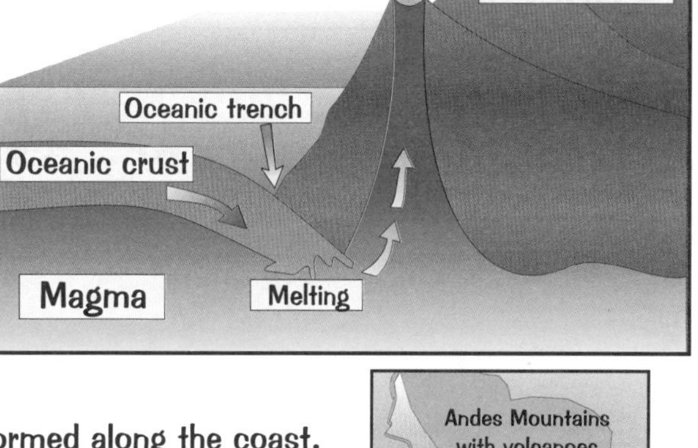

1) Oceanic crust is denser than continental crust. When the two types of crust collide, the oceanic crust is always forced underneath the continental crust. This is called subduction.
2) As the oceanic crust is pushed down it melts and starts to rise.
3) If this molten rock finds its way to the surface, volcanoes form.
4) There are also earthquakes as the two plates slowly grind past each other.
5) Where the oceanic crust is forced down, you get a deep trench on the ocean floor.
6) And as the continental crust crumples, mountains are formed along the coast.
7) The classic example of all this is the west coast of South America where the Andes mountains are. That region has all the features:

Volcanoes, earthquakes, an oceanic trench and mountains.

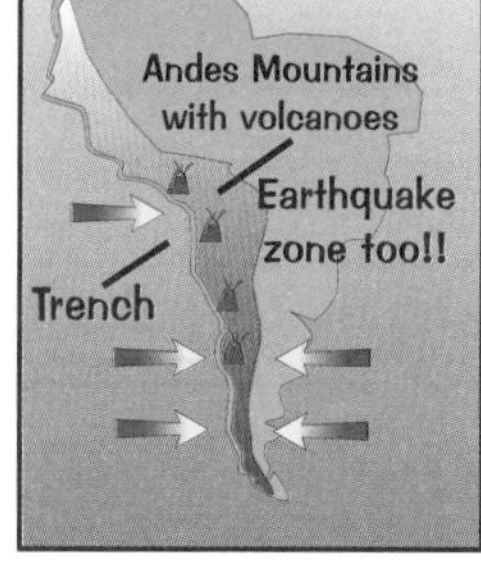

Volcanic Activity Forms Igneous Rock

1) Igneous rock is made when any sort of molten rock cools down and solidifies. Lots of rocks on the surface of the Earth were formed this way (see also p.26).
2) The type of igneous rock (and the behaviour of the volcano) depends on the composition of the magma and how quickly the magma cools.
3) Some volcanoes produce magma that forms iron-rich basalt. The lava from the eruption is runny, and the eruption is fairly safe. (As safe as you can be with molten rock at 1200 °C, I suppose.)
4) But if the magma is silica-rich rhyolite, the eruption is explosive. It produces pumice, volcanic ash and "bombs" (lumps of magma that get violently blown out of the volcano). Crikey.
5) Sometimes the lumps of pumice and ash that come from a volcanic explosion form layers of different sized pieces. Bigger fragments are usually on the bottom, and smaller fragments are on the top. These layers are called graded beds.

Make the Earth move for you — stand next to a volcano...

It might seem silly that some people choose to live close to volcanoes, but there are benefits — volcanic ash creates very fertile soil that's great for farming. It would be safer if eruptions could be predicted really accurately, but geologists aren't there yet. However, they have got much better recently — their computer models describing eruptions are much more sophisticated than in the old days, which helps.

The Evolution of the Atmosphere

The atmosphere wasn't always like it is today. It's gradually evolved over billions of years and we have evolved with it. All very slowly. Here's one theory for how the first 4.5 billion years have gone:

Phase 1 — Volcanoes Gave Out Steam and CO_2

1) The Earth's surface was originally molten for many millions of years. Any atmosphere boiled away.
2) Eventually it cooled and a thin crust formed, but volcanoes kept erupting, releasing many gases. This 'degassing' released mainly carbon dioxide, but also steam and ammonia.
3) When things eventually settled down, the early atmosphere was mostly CO_2 and water vapour (the water vapour later condensed to form the oceans). There was very little oxygen.

Holiday report: Not a nice place to be. Take strong walking boots and a good coat.

Phase 2 — Green Plants Evolved and Produced Oxygen

1) A lot of the early CO_2 dissolved into the oceans.
2) Green plants later evolved over most of the Earth. As they photosynthesised, they helped to steadily remove CO_2 and produce O_2.
3) Much of the CO_2 from the air thus became locked up in fossil fuels and sedimentary rocks.
4) Nitrogen gas was put into the atmosphere in two ways — it was formed by ammonia reacting with oxygen, and was released by denitrifying bacteria.

Holiday Report: A bit slimy underfoot. Take wellies and a lot of suncream.

Phase 3 — Ozone Layer Allows Evolution of Complex Animals

1) The build-up of oxygen in the atmosphere killed off early organisms that couldn't tolerate it.
2) But it did allow the evolution of more complex organisms that made use of the oxygen.
3) The oxygen also created the ozone layer (O_3), which blocked harmful rays from the Sun and enabled even more complex organisms to evolve.
4) There is virtually no CO_2 left now.

Holiday report: A nice place to be. Get there before the crowds ruin it.

Today's Atmosphere is Just Right for Us

The present composition of the atmosphere is:

78% nitrogen, 21% oxygen and 0.035% carbon dioxide

There are also: 1) Varying amounts of water vapour,
2) And noble gases (mainly argon).

4 billion years ago, it was a whole other world...

It's amazing how much the atmosphere has changed. The climate change we talk about nowadays is small beer in comparison (though massively important to us).

The Carbon Cycle

It's all over the news — you can't miss it. Environmentalists, scientists and even the Government now believe that human activities are changing the proportion of carbon dioxide in the atmosphere — and that that's having massive effects on life as we know it on Planet Earth.

You need to understand all the science behind the headlines — starting with the carbon cycle.

Carbon is Constantly Being Recycled

Carbon is the key to the greenhouse effect — it exists in the atmosphere as carbon dioxide gas, and is also present in many other greenhouse gases (e.g. methane).

1) The carbon on Earth moves in a big cycle — the diagram below is a pretty good summary.
2) Respiration, combustion (p.16) and decay of plants and animals add carbon dioxide to the air and remove oxygen.
3) Photosynthesis does the opposite — it removes carbon dioxide and adds oxygen.
4) These processes should balance out. However, humans have upset the natural carbon cycle, which has affected the balance of gases in the atmosphere.

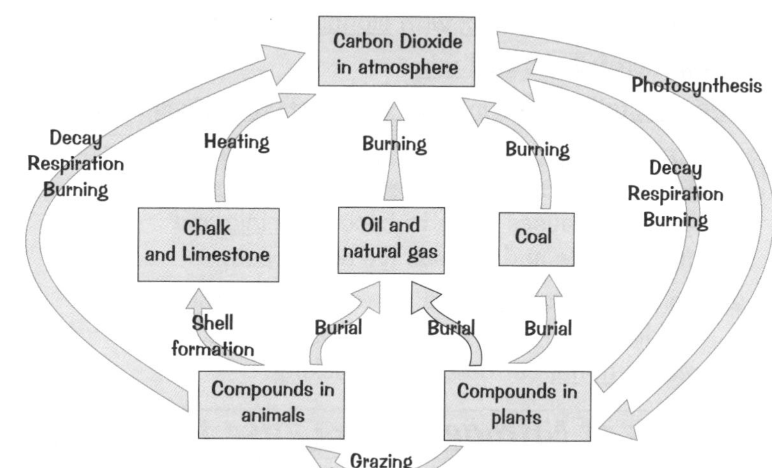

Human Activity Affects the Composition of Air

1) The human population is increasing. This means there are more people respiring — giving out more carbon dioxide. But that's not the half of it...
2) More people means that more energy is needed for lighting, heating, cooking, transport and so on. And people's lifestyles are changing too. More and more countries are becoming industrialised and well-off. This means the average energy demand per person is also increasing (since people have more electrical gadgets at home, more people have cars, and more people travel on planes, etc.). This increased energy consumption comes mainly from the burning of fossil fuels, which releases more carbon dioxide.

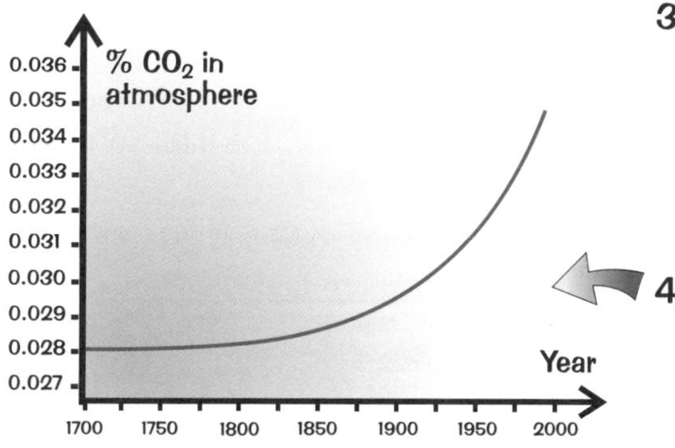

3) More people also means more land is needed to build houses and grow food. This space is often made by chopping down trees. But plants are the main things taking carbon dioxide out of the atmosphere (as they photosynthesise) — so fewer plants means less carbon dioxide is taken out of the atmosphere.
4) The graph shows how CO_2 levels in the atmosphere have risen over the last 150 years.

Eeeek — the carbon cycle's got a puncture...

For each person on a one-way flight from London to New York, a whopping 600 kg of carbon dioxide is added to the air. If you feel bad about the amount of carbon dioxide that flying off on your holidays releases, you can balance it by paying for trees to be planted. There are companies that'll tell you just how many trees need to be planted to balance the carbon dioxide released by your flight.

Air Pollution and Acid Rain

Carbon dioxide levels are causing climate change. But CO_2 isn't the only gas released when fossil fuels burn — you also get other nasties like carbon monoxide, oxides of nitrogen and sulfur dioxide.

Acid Rain is Caused by Sulfur Dioxide and Oxides of Nitrogen

1) When fossil fuels are burned they release mostly CO_2 (a big cause of the greenhouse effect).
2) But they also release other harmful gases — especially sulfur dioxide and various nitrogen oxides.
3) The sulfur dioxide (SO_2) comes from sulfur impurities in the fossil fuels.
4) However, the nitrogen oxides are created from a reaction between the nitrogen and oxygen in the air, caused by the heat of the burning. (This can happen in the internal combustion engines of cars.)
5) When these gases mix with clouds they form dilute sulfuric acid and dilute nitric acid.
6) This then falls as acid rain.
7) Power stations and internal combustion engines in cars are the main causes of acid rain.

Acid Rain Kills Fish, Trees and Statues

1) Acid rain causes lakes to become acidic and many plants and animals die as a result.
2) Acid rain kills trees and damages limestone buildings and ruins stone statues. It also makes metal corrode. It's shocking.

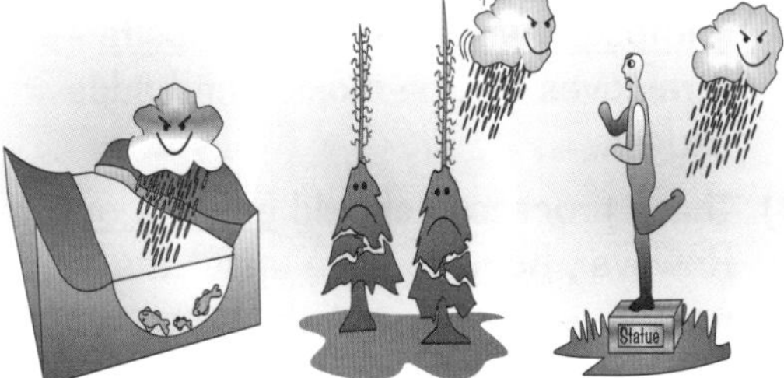

Oxides of Nitrogen Also Cause Photochemical Smog

Photochemical smog is a type of air pollution caused by sunlight acting on oxides of nitrogen. These oxides combine with oxygen in the air to produce ozone (O_3). Ozone can cause breathing difficulties, headaches and tiredness. (Don't confuse ground-level ozone with the useful ozone layer high up in the atmosphere.)

Carbon Monoxide is a Poisonous Gas

1) Carbon monoxide (CO) can stop your blood doing its proper job of carrying oxygen around the body.
2) A lack of oxygen in the blood can lead to fainting, a coma or even death.
3) Carbon monoxide is formed when petrol or diesel in car engines is burnt without enough oxygen — this is incomplete combustion (see page 16 for more details).

It's Important That Atmospheric Pollution is Controlled

1) The build-up of all these pollutants can make life unhealthy and miserable for many humans, animals and plants. The number of cases of respiratory illnesses (e.g. asthma) has increased in recent years — especially among young people. Many people blame atmospheric pollution for this, so efforts are being made to improve things.
2) Catalytic converters on motor vehicles reduce the amount of carbon monoxide and nitrogen oxides getting into the atmosphere. The catalyst is normally a mixture of platinum and rhodium.
   It helps unpleasant exhaust gases from the car react to make things that are less immediately dangerous (though more CO_2 is still not exactly ideal).

   Carbon monoxide + Nitrogen oxide → nitrogen + carbon dioxide

   $$2CO + 2NO \rightarrow N_2 + 2CO_2$$
3) And Flue Gas Desulfurisation (FGD) technology in some fossil-fuel power stations removes sulfur dioxide from the exhaust gases.

Revision and pollution — the two bugbears of modern life...

Eeee.... cars and fossil fuels — they're nowt but trouble. But at least this topic is kind of interesting, what with its relevance to everyday life and all. Just think... you could see this kind of stuff on TV.

Chemical Reaction Rates

The rate of a chemical reaction is how fast the reactants are changed into products (the reaction is over when one of the reactants is completely used up). Scientists like to know what affects the rate of a reaction — if they can understand it, then maybe they can control it. This knowledge is particularly useful in the chemical industry — the faster you make chemicals, the faster you make money.

Reactions Can Go at All Sorts of Different Rates

1) One of the slowest is the rusting of iron (it's not slow enough though — what about my little MGB).
2) Other slow reactions include chemical weathering — like acid rain damage to limestone buildings.
3) An example of a moderate speed reaction is a metal (e.g. magnesium) reacting with acid to produce a gentle stream of bubbles.
4) Burning is a fast reaction, but an explosion is really fast and releases a lot of gas. Explosive reactions are all over in a fraction of a second.

You Can Do an Experiment to Follow a Reaction

The rate of a reaction that produces a gas can be observed by measuring how quickly the gas is produced. There are two ways of doing this:

MEASURE THE CHANGE IN MASS

If you carry out the reaction on a balance, the mass will fall as the gas is released. You need to take readings of the mass at regular time intervals.

MEASURE THE VOLUME OF GAS GIVEN OFF

This method is pretty similar, except you use a gas syringe to measure the volume of gas given off after regular time intervals.

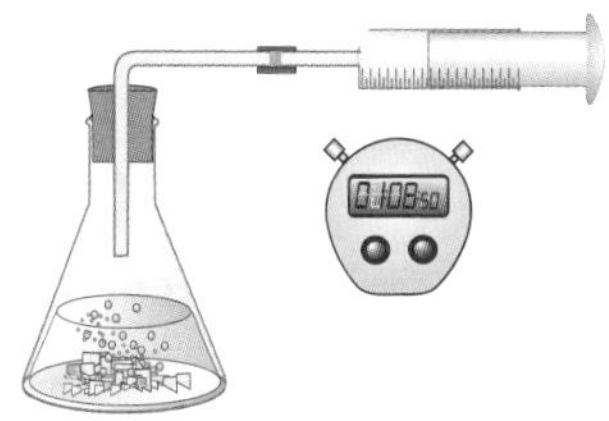

Whichever of these methods you use, you can plot your results on a graph. P.35 shows you the type of graph you'll get and what it shows.

Particles Must Collide with Enough Energy in Order to React

Reaction rates are explained perfectly by collision theory. It's really simple.

It just says that the rate of a chemical reaction simply depends on how often and how hard the reacting particles collide with each other. The basic idea is that particles have to collide in order to react, and they have to collide with enough energy as well.

The Rate of a Reaction Depends on Four Things

1) TEMPERATURE
2) CONCENTRATION — (or PRESSURE for gases)
3) CATALYST
4) SIZE OF PARTICLES — (or SURFACE AREA)

LEARN THEM!

And then read the next page to find out more about them.

Get a fast, furious reaction — tickle your teacher...

First off... remember that the amount of product you get depends on the amount of reactants you start with. So all this stuff about the rate of a reaction is only talking about how quickly your products form — not how much of them you get. It's an important difference — so get your head round it asap.

Collision Theory

The last page told you the four things the rate of a reaction depends on — temperature, concentration (or pressure for gases), the presence of a catalyst and the size of the particles. This page tells you the theory explaining why these things affect the reaction rate. Wowzers.

More Collisions Increases the Rate of Reaction

Reactions happen if particles collide. So if you increase the number of collisions, the reaction happens more quickly. Now then... all four factors from p.33 lead to more collisions... (Well, a catalyst's a bit different, I guess — there are the same number of collisions, it's just that more of them lead to a reaction.)

1) Increasing the TEMPERATURE Means the Particles are Going Faster

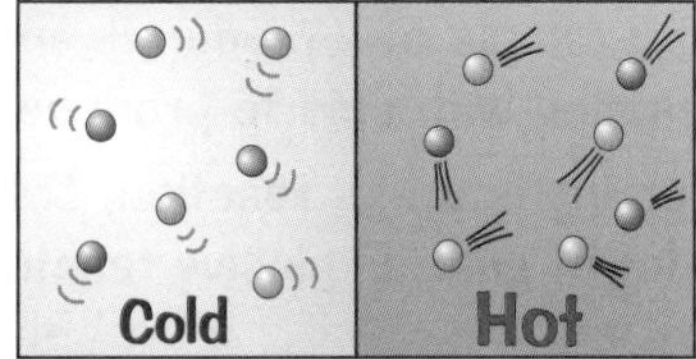

When the temperature is increased the particles all move quicker. If they're moving quicker, they're going to have more collisions.

2) Increasing the CONCENTRATION (or PRESSURE) Means the Particles are More Crowded Together

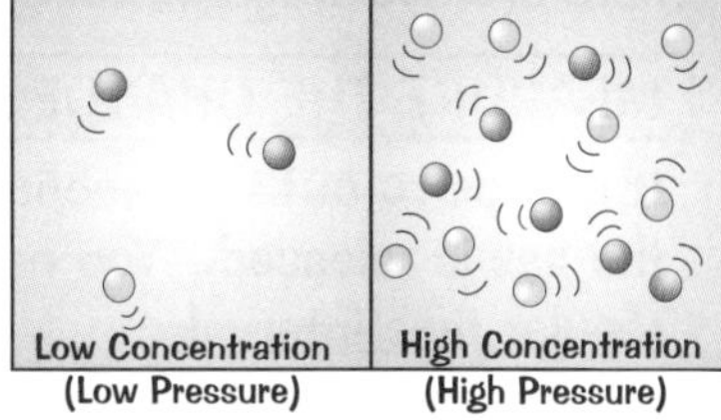

If a solution is made more concentrated it means there are more particles of reactant knocking about between the water molecules, which makes collisions between the important particles more likely. In a gas, increasing the pressure means the molecules are more squashed up together, so there are going to be more collisions.

3) SMALLER SOLID PARTICLES (or MORE SURFACE AREA) Means Other Particles Can Get to It More Easily

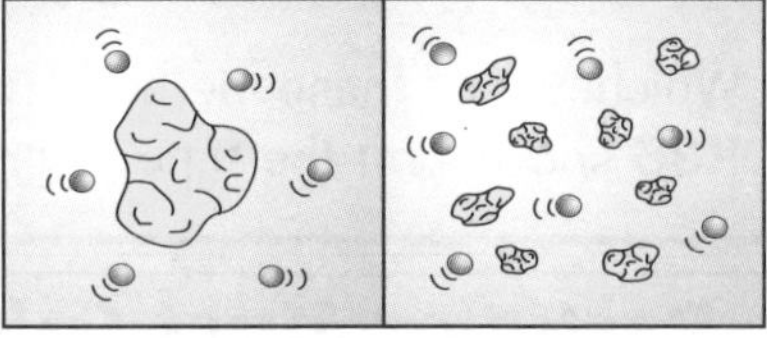

If one of the reactants is a solid then breaking it up into smaller pieces will increase its surface area. This means the particles around it will have more area to work on so there'll be more useful collisions. For example, soluble pain killers dissolve faster when they're broken into bits.

Fine powders of combustible materials dispersed in the air burn very very fast because they have such a big surface area. In fact, if there's a spark, they'll EXPLODE (an explosion is basically a very fast reaction that releases a lot of gaseous products very quickly). That's why factories that make custard powder, flour and powdered sulfur have to be careful.

The Great Fire of London started in a bakery — some people reckon it started when sparks ignited some flour dust, which exploded.

4) A CATALYST Increases the Number of Successful Collisions

A catalyst is a substance which increases the speed of a reaction, without being changed or used up in the reaction — and because it isn't used up, you only need a tiny bit of it to catalyse large amounts of reactants. Catalysts tend to be very fussy about which reactions they catalyse though — you can't just stick any old catalyst in a reaction and expect it to work.

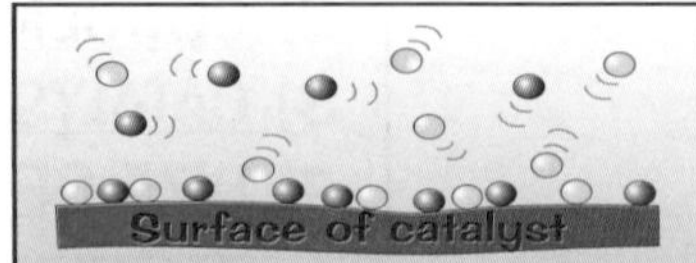

A catalyst works by giving the reacting particles a surface to stick to where they can bump into each other — and reduces the energy needed by the particles before they react. So the overall number of collisions isn't increased, but the number of successful collisions is.

Collision theory — it's always the other driver...

Industries that use chemical reactions to make their products have to think carefully about reaction rates. Ideally, they want to speed up the reaction to get the products quickly, but high temperatures and pressures are expensive. So they compromise — they use a slower reaction but a cheaper one.

Collision Theory

Higher temperatures increase the number of collisions. Easy.
But higher temperatures also have another speeding-up effect. Smashing.

Faster Collisions Also Increase the Rate of Reaction

Higher temperatures increase the energy of the collisions, since the particles are moving faster.

Faster Collisions are ONLY Caused by Increasing the Temperature

Reactions only happen if the particles collide with enough energy. At a higher temperature there'll be more particles colliding with enough energy to make the reaction happen.

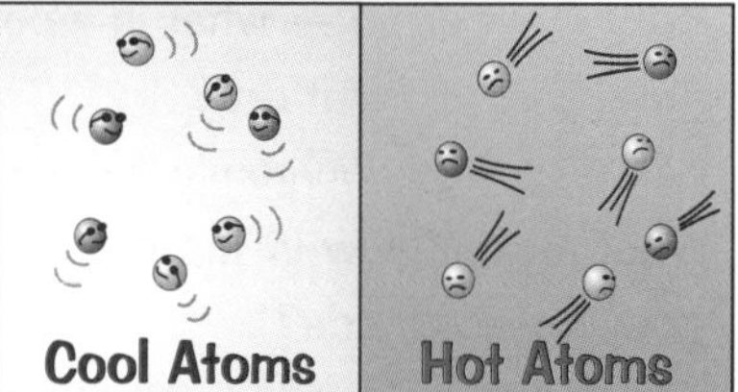

That's all very nice. But in the exam they might ask you to interpret rate-of-reaction data. Read on...

Changing Any of These Factors Alters the Reaction Rate Graph

(A) When marble chips are added to hydrochloric acid, CO_2 is given off. In this experiment, 5 g of marble chips were added to hydrochloric acid, and the volume of CO_2 measured every 10 seconds. The results are plotted below. Line 1 is for small chips and line 2 is for large chips.

1) Both reactions finish (the line goes flat) when 80 cm³ of CO_2 are produced.
2) Reaction 1 takes about 60 s, Reaction 2 about 90 s — Reaction 1 is faster.
3) Another way to tell the rate of reaction is to look at the slope of the graph — the steeper the graph, the faster the reaction.
   Reaction 1 is faster than Reaction 2 — the slope of its graph is steeper.
   Also, the rate of reaction slows down as the reaction goes on — the slope of each line gets smaller.
   The reaction is finished when the line is horizontal.
4) Reaction 1 is faster because small chips have a larger surface area than the same mass of large chips.

(B)

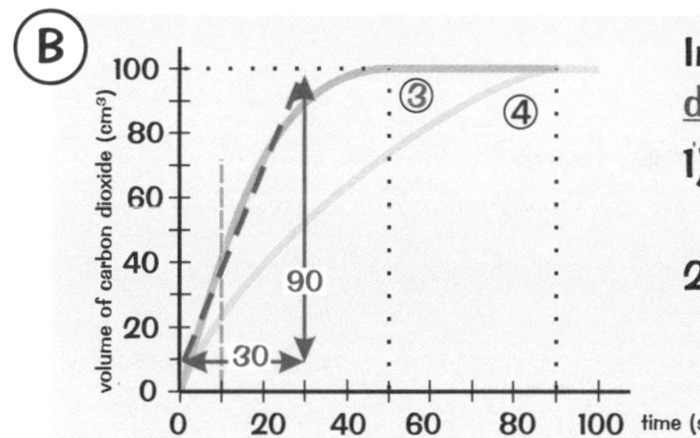

In this version of the experiment the size of the chips is the same but two different temperatures of acid are used.

1) Both reactions finish when 100 cm³ of CO_2 have been produced. Reaction 3 is faster (about 50 s, compared to Reaction 4's 90 s or so).
2) You can calculate the rate of reaction by calculating the slope of the line. To find the rate after 10 s, draw a line with the same slope as the curve at 10 s and work out its slope. For Reaction 3, the slope is $90 \div 30 = 3$. This means that you're getting 3 cm³ of CO_2 per second.

(C) This time, a piece of magnesium has been added to hydrochloric acid. The graphs show the volume of hydrogen produced when two different concentrations of acid are used.

1) Reaction 5 is faster than Reaction 6 — its slope is steeper (or use the fact that Reaction 5 takes about 30 s, and Reaction 6 about 50 s).
2) Since Reaction 5 is faster, it must use the more concentrated acid.

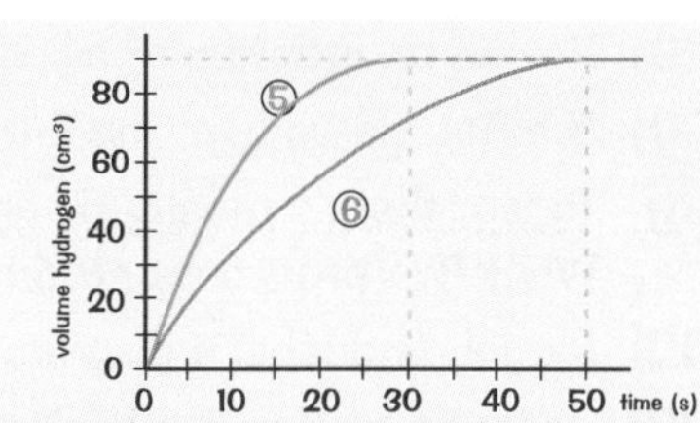

(D) This graph shows the effect of adding a catalyst.
Line 7 is the catalysed reaction, line 8 is the uncatalysed reaction.
The graph tells you that the catalyst speeds up the reaction because line 7 is steeper than line 8 (but the total volume of gas produced is the same in each reaction).

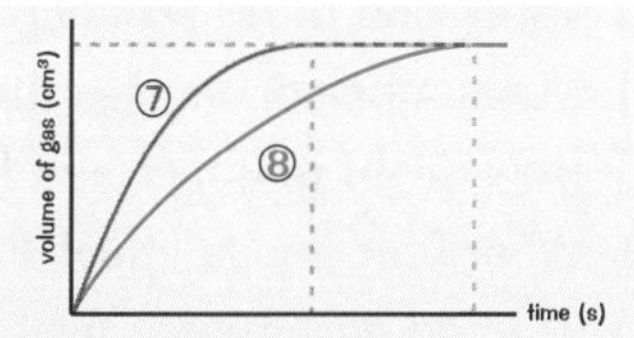

My reactions slow down when it gets hot — I get sleepy...

So reaction rate depends on two things: 1) the number of collisions, and 2) how many of those collisions have enough energy. Remember, temperature's the only thing that affects how fast the particles collide.

Revision Summary for Module C2

The only way that you can tell if you've learned this module is to test yourself. Try these questions, and if there's something you don't know, it means you need to go back and learn it. Even if it is all that tricky business about rates of reaction. And don't miss any questions out — you don't get a choice about what comes up on the exam so you need to be sure that you've learnt it all.

1) What is the name for the substance that gives a paint its colour?
2) Paint is a colloid — what is a colloid?
3) How does oil paint dry?
4) What are thermochromic pigments? How might these be used commercially?
5) What makes glow-in-the-dark watches glow in the dark?
6) How is glass made?
7) How is cement made? What about concrete?
8) Why is reinforced concrete better than non-reinforced concrete as a building material?
9) List three environmental impacts of extracting rocks from the Earth.
10) How is copper obtained from malachite?
11) Draw and label the apparatus used to purify copper. Label the anode, the cathode and the electrolyte.
12) During the purification process, which electrode gets bigger — the cathode or the anode? Write down the equation for the reaction at the anode, and the equation for the reaction at the cathode.
13) Give an example of a large-scale use of each of the following: brass, solder, amalgam.
14) What two metals is brass made from? How are its physical properties different from those metals?
15) Give an example of a smart alloy. What is it used for?
16) Write down the word equation for the corrosion of iron.
17) Explain why a car parked on the Brighton seafront rusts more than a car parked in hot, dry Cairo.
18) Why doesn't aluminium corrode when it's wet?
19) Give two advantages of using aluminium instead of steel for car bodywork.
20) Polypropylene fibres are cheap and hardwearing. What might they be used for when building a car?
21) Draw diagrams to show how sedimentary rocks form.
22) Draw a diagram to show how metamorphic rocks form.
23) Give an example of a metamorphic rock and say what material it formed from.
24) What is the lithosphere?
25) What causes the Earth's tectonic plates to move?
26) Describe four pieces of evidence for the theory of plate tectonics.
27) What is meant by 'subduction'?
28) How does tectonic plate movement cause: a) earthquakes? b) volcanoes?
29) How is an eruption of silica-rich rhyolitic lava different from an eruption of iron-rich basaltic lava?
30) 3 billion years ago, the Earth's atmosphere was mostly CO_2. Where did this CO_2 come from?
31) Today, there's mostly O_2 and N_2 in the Earth's atmosphere. What process produced the O_2? What two processes produced the N_2?
32) Sketch and label a diagram of the carbon cycle.
33) Describe how an increasing human population affects the composition of the air.
34) What kind of air pollution makes limestone buildings and statues look worn?
35) Name a poisonous gas that catalytic converters help to remove from car exhausts.
36) How might you measure the rate of the reaction between calcium carbonate and hydrochloric acid?
37) What four things affect the rate of a reaction?
38) Why do gases react faster when they're under higher pressure?
39) Why do fine combustible powders sometimes explode?
40)* A piece of magnesium is added to a dilute solution of hydrochloric acid, and hydrogen gas is produced. The experiment is repeated with a more concentrated hydrochloric acid. How can you tell from the experiment which concentration of acid produces a faster rate of reaction?

* Answers on page 108.

Atoms

There are quite a few different (and equally useful) models of the atom — but chemists tend to like this model best. You can use it to explain pretty much the whole of chemistry... which is nice.

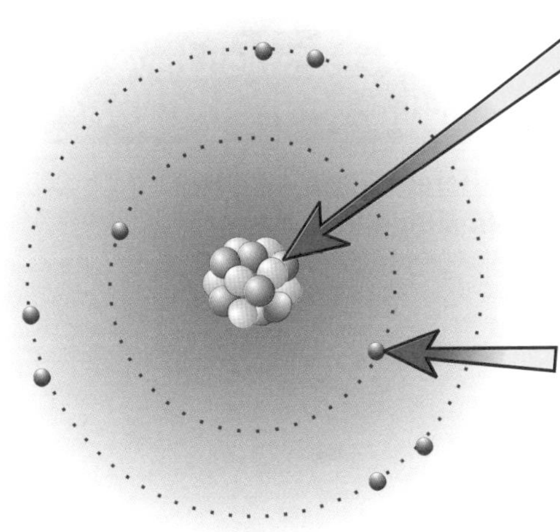

Atoms are really tiny, don't forget. They're too small to see, even with a very high power microscope.

The Nucleus

1) It's in the middle of the atom.
2) It contains protons and neutrons.
3) It has a positive charge because of the protons.
4) Almost the whole mass of the atom is concentrated in the nucleus.
5) But size-wise it's tiny compared to the rest of the atom.

The Electrons

1) Move around the nucleus.
2) They're negatively charged.
3) They're tiny, but they cover a lot of space.
4) The volume of their orbits determines how big the atom is.
5) They have virtually no mass.
6) They occupy shells around the nucleus.
7) These shells explain the whole of chemistry.

PARTICLE	MASS	CHARGE
Proton	1	+1
Neutron	1	0
Electron	0.0005	–1

Protons are heavy and positively charged
Neutrons are heavy and neutral
Electrons are tiny and negatively charged (Electron mass is often taken as zero.)

Number of Protons Equals Number of Electrons

1) Neutral atoms have no charge overall.
2) The charge on the electrons is the same size as the charge on the protons — but opposite.
3) This means the number of protons always equals the number of electrons in a neutral atom.
4) If some electrons are added or removed, the atom becomes charged and is then an ion.

Atomic Number and Mass Number Describe an Atom

These two numbers tell you how many of each kind of particle an atom has.

The Mass Number — Total of protons and neutrons → 23

$^{23}_{11}Na$

The Atomic Number — Number of protons → 11

1) The atomic (proton) number tells you how many protons there are.
2) Atoms of the same element all have the same number of protons — so atoms of different elements will have different numbers of protons.
3) To get the number of neutrons, just subtract the atomic number from the mass number.
4) The mass (nucleon) number is always the biggest number. On a periodic table the mass number is actually the relative atomic mass.
5) The mass number tends to be roughly double the proton number.
6) Which means there's about the same number of protons as neutrons in most nuclei.

Number of protons = number of electrons...

This stuff might seem a bit useless at first, but it should be permanently engraved into your mind. If you don't know these basic facts, you've got no chance of understanding the rest of chemistry. So learn it now, and watch as the Universe unfolds and reveals its timeless mysteries to you...

Isotopes, Elements and Compounds

And the question on everybody's lips is — what are isotopes...

Isotopes are the Same Except for an Extra Neutron or Two

Isotopes are: different atomic forms of the same element, which have the SAME number of PROTONS but a DIFFERENT number of NEUTRONS.

1) The upshot is: isotopes must have the same atomic number but different mass numbers.
2) If they had different atomic numbers, they'd be different elements altogether.
3) A very popular pair of isotopes are carbon-12 and carbon-14.

Carbon-12

$^{12}_{6}C$

6 PROTONS
6 ELECTRONS
6 NEUTRONS

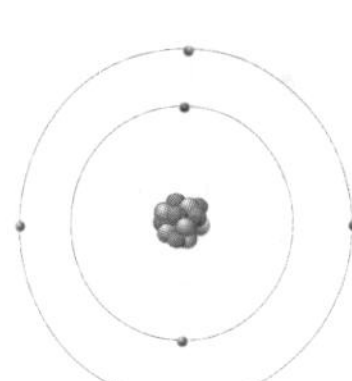

Carbon-14

$^{14}_{6}C$

6 PROTONS
6 ELECTRONS
8 NEUTRONS

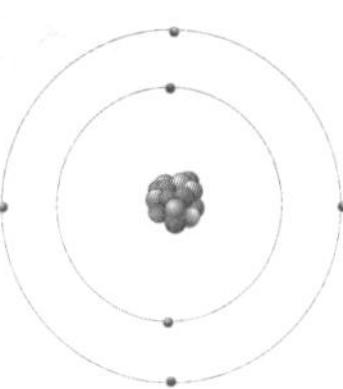

The number of electrons decides the chemistry of the element. If the atomic number is the same, then the number of protons is the same, so the number of electrons is the same, so the chemistry is the same. The different number of neutrons in the nucleus doesn't affect the chemical behaviour at all.

Elements Consist of One Type of Atom Only

Elements cannot be broken down chemically. Quite a lot of everyday substances are elements:

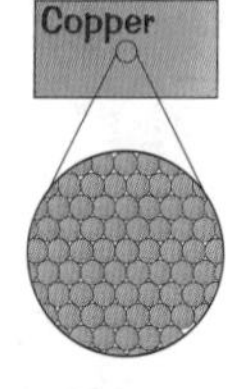

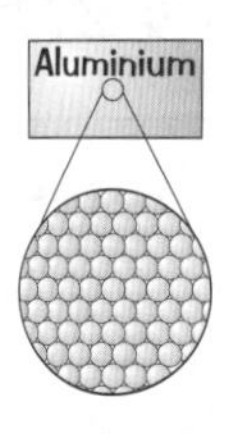

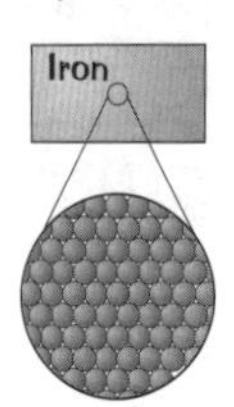

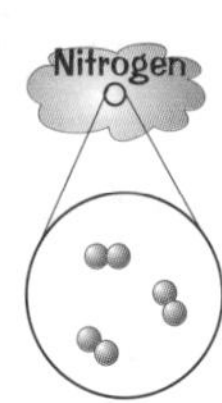

Compounds are Chemically Bonded

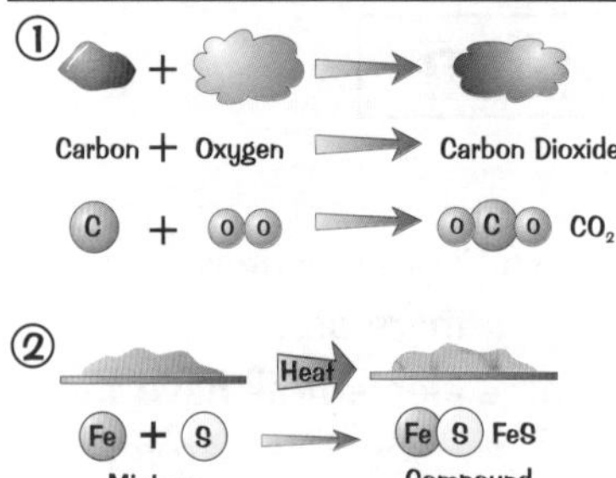

1) Carbon dioxide is a compound formed from a chemical reaction between carbon and oxygen.
2) It's very difficult to separate the two original elements again.
3) The properties of a compound are totally different from the properties of the original elements.
4) If iron and sulfur react to form iron sulfide, the compound formed is a grey solid lump, and doesn't behave anything like either iron or sulfur.

There are two types of chemical bonding:

1) Ionic Bonding — the attraction between positive and negative particles called ions.
2) Covalent Bonding — sharing a pair of electrons.

You'll find out more about these types of bond later in this section.
Until then, you'll just have to hold your breath...

Don't mix these up — it'll only compound your problems...

There are loads of natural isotopes out there. Radioactive ones, non-radioactive ones... they have their uses as well. Carbon's in every living organism, carbon-13 and carbon-14 are both radioactive (great stuff), and what's more, carbon-14's used to date old materials... wonder if it'd work on my Dad...

The Periodic Table

The periodic table is a chemist's bestest friend — start getting to know it now... seriously...

The Periodic Table is a Table of All Known Elements

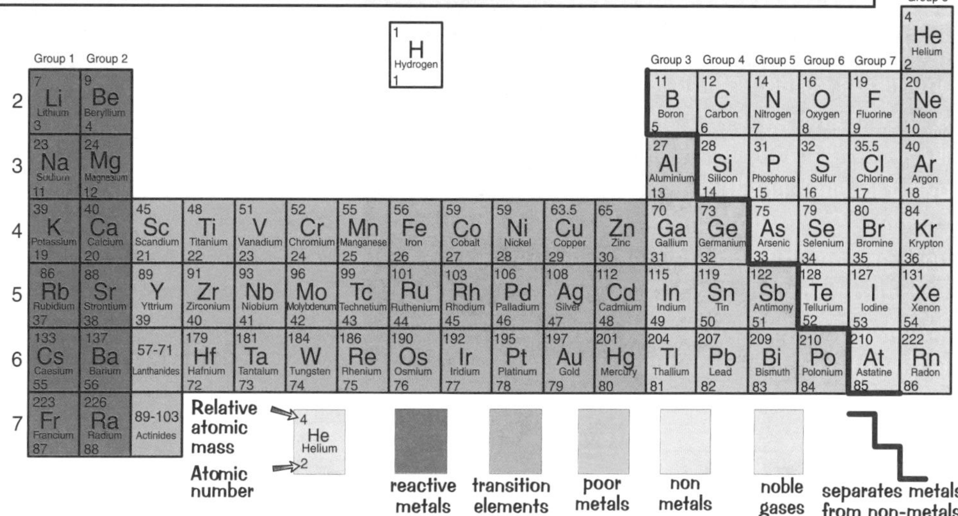

1) There are 100ish elements, which all materials are made of. More are still being 'discovered'.
2) The modern periodic table shows the elements in order of ascending atomic number.
3) The periodic table is laid out so that elements with similar properties form columns.
4) These vertical columns are called groups and roman numerals are often (but not always) used for them.
5) The group to which the element belongs corresponds to the number of electrons it has in its outer shell. E.g. Group 1 elements have 1 outer shell electron, Group 7 elements have 7 outer shell electrons, and so on.
6) Some of the groups have special names. Group 1 elements are called alkali metals. Group 7 elements are called halogens, and Group 8 elements are called the noble gases.
7) The rows are called periods. Each new period represents another full shell of electrons (see page 40).
8) The period to which the element belongs corresponds to the number of shells of electrons it has.

Elements in a Group Have the Same Number of Outer Electrons

1) The elements in each group all have the same number of electrons in their outer shell.
2) That's why they have similar properties. And that's why we arrange them in this way.
3) When only a small number of elements were known, the periodic table was made by looking at the properties of the elements and arranging them in groups — the same groups that they are in today.
4) This idea is extremely important to chemistry — so make sure you understand it.

The properties of the elements are decided entirely by how many electrons they have.
Atomic number is therefore very significant because it is equal to the number of electrons each atom has.
But it's the number of electrons in the outer shell which is the really important thing.

Electron Shells are Just Totally Brill

The fact that electrons form shells around atoms is the basis for the whole of chemistry.
If they just whizzed round the nucleus any old how and didn't care about shells or any of that stuff there'd be no chemical reactions. No nothing in fact — because nothing would happen.
The atoms would just slob about, all day long. Just like teenagers.
But amazingly, they do form shells (if they didn't, we wouldn't even be here to wonder about it), and the electron arrangement of each atom determines the whole of its chemical behaviour.
Phew. I mean electron arrangements explain practically the whole Universe. They're just totally brill.

This table comes up periodically...

Physicists are still producing new elements in particle accelerators, but they're all radioactive.
Most only last a fraction of a second before they decay — they're up to element 118 at the moment.

Electron Shells

Electron shells... orbits electrons zoom about in.

Electron Shell Rules:

1) Electrons always occupy shells (sometimes called energy levels).
2) The lowest energy levels are always filled first.
3) Only a certain number of electrons are allowed in each shell:
   1st shell: 2 2nd Shell: 8 3rd Shell: 8
4) Atoms are much happier when they have full electron shells.
5) In most atoms the outer shell is not full and this makes the atom want to react.

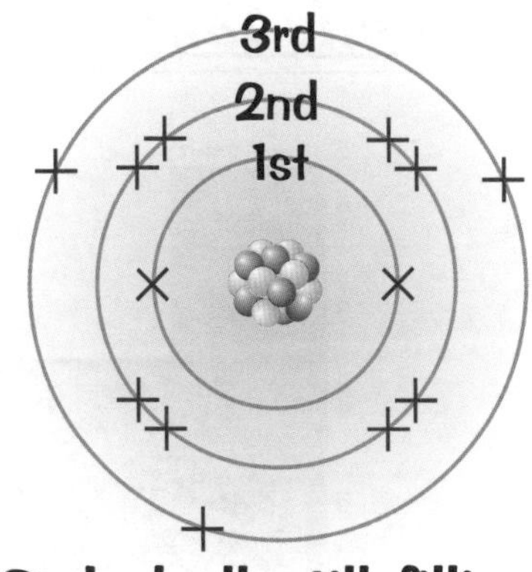

3rd shell still filling

Working Out Electron Configurations

You need to know the electron configurations for the first 20 elements. They're shown in the diagram below — but they're not hard to work out. For a quick example, take nitrogen. Follow the steps...

1) The periodic table tells you that nitrogen has seven protons... so it must have seven electrons.
2) Follow the 'Electron Shell Rules' above. The first shell can only take 2 electrons and the second shell can take a maximum of 8 electrons.
3) So the electron configuration for nitrogen must be 2,5 — easy peasy.
4) Now you try it for argon.

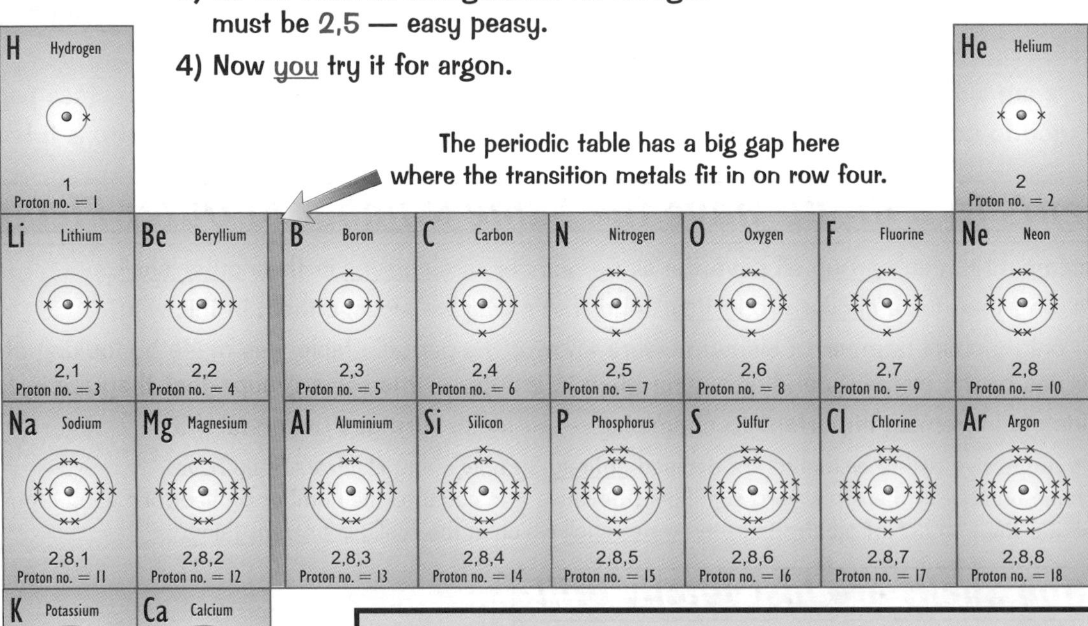

Answer: To calculate the electron configuration of argon, follow the rules. It's got 18 protons, so it must have 18 electrons. The first shell must have 2 electrons, the second shell must have 8, and so the third shell must have 8 as well. It's as easy as 2, 8, 8.

One little duck and two fat ladies — 2, 8, 8...

You need to know enough about electron shells to draw out that whole diagram at the bottom of the page without looking at it. Obviously, you don't have to learn each element separately, just learn the pattern. Cover the page: using a periodic table, find the atom with the electron configuration 2, 8, 6.

Ionic Bonding

Ionic Bonding — Swapping Electrons

In ionic bonding, atoms lose or gain electrons to form charged particles (or ions) which are then strongly attracted to one another (because of the attraction of opposite charges, + and –).

A Shell with Just One Electron is Well Keen to Get Rid...

All the atoms over at the left-hand side of the periodic table, such as sodium, potassium, calcium etc., have just one or two electrons in their outer shell. And basically they're pretty keen to get shot of them, because then they'll only have full shells left, which is how they like it.
So given half a chance they do get rid, and that leaves the atom as an ion instead.
Now ions aren't the kind of things to sit around quietly watching the world go by.
They tend to leap at the first passing ion with an opposite charge and stick to it like glue.

A Nearly Full Shell is Well Keen to Get That Extra Electron...

On the other side of the periodic table the elements in Group 6 and Group 7, such as oxygen and chlorine, have outer shells which are nearly full. They're obviously pretty keen to gain that extra one or two electrons to fill the shell up. When they do of course they become ions — you know, not the kind of things to sit around, and before you know it, pop, they've latched onto the atom (ion) that gave up the electron a moment earlier. The reaction of sodium and chlorine is a classic case:

1. The sodium atom gives up its outer electron and becomes an Na^+ ion.
2. The chlorine atom picks up the spare electron and becomes a Cl^- ion.

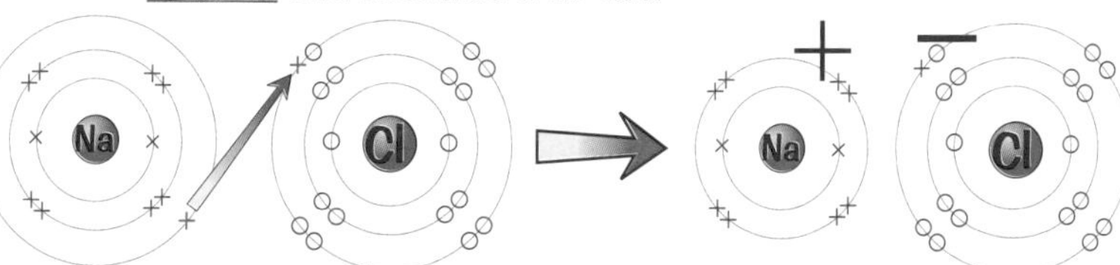

3. **POP!** An ionic bond is formed.

Simple Ions — Groups 1 & 2 and 6 & 7

1) Ions are charged particles — they can be single atoms (e.g. Cl^-) or groups of atoms (e.g. NO_3^-).
2) When atoms lose or gain electrons to form ions, all they're trying to do is get a full outer shell (a stable octet). Atoms like full outer shells — it's atom heaven.
3) When metals form ions, they lose electrons to form positive ions. Loss of electrons is called oxidation.
4) When non-metals form ions, they gain electrons to form negative ions. Gain of electrons is called reduction.
5) So when a metal and a non-metal combine, they form ionic bonds.
6) You need to know the positive and negative ions in the table on the right.
7) To work out the formula of an ionic compound, you have to balance the +ve and the –ve charges.

Positive (+ve) ions		Negative (–ve) ions	
Group 1	Group 2	Group 6	Group 7
Li^+	Be^{2+}	O^{2-}	F^-
Na^+	Mg^{2+}		Cl^-
K^+	Ca^{2+}		

Lithium fluoride

$Li^+ + F^- \longrightarrow LiF$

The lithium ion is 1+, and the fluoride ion is 1–, so they balance.

Potassium oxide

$2K^+ + O^{2-} \longrightarrow K_2O$

The potassium ion is 1+, and the oxygen ion is 2–, so you need two K^+ ions to balance the O^{2-} ion.

Magnesium chloride

$Mg^{2+} + 2Cl^- \longrightarrow MgCl_2$

The magnesium ion is 2+, and the chloride ion is 1–, so you need two Cl^- ions to balance the Mg^{2+} ion.

Full Shells — it's the name of the game...

Here's where you can get a little practice working out formulas for molecules. Remember to balance them, or you'll lose marks. Some elements like to gain electrons, some like to lose electrons, but they all want to have a full outer shell. Poor little electron shells, all they want in life is to be full...

Ions and Ionic Compounds

Electronic Structure of Some Simple Ions

'Dot and cross' diagrams show what happens to the electrons in an ionic bond:

Sodium Chloride (NaCl)

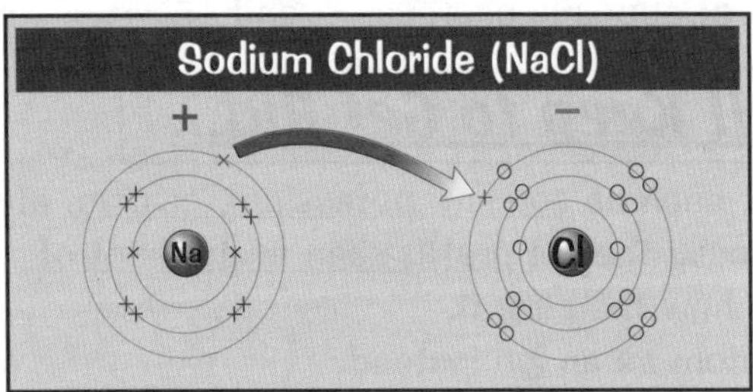

The sodium atom gives up its outer electron, becoming an Na^+ ion. The chlorine atom picks up the electron, becoming a Cl^- (chloride) ion.

Magnesium Oxide (MgO)

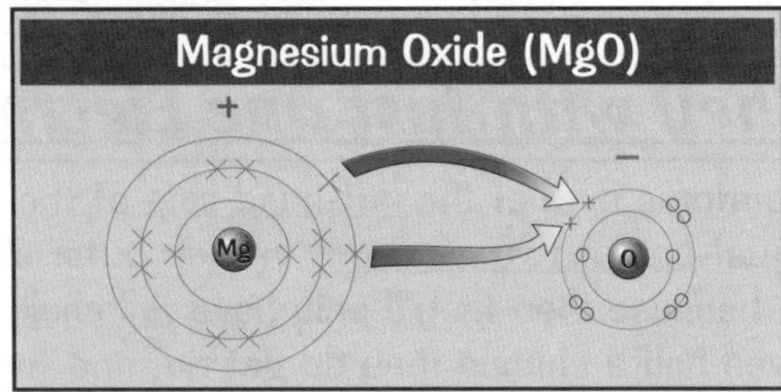

The magnesium atom gives up its two outer electrons, becoming an Mg^{2+} ion. The oxygen atom picks up the electrons, becoming an O^{2-} (oxide) ion.

Sodium Oxide (Na_2O)

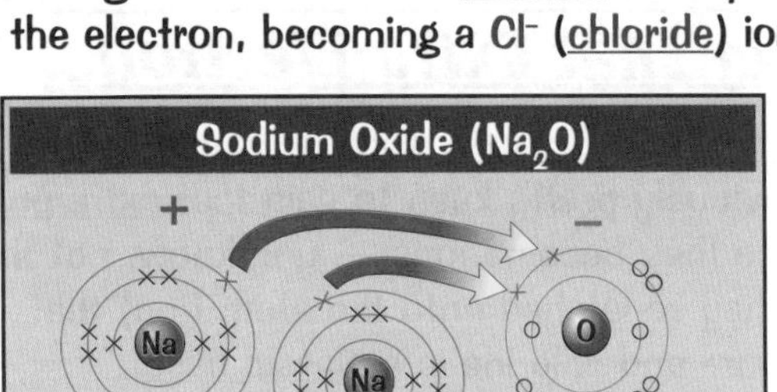

Two sodium atoms give up their outer electrons, becoming two Na^+ ions. The oxygen atom picks up the two electrons, becoming an O^{2-} ion.

Magnesium Chloride ($MgCl_2$)

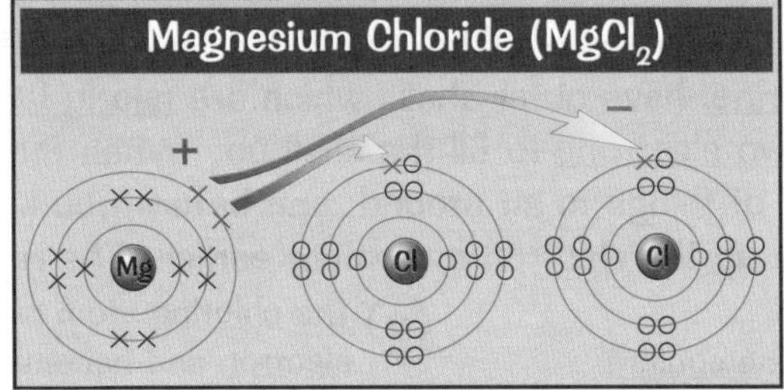

The magnesium atom gives up its two outer electrons, becoming an Mg^{2+} ion. The two chlorine atoms pick up one electron each, becoming two Cl^- (chloride) ions.

Notice that all the atoms end up with full outer shells as a result of this giving and taking of electrons.

NaCl and MgO Form Giant Ionic Lattices

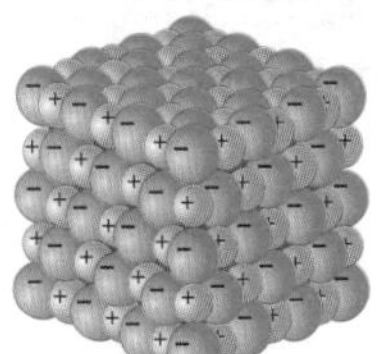

1) Ionic bonds always produce giant ionic structures.
2) The ions form a closely packed regular lattice arrangement. The ions are not free to move though, so these compounds do not conduct electricity when solid.
3) There are very strong chemical bonds between all the ions.
4) A single crystal of sodium chloride (salt) is one giant ionic lattice, which is why salt crystals tend to be cuboid in shape.

1) They Have High Melting Points and Boiling Points...

...due to the very strong chemical bonds between all the ions in the giant structure.

2) NaCl Dissolves to Form a Solution That Conducts Electricity

When dissolved the ions separate and are all free to move in the solution, so obviously they'll carry electric current.
(Not all ionic compounds dissolve in water — MgO is insoluble.)

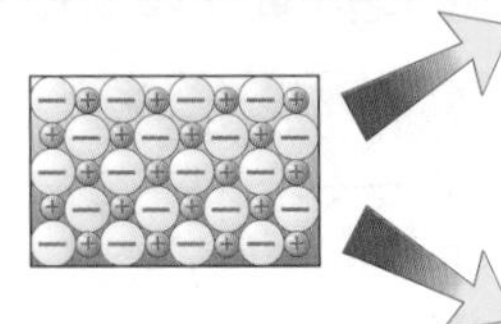

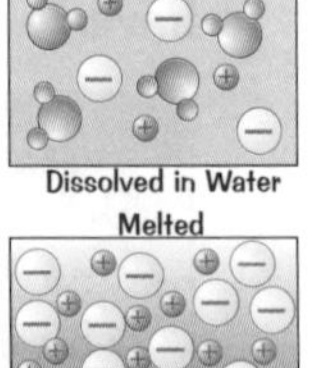

3) They Conduct Electricity When Molten

When it melts, the ions are free to move and they'll carry electric current.

Giant ionic lattices — all over your chips...

Because they conduct electricity when they're dissolved in water, ionic compounds are used to make some types of battery. In the olden days, most batteries had actual liquid in, so they tended to leak all over the place. Now they've come up with a sort of paste that doesn't leak but still conducts. Clever.

Group 1 — Alkali Metals

Group 1 Metals are Known as the 'Alkali Metals'

Group 1 metals include lithium, sodium and potassium... know those three names real well. They could also ask you about rubidium and caesium.

Group I

Mass	Symbol	Name	Atomic no.
7	Li	Lithium	3
23	Na	Sodium	11
39	K	Potassium	19
85.5	Rb	Rubidium	37
133	Cs	Caesium	55
223	Fr	Francium	87

As you go DOWN Group 1, the alkali metals become more reactive — the outer electron is more easily lost, because it's further from the nucleus.

1) The alkali metals all have ONE outer electron.
   This makes them very reactive and gives them all similar properties.
2) They all have the following physical properties:
   - Low melting point and boiling point (compared with other metals),
   - Low density — lithium, sodium and potassium float on water,
   - Very soft — they can be cut with a knife.
3) The alkali metals always form ionic compounds. They are so keen to lose the outer electron there's no way they'd consider sharing, so covalent bonding is out of the question.

Oxidation is the Loss of Electrons

1) Group 1 metals are keen to lose an electron to form a 1^+ ion with a stable electronic structure.
2) The more reactive the metal the happier it is to lose an electron.
3) Loss of electrons is called OXIDATION.

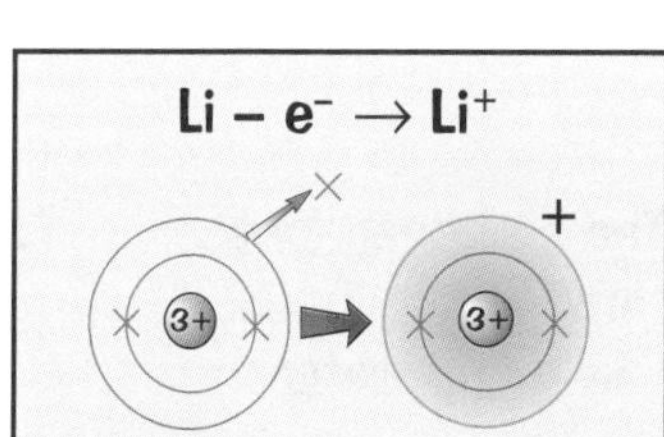

Reaction with Cold Water Produces Hydrogen Gas

1) When lithium, sodium or potassium are put in water, they react very vigorously.
2) They move around the surface, fizzing furiously.
3) They produce hydrogen.
4) The reactivity with water increases down the group — the reaction with potassium gets hot enough to ignite it.
5) Sodium and potassium melt in the heat of the reaction.
6) They form a hydroxide in solution, i.e. aqueous OH^- ions.

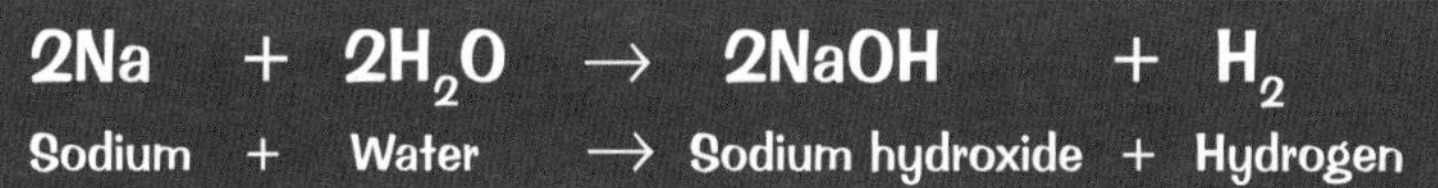

$$2Na + 2H_2O \rightarrow 2NaOH + H_2$$

Sodium + Water → Sodium hydroxide + Hydrogen

A lighted splint will indicate hydrogen by producing the notorious "squeaky pop" as the H_2 ignites.

The solution becomes alkaline, which changes the colour of the pH indicator (see C4, page 52) to purple.

Alkali Metal Compounds Burn with Characteristic Colours

1) Dip a wire loop into some hydrochloric acid to clean it.
2) Put the loop into a powdered sample of the compound to be tested, then place the end in a blue Bunsen flame.
3) Alkali metal ions will give pretty coloured flames — the colour of the flame tells you which alkali metal is present.

Lithium:	Red flame
Sodium:	Yellow/orange flame
Potassium:	Lilac flame

Red and orange and pink and green — or something like that...

Alkali metals are really reactive. They're so reactive in fact they have to be stored in oil — otherwise they just react with the air. Learn the trends and characteristics of alkali metals before turning over.

Electrolysis and the Half-Equations

Electrolysis Means 'Splitting Up with Electricity'

1) Electrolysis is the breaking down of a substance using electricity.
2) It needs a liquid to conduct the electricity, called the electrolyte.
3) Electrolytes are usually free ions dissolved in water, e.g. dilute acids like H_2SO_4, and dissolved salts like NaCl.
4) It's the free ions which conduct the electricity and allow the whole thing to work.
5) For an electrical circuit to be complete, there's got to be a flow of electrons. In electrolysis, electrons are taken away from ions at the positive anode and given to other ions at the negative cathode. As ions gain or lose electrons they become atoms or molecules and are released.

The Electrolysis of Sulfuric Acid Solution

Water contains hydrogen and oxygen — two elements that are very useful gases.

But, pure water doesn't conduct electricity very well, which makes its electrolysis difficult. If you add a little sulfuric acid it conducts a lot better.

In solution, the molecules will split into their ions:

$$H_2O \rightleftharpoons H^+ + OH^-$$
$$H_2SO_4 \rightleftharpoons H^+ + SO_4^{2-}$$

The hydrogen ions are from sulfuric acid and water.

+ve ions are called CATIONS because they're attracted to the –ve cathode.

Hydrogen is produced at the –ve cathode.

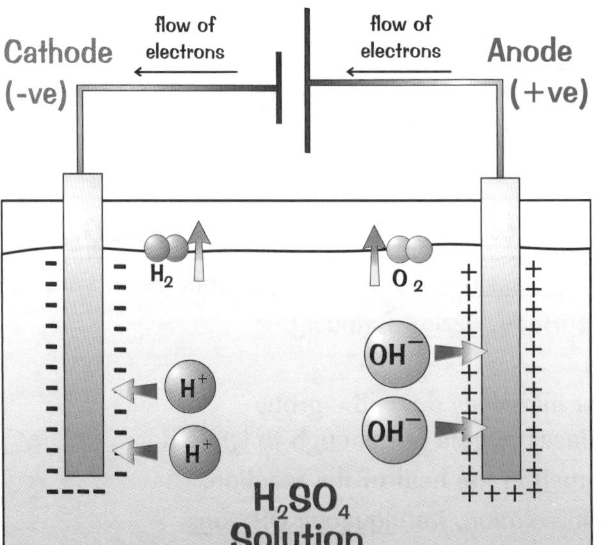

All the hydroxide ions come from water.

–ve ions are called ANIONS because they're attracted to the +ve anode.

Oxygen is produced at the +ve anode.

1) At the cathode, two hydrogen ions accept two electrons to become one hydrogen molecule.
2) At the anode, four hydroxide (OH^-) ions lose their electrons and become one oxygen molecule and two water molecules.

The Half-Equations — Make Sure the Electrons Balance

The main thing is to make sure the charges balance on each side of each half-equation.
For the above cell the half-equations are:

Cathode:	$2H^+ + 2e^- \rightarrow H_2$
Anode:	$4OH^- \rightarrow 2H_2O + O_2 + 4e^-$

Cations — sounds like a useful form of pet control...

So you need a bit of acid to split water into hydrogen and oxygen. Hydrogen gas is used in the Haber process, which makes ammonia — you'll learn all about this on page 59. Oxygen is just generally great, you know, for breathing and stuff...

Extracting Aluminium

Electrolysis Removes Aluminium from Its Ore

1) Aluminium's a very abundant metal, but it is always found naturally in compounds.
2) The main ore is bauxite, and after mining and purifying, a white powder is left.
3) This is pure aluminium oxide, Al_2O_3.
4) As aluminium's more reactive than carbon, it has to be extracted from its ore using electrolysis.

Cryolite is Used to Lower the Temperature (and Costs)

1) Al_2O_3 has a very high melting point of over 2000 °C — so melting it would be very expensive.
2) Instead the aluminium oxide is dissolved in molten cryolite (a less common ore of aluminium).
3) This brings the temperature down to about 900 °C, which makes it much cheaper and easier.
4) The electrodes are made of graphite, a good conductor of electricity.

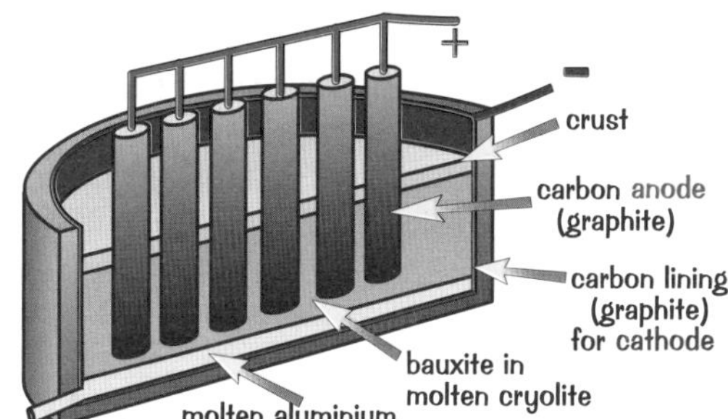

Electrolysis — Turning IONS into the ATOMS You Want

1) Molten aluminium oxide contains free ions — so it'll conduct electricity.
2) The positive Al^{3+} ions are attracted to the cathode where they pick up electrons and "zup", they turn into aluminium atoms. These then sink to the bottom.
3) The negative O^{2-} ions are attracted to the anode where they lose electrons. The oxygen atoms will then react together to form O_2, or with the carbon anode as well to form CO_2.
4) As the carbon anode is constantly getting worn down, it often needs replacing.

Overall, this is a REDOX reaction and you need to know the reactions at both electrodes:

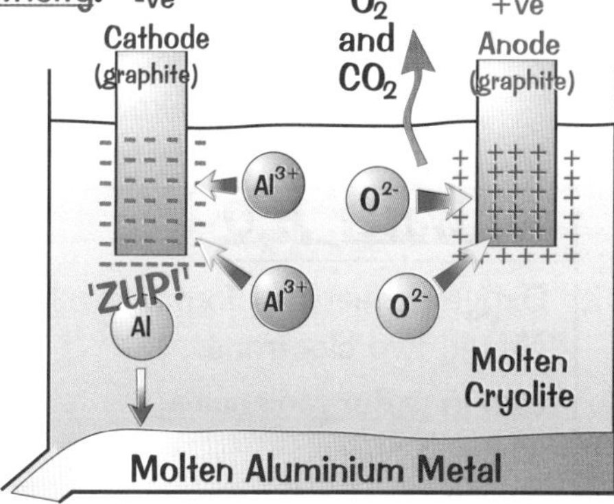

At the Cathode (-ve):

$$Al^{3+} + 3e^- \rightarrow Al$$

(Reduction — a gain of electrons)

At the Anode (+ve):

$$2O^{2-} \rightarrow O_2 + 4e^-$$

(Oxidation — a loss of electrons)

The complete equation for the decomposition of aluminium oxide is then:

Aluminium oxide → Aluminium + Oxygen

Electrolysis is Expensive — It's All That Electricity...

1) Electrolysis uses a lot of electricity and that can make it pretty expensive.
2) Energy is also needed to heat the electrolyte mixture to 900 °C. This is expensive too.
3) The disappearing anodes need frequent replacement. That costs money as well.
4) But in the end, aluminium now comes out as a reasonably cheap and widely-used metal. A hundred years ago it was a very rare metal, simply because it was so hard to extract.

Faster shopping at Tesco — use Electrolleys...

Electrolysis is fantastic for removing any unwanted hairs from your body. Great for women with moustaches, or men with hairy backs. And even better for the beauty clinic, as they'll get to charge a small fortune for the treatment. After all it's a very expensive process...

Covalent Bonding

Covalent Bonds — Sharing Electrons

1) Sometimes atoms prefer to make covalent bonds by sharing electrons with other atoms.
2) This way both atoms feel that they have a full outer shell, and that makes them happy.
3) Each covalent bond provides one extra shared electron for each atom.
4) Each atom involved has to make enough covalent bonds to fill up its outer shell.
5) Learn these important examples:

1) Hydrogen Gas, H_2

Hydrogen atoms have just one electron. They only need one more to complete the first shell...

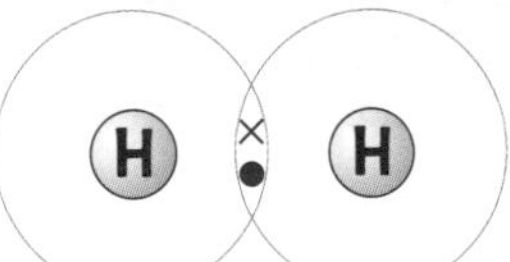

...so they often form single covalent bonds to achieve this.

2) Chlorine Gas, Cl_2

Each chlorine atom needs just one more electron to complete the outer shell...

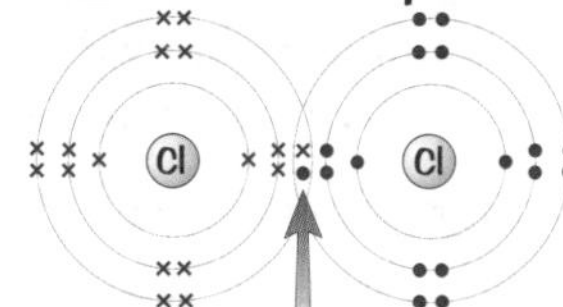

...so they form a single covalent bond and together share one pair of electrons.

3) Methane, CH_4

Carbon has four outer electrons, which is a half full shell.

To become a 4+ or a 4– ion is hard work so it forms four covalent bonds to make up its outer shell.

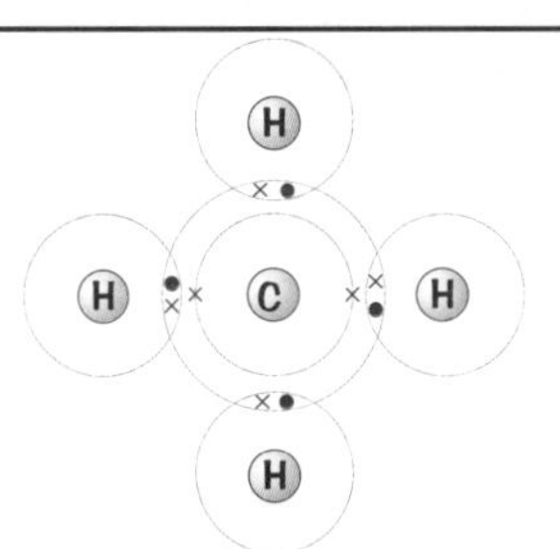

4) Water, H_2O

Oxygen cheerfully forms covalent bonds and shares two electrons.

Like in water molecules, where it shares electrons with the hydrogen atoms.

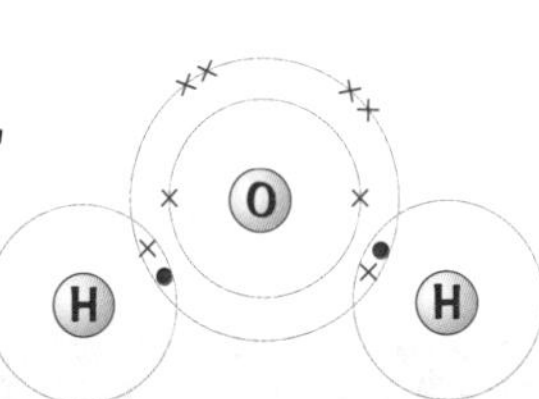

5) Carbon Dioxide, CO_2

Carbon needs four more electrons to fill it up, oxygen needs two. So two double covalent bonds are formed.

A double covalent bond has two shared pairs of electrons.

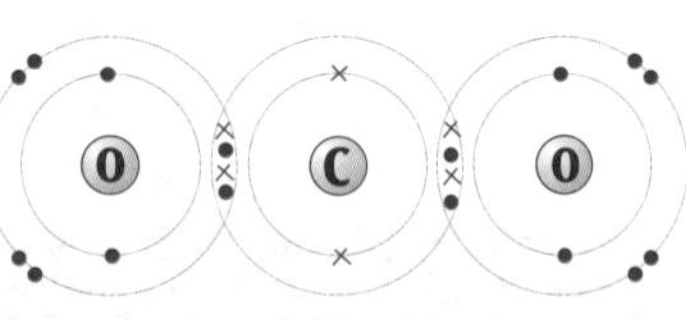

Simple Molecular Substances

weak intermolecular forces

Carbon dioxide

Water

1) Substances formed from covalent bonds usually have simple molecular structures, like CO_2 and H_2O.
2) The atoms within the molecules are held together by very strong covalent bonds.
3) By contrast, the forces of attraction between these molecules are very weak.
4) The result of these feeble intermolecular forces is that the melting and boiling points are very low, because the molecules are easily parted from each other.
5) Most molecular substances are gases or liquids at room temperature.
6) Molecular substances don't conduct electricity, simply because there are no free electrons or ions.

It's good to share — especially when it's somebody else's...

Make sure you can draw all five of those examples. You never know when they'll come in handy... (hint: in your exam). You also get giant covalent structures (see page 64) — they're totally different from the simple molecular ones. You've got to know the details, and examples. Learn them now.

Group 7 — Halogens

Group 7 Elements are Known as the 'Halogens'

Group 7 is made up of fluorine, chlorine, bromine, iodine and astatine.

All Group 7 elements have 7 electrons in their outer shell — so they've all got similar properties.

As you go DOWN Group 7, the halogens become less reactive — there's less inclination to gain the extra electron to fill the outer shell when it's further out from the nucleus.

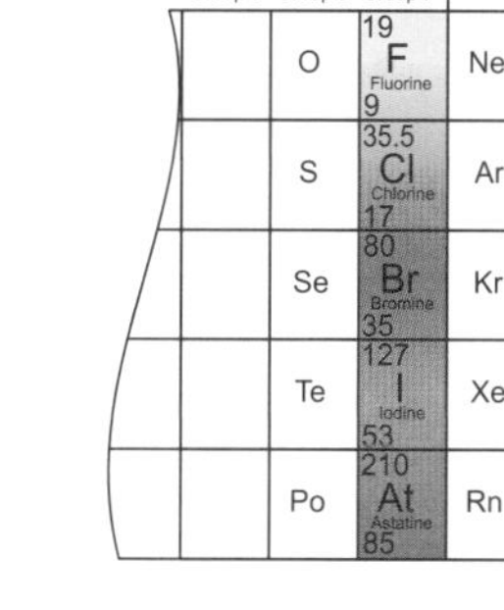

Chlorine is a fairly reactive, poisonous, dense green gas.
Bromine is a dense, poisonous, orange liquid.
Iodine is a dark grey crystalline solid.

Halogens Do Both Covalent and Ionic Bonding

Halogens form covalent bonds with themselves and in various molecular compounds like this:

Cl_2 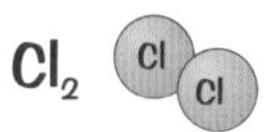

Br_2 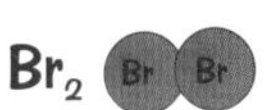

I_2 

Hydrogen chloride 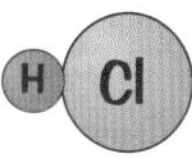

Or, they can form ionic bonds with other elements like the alkali metals to form ions with a 1– charge: Cl^- Br^- I^- as in Na^+Cl^- or $Fe^{3+}Br_3^-$

Reduction is the Gain of Electrons

1) Halogens are keen to gain an electron to form a 1^- ion with a stable electronic structure.
2) The more reactive the halogen the happier it is to gain an electron.
3) Gain of electrons is called REDUCTION.

$$Cl_2 + 2e^- \rightarrow 2Cl^-$$

Halogen molecule — Halide ion

The Halogens React with Alkali Metals to Form Salts

They react vigorously with alkali metals to form salts called 'metal halides'.

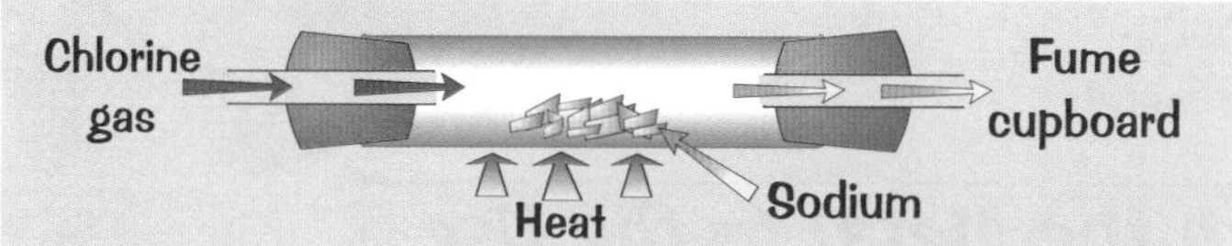

$$2Na + Cl_2 \rightarrow 2NaCl$$
Sodium + Chlorine → Sodium chloride

$$2K + Br_2 \rightarrow 2KBr$$
Potassium + Bromine → Potassium bromide

More Reactive Halogens Will Displace Less Reactive Ones

Chlorine can displace bromine and iodine from a solution of bromide or iodide.
Bromine will also displace iodine because of the trend in reactivity.

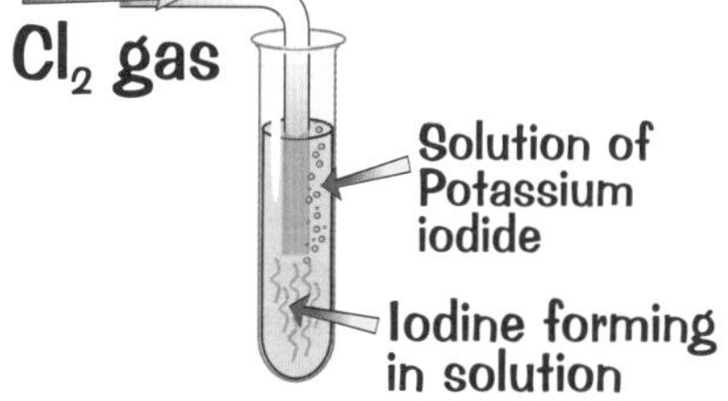

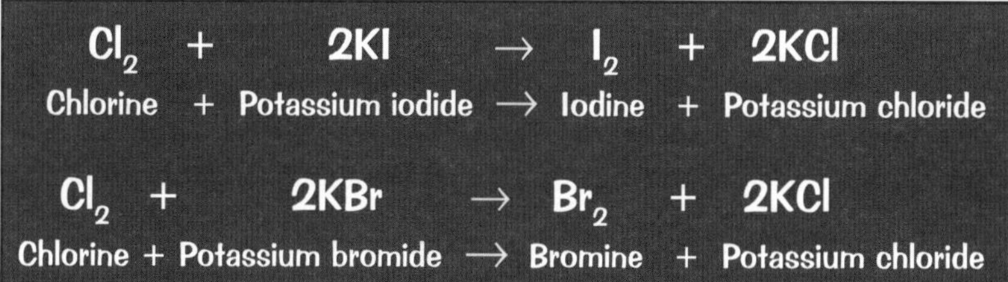

$$Cl_2 + 2KI \rightarrow I_2 + 2KCl$$
Chlorine + Potassium iodide → Iodine + Potassium chloride

$$Cl_2 + 2KBr \rightarrow Br_2 + 2KCl$$
Chlorine + Potassium bromide → Bromine + Potassium chloride

Halogens — one electron short of a full shell...

The halogens are another group from the periodic table, and just like the alkali metals (p.43) you've got to learn their trends and the equations on this page. Learn them, cover up the page, scribble, check.

Metals

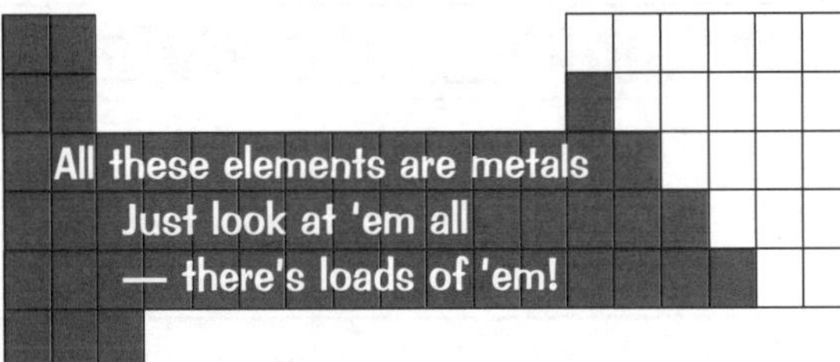

Metals Have a Crystal Structure

1) All metals have the same basic properties.
2) These are due to the special type of bonding that exists in metals.
3) Metals consist of a giant structure of atoms held together with metallic bonds.
4) These special bonds allow the outer electron(s) of each atom to move freely.
5) This creates a 'sea' of free electrons throughout the metal which is what gives rise to many of the properties of metals.

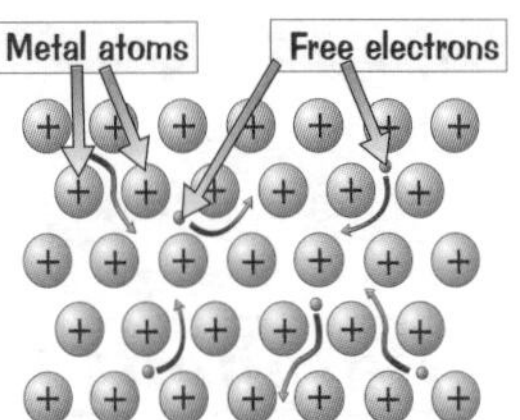

Most Have High Melting and Boiling Points, and High Density

1) Metals are very dense and lustrous (i.e. shiny).
2) There's a strong attraction between the free electrons and the closely packed positive ions — causing very strong metallic bonding.
3) You're going to have to get them pretty hot to melt them, e.g. iron melts at 1538 °C and boils at 2860 °C. (Mercury is an exception — it's liquid at room temp.)

They're Strong, but Also Bendy and Malleable

1) Metals have a high tensile strength — in other words they're strong and hard to break.
2) But they can also be hammered into a different shape (they're malleable).

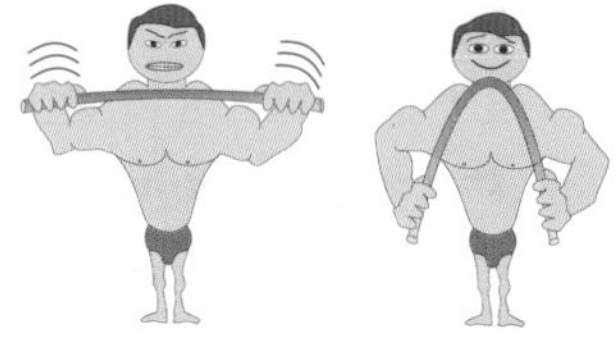

They're Good Conductors of Heat and Electricity

This is entirely due to the sea of free electrons.

1) They carry the current — so conduct electricity.
2) They also carry the heat energy through the metal.

You've Got to be Able to Match the Metal to the Use

Use	Properties	Metal
Saucepans	Good conductor of heat, doesn't rust easily	Stainless Steel — and it's cheap too.
Electrical Wiring	Good conductor of electricity, easily bent	Copper. One of the best conductors around.
Aeroplanes	Low density (light), strong, doesn't corrode	Aluminium. Titanium's sometimes used, but it's a lot more expensive.
Bridges	Strong	Steel — this is mostly iron, but it's got a little bit of carbon in it, which makes it a lot less brittle.

Metal Fatigue? — yeah, we've all had enough of this page now...

It's not just the main structure of an aeroplane that's made of aluminium — parts of the engines, the seat supports and even the cabin crew's trolleys are all made of aluminium. And because aluminium doesn't corrode, planes don't have to be painted, saving hundreds of kilograms on a big commercial jet.

Superconductors and Transition Metals

Oooooo, some interesting stuff...

At Very Low Temperatures, Some Metals are Superconductors

1) Normally, all metals have some electrical resistance — even really good conductors like copper.
2) That resistance means that whenever electricity flows through them, they heat up, and some of the electrical energy is wasted as heat.
3) If you make some metals cold enough, though, their resistance disappears completely. The metal becomes a superconductor.
4) Without any resistance, none of the electrical energy is turned into heat, so none of it's wasted.
5) That means you could start a current flowing through a superconducting circuit, take out the battery, and the current would carry on flowing forever.

So What's the Catch...

1) Using superconducting wires you can make:
   a) Power cables that transmit electricity without any loss of power.
   b) Really strong electromagnets that don't need a constant power source.
   c) Electronic circuits that work really fast, because there's no resistance to slow them down.
2) But here's the catch — when I said cold, I meant REALLY COLD. Metals only start superconducting at less than –265 °C! Getting things that cold is very hard, and very expensive.
3) Scientists are trying to develop room temperature superconductors now. So far, they've managed to get some weird metal oxide things to superconduct at about –135 °C, which is a much cheaper temperature to get down to. They've still got a long way to go, though.

Metals in the Middle of the Periodic Table are Transition Metals

A lot of everyday metals are transition metals (e.g. copper, iron, zinc, gold, silver, platinum) — but there are loads of others as well. Transition metals have typical 'metallic' properties.

If you get asked about a transition metal you've never heard of — don't panic. These 'new' transition metals follow all the properties you've already learnt for the others. It's just that some folk get worried by the unfamiliar names.

These are the transition metals

Sc Ti V Cr Mn Fe Co Ni Cu Zn

Transition Metals and Their Compounds Make Good Catalysts

1) Iron is the catalyst used in the Haber process for making ammonia.
2) Nickel is useful for the hydrogenation of alkenes (e.g. to make margarine).

The Compounds are Very Colourful

The compounds are colourful due to the transition metal ion they contain.

e.g. Iron(II) compounds are usually light green.
Iron(III) compounds are usually orange/brown (e.g. rust).
Copper compounds are often blue.

Mendeleev and his amazing technicoloured periodic table...

Superconducting magnets are used in magnetic resonance image (MRI) scanners in hospitals. That way, the huge magnetic fields they need can be generated without using up a load of electricity. Great stuff...

Thermal Decomposition and Precipitation

1) Thermal Decomposition — Breaking Down with Heat

1) Thermal decomposition is when a substance breaks down into simpler substances when heated.
2) Transition metal carbonates break down on heating. Transition metal carbonates are things like copper carbonate ($CuCO_3$), iron(II) carbonate ($FeCO_3$), zinc carbonate ($ZnCO_3$) and manganese carbonate ($MnCO_3$), i.e. they've all got a CO_3 bit in them.
3) They break down into a metal oxide (e.g. copper oxide, CuO) and carbon dioxide. This usually results in a colour change.

EXAMPLE: The thermal decomposition of copper carbonate.

copper carbonate → copper oxide + carbon dioxide

$$CuCO_3 \rightarrow CuO + CO_2$$

This is green... ...and this is black.

The reactions for the thermal decomposition of:
(i) iron(II) carbonate,
(ii) manganese carbonate,
(iii) zinc carbonate,
are the same — although the colours are different.

Use Limewater to Test for Carbon Dioxide

1) You can easily check that the gas given off is carbon dioxide.
2) Bubble the gas through limewater — if it is carbon dioxide, the limewater turns milky.

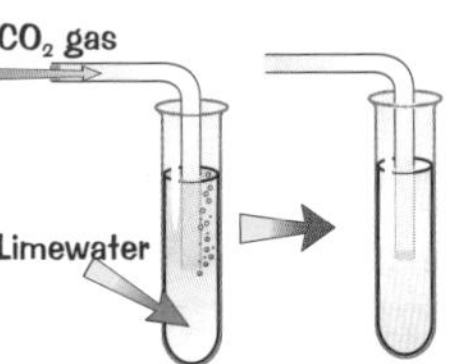

2) Precipitation — A Solid Forms in Solution

1) A precipitation reaction is where two solutions react and an insoluble solid forms in the solution.
2) The solid is said to 'precipitate out' and, confusingly, the solid is also called 'a precipitate'.
3) Some soluble transition metal compounds react with sodium hydroxide to form an insoluble hydroxide, which then precipitates out.

EXAMPLE: Soluble copper sulfate reacts with sodium hydroxide to form insoluble copper hydroxide.

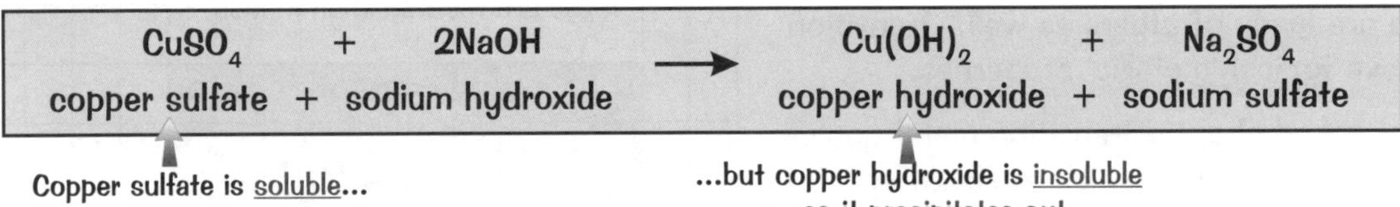

Copper sulfate is soluble... ...but copper hydroxide is insoluble — so it precipitates out.

4) Since copper hydroxide is blue, you get a distinctive blue precipitate forming in the test tube.
5) You can also write the above equation in terms of ions:

$$Cu^{2+} + 2OH^- \rightarrow Cu(OH)_2$$

The Cu^{2+} ions and the hydroxide ions combine to give you the insoluble copper hydroxide.

Use Precipitation to Test for Transition Metal Ions

1) Some insoluble transition metal hydroxides have distinctive colours.
2) You can use this fact to test which transition metal ions a solution contains.

Copper hydroxide is a blue solid.
Iron(II) hydroxide is a dark grey/green solid.
Iron(III) hydroxide is an orange solid.

3) For example, if you add sodium hydroxide to an unknown soluble salt, and an orange precipitate forms, you know you had iron(III) ions in the solution.

My duffel coat's worn out — thermal decomposition...

Limewater isn't actually water with limes dissolved in it. Disappointing isn't it. It's named because it's made from treating quicklime with water, which is named from... umm... well definitely not the fruit. Impress the examiner by learning these equations and the colours of the precipitates.

Revision Summary for Module C3

These certainly aren't the easiest questions you're going to come across. That's because they test what you know without giving you any clues. At first you might think they're impossibly difficult. Eventually you'll realise that they simply test whether you've learnt the stuff or not.
If you're struggling to answer these then you need to do some serious learning.

1)* Give three rules for balancing equations, then try balancing these equations:
   a) $CaCO_3 + HCl \rightarrow CaCl_2 + H_2O + CO_2$ b) $Ca + H_2O \rightarrow Ca(OH)_2 + H_2$
   c) $H_2SO_4 + KOH \rightarrow K_2SO_4 + H_2O$ d) $Fe_2O_3 + H_2 \rightarrow Fe + H_2O$
2) What are the three particles found in an atom? What are their relative masses and charges?
3) What do the mass number and atomic number represent?
4) Explain what an isotope is. Give a well-known example.
5) What's the difference between elements and compounds?
6) What feature of atoms determines the order of the modern periodic table?
7) What are the periods and groups? Explain their significance in terms of electrons.
8) List five facts (or 'rules') about electron shells.
9) Calculate the electron configuration for each of the following elements: $^{4}_{2}He$, $^{12}_{6}C$, $^{31}_{15}P$, $^{39}_{19}K$.
10) Draw diagrams to show the electron arrangements for the first 20 elements.
11) What is ionic bonding? Which kind of atoms like to do ionic bonding? Why is this?
12) The atoms of which groups form 1+, 1–, 2+ and 2– ions?
13) Sketch dot and cross diagrams for:
   a) sodium chloride
   b) magnesium oxide
   c) sodium oxide
   d) magnesium chloride
14) Draw a diagram of a giant ionic lattice and give three features of giant ionic structures.
15) Which group are the alkali metals? What is their outer shell like?
16) Give details of the reactions of the alkali metals with water.
17) List four physical properties and two chemical properties of the alkali metals.
18) How is aluminium extracted from its ore?
   Give four operational details, draw a diagram and give the two equations.
19) Explain three reasons why this process is so expensive.
20) Describe the trends in appearance and reactivity of the halogens as you go down the group.
21)* Write word equations and balanced symbol equations for the reactions between:
   a) bromine and lithium, b) chlorine and potassium, c) iodine and sodium.
22) Give details, with an equation, of a displacement reaction involving the halogens.
23) What is oxidation? What is reduction?
24) What is a superconductor? Describe some useful applications of superconductors.
25) List two properties of transition metal compounds.
26) Name six transition metals, and give uses for two of them.
27) What are thermal decomposition reactions?
28) What type of reaction between two liquids results in the formation of a solid?
   What are these solid products called?
29) Describe a way to test solutions for transition metal ions.

* Answers on page 108.

Acids and Bases

You'll find acids and bases at home, in industry and in the lab — they're an important set of chemicals.

The pH Scale and Universal Indicator

pH 0 1 2 3 4 5 6 7 8 9 10 11 12 13 14

An Indicator is Just a Dye That Changes Colour

The dye in the indicator changes colour depending on whether it's above or below a certain pH. Universal indicator is a very useful combination of dyes which gives the colours shown above.

It's very useful for estimating the pH of a solution.

The pH Scale Goes from 0 to 14

1) A very strong acid has pH 0. A very strong alkali has pH 14.
2) A neutral substance has pH 7 (e.g. pure water).

Acids and Bases Neutralise Each Other

An ACID is a substance with a pH of less than 7. Acids form H^+ ions in water.
A BASE is a substance with a pH of greater than 7.
An ALKALI is a base that DISSOLVES IN WATER. Alkalis form OH^- ions in water.

The reaction between acids and bases is called neutralisation. Make sure you learn it:

acid + base → salt + water

Neutralisation can also be seen in terms of H^+ and OH^- ions like this, so learn it too:

$$H^+ + OH^- \rightarrow H_2O$$

When an acid neutralises a base (or vice versa), the products are neutral, i.e. they have a pH of 7.

Modern Industry Uses Tonnes of Sulfuric Acid

1) Sulfuric acid is used in car batteries, where it's concentrated enough to cause severe burns.
2) It's also used in many manufacturing processes, such as making fertilisers and detergents.
3) You can also use it to clean and prepare metal surfaces, e.g. before painting or welding. A metal surface is usually covered with a layer of insoluble metal oxide. Sulfuric acid reacts with these, forming soluble metal salts which wash away, nice and easily.

This'll give you a firm base for Chemistry...

There's no getting away from acids and bases in Chemistry, or even in real life. They are everywhere — acids are found in loads of foods, like vinegar and fruit, and as food flavourings and preservatives, whilst alkalis (particularly sodium hydroxide) are used to help make all sorts of things from soaps to ceramics.

Reactions of Acids

Metal Oxides and Metal Hydroxides are Bases

1) Some metal oxides and metal hydroxides dissolve in water. These soluble compounds are alkalis.
2) Even bases that won't dissolve in water will still react with acids.
3) So, all metal oxides and metal hydroxides react with acids to form a salt and water.

Acid + Metal Oxide → Salt + Water

Acid + Metal Hydroxide → Salt + Water

(These are neutralisation reactions, of course.)

Hydrochloric acid	+	Copper oxide	→	Copper chloride	+	water
2HCl	+	CuO	→	$CuCl_2$	+	H_2O
Sulfuric acid	+	Potassium hydroxide	→	Potassium sulfate	+	water
H_2SO_4	+	2KOH	→	K_2SO_4	+	$2H_2O$
Nitric acid	+	Sodium hydroxide	→	Sodium nitrate	+	water
HNO_3	+	NaOH	→	$NaNO_3$	+	H_2O

Acids and Carbonates Produce Carbon Dioxide

These are very like the ones above — they just produce carbon dioxide as well.

Acid + Carbonate → Salt + Water + Carbon dioxide

Hydrochloric acid	+	Sodium carbonate	→	Sodium chloride	+	water	+	carbon dioxide
2HCl	+	Na_2CO_3	→	2NaCl	+	H_2O	+	CO_2
Hydrochloric acid	+	Calcium carbonate	→	Calcium chloride	+	water	+	carbon dioxide
2HCl	+	$CaCO_3$	→	$CaCl_2$	+	H_2O	+	CO_2

Acids and Ammonia Produce Ammonium Salts

And lastly...

Acid + Ammonia → Ammonium salt

Hydrochloric acid	+	Ammonia	→	Ammonium chloride
HCl	+	NH_3	→	NH_4Cl
Sulfuric acid	+	Ammonia	→	Ammonium sulfate
H_2SO_4	+	$2NH_3$	→	$(NH_4)_2SO_4$
Nitric acid	+	Ammonia	→	Ammonium nitrate
HNO_3	+	NH_3	→	NH_4NO_3

This last reaction with nitric acid produces the famous ammonium nitrate fertiliser, much appreciated for its double dose of essential nitrogen (see p.57).

Acid + Revision → Insomnia Cure...

Some of these reactions are really useful, and some are just for fun (who said chemistry was dull). Try doing different combinations of acids and alkalis, acids and carbonates, acids and ammonia. Balance them. Cover the page and scribble all the equations down. If you make any mistakes, try again...

Relative Formula Mass

The biggest trouble with relative atomic mass and relative formula mass is that they sound so blood-curdling. You need them for the calculations on the next page though, so take a few deep breaths, and just enjoy, as the mists slowly clear...

Relative Atomic Mass, A_r — Easy Peasy

1) This is just a way of saying how heavy different atoms are compared with the mass of an atom of carbon-12. So carbon-12 has A_r of exactly 12.
2) It turns out that the relative atomic mass A_r is usually just the same as the mass number of the element.
3) In the periodic table, the elements all have two numbers. The smaller one is the atomic number (how many protons it has). The bigger one is the relative atomic mass. Easy peasy, I'd say.

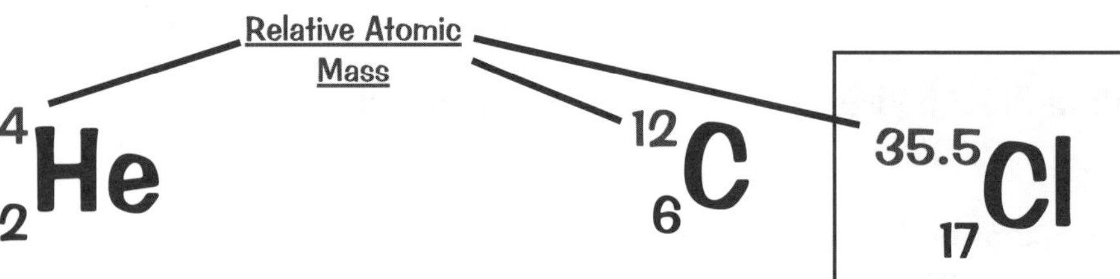

When an element has more than one stable isotope, the relative atomic mass is an average value of all the different isotopes (taking into account how much there is of each isotope).

Helium has $A_r = 4$. Carbon has $A_r = 12$. Chlorine has $A_r = 35.5$.

Relative Formula Mass, M_r — Also Easy Peasy

If you have a compound like $MgCl_2$ then it has a relative formula mass, M_r, which is just all the relative atomic masses added together.

For $MgCl_2$ it would be:

$$MgCl_2$$

$$24 + (35.5 \times 2) = 95$$

So M_r for $MgCl_2$ is simply 95.

You can easily get A_r for any element from the periodic table (see inside front cover), but in a lot of questions they give you them anyway. I tell you what, since it's nearly Christmas I'll run through another example for you:

Compounds with Brackets in...

Find the relative formula mass for calcium hydroxide, $Ca(OH)_2$

ANSWER: The small number 2 after the bracket in the formula $Ca(OH)_2$ means that there's two of everything inside the brackets. But that doesn't make the question any harder really.

The brackets in the sum are in the same place as the brackets in the chemical formula.

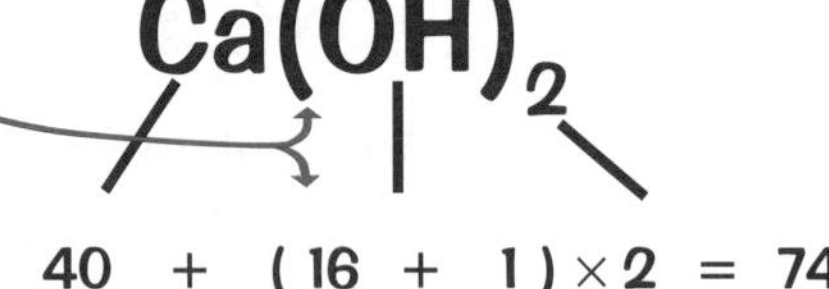

$$Ca(OH)_2$$

$$40 + (16 + 1) \times 2 = 74$$

So the Relative Formula Mass for $Ca(OH)_2$ is 74.

Phew, Chemistry — scary stuff sometimes, innit...

Learn the definitions of relative atomic mass and relative formula mass, then have a go at these:

1) Use the periodic table to find the relative atomic mass of these elements: Cu, K, Kr, Cl
2) Find the relative formula mass of: NaOH, Fe_2O_3, C_6H_{14}, $Mg(NO_3)_2$

Answers on page 108.

Calculating Masses in Reactions

These can be kinda scary too, but chill out, little trembling one — just relax and enjoy.

The Three Important Steps — Not to Be Missed...

(Miss one out and it'll all go horribly wrong, believe me.)

1) Write out the balanced equation
2) Work out M_r — just for the two bits you want
3) Apply the rule: Divide to get one, then multiply to get all
   (But you have to apply this first to the substance they give information about, and then the other one!)

Don't worry — these steps should all make sense when you look at the example below.

Example: What mass of magnesium oxide is produced when 60 g of magnesium is burned in air?

Answer:

1) Write out the balanced equation:

$$2Mg + O_2 \rightarrow 2MgO$$

2) Work out the relative formula masses:

(don't do the oxygen — we don't need it)

$$2 \times 24 \rightarrow 2 \times (24 + 16)$$
$$48 \rightarrow 80$$

3) Apply the rule: Divide to get one, then multiply to get all

The two numbers, 48 and 80, tell us that 48 g of Mg react to give 80 g of MgO.
Here's the tricky bit. You've now got to be able to write this down:

48 g of Mg ......reacts to give.....80 g of MgO
1 g of Mg ......reacts to give.....
60 g of Mg .....reacts to give......

The big clue is that in the question they've said we want to burn '60 g of magnesium', i.e. they've told us how much magnesium to have, and that's how you know to write down the left-hand side of it first, because:

We'll first need to divide by 48 to get 1 g of Mg
and then need to multiply by 60 to get 60 g of Mg.

Then you can work out the numbers on the other side (shown in orange below) by realising that you must divide both sides by 48 and then multiply both sides by 60. It's tricky.

÷48 48 g of Mg .... 80 g of MgO ÷48
1 g of Mg .... 1.67 g of MgO
×60 60 g of Mg .... 100 g of MgO ×60

The mass of product is called the yield of a reaction. You should realise that in practice you never get 100% of the yield, so the amount of product will be slightly less than calculated (see p.56).

This finally tells us that 60 g of magnesium will produce 100 g of magnesium oxide.
If the question had said 'Find how much magnesium gives 500 g of magnesium oxide', you'd fill in the MgO side first, because that's the one you'd have the information about. Got it? Good-O!

Reaction mass calculations? — no worries, matey...

Calculating masses is a very useful skill to have. If you're trying to get 10 g of magnesium oxide, say, for use in a medicine or fertiliser, you're going to need to be able to work out how much magnesium to use, or you could get too much or too little. A wrong calculation could be an expensive mistake...

Percentage Yield

Of course, things are never simple. Not even the most efficient reaction will have a 100% yield.

Percentage Yield Compares Actual and Predicted Yield

The more reactants you start with, the higher the actual yield will be — that's pretty obvious. But the percentage yield doesn't depend on the amount of reactants you started with — it's a percentage.

1) The predicted yield of a reaction can be calculated from the balanced reaction equation (see page 55).
2) Percentage yield is given by the formula:

$$\text{percentage yield} = \frac{\text{actual yield (grams)}}{\text{predicted yield (grams)}} \times 100$$

3) Percentage yield is always somewhere between 0 and 100%.
4) 100% yield means that you got all the product you expected to get.
5) 0% yield means that no reactants were converted into product, i.e. no product at all was made.

Yields are Always Less Than 100%

In real life, you never get a 100% yield. Some product or reactant always gets lost along the way — and that goes for big industrial processes as well as school lab experiments.
How this happens depends on what sort of reaction it is and what apparatus is being used.

Lots of things can go wrong, but the four you need to know about are:

1) Evaporation

Liquids evaporate all the time — not just while they're being heated.

2) Heating

Losses while heating can be due to evaporation, or for more complicated reasons.

In reversible reactions, increasing the temperature moves the equilibrium position.

So heating the reaction to speed it up might mean a lower yield.

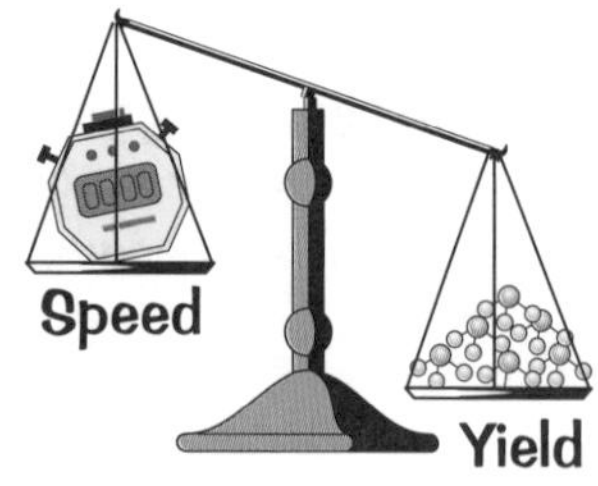

3) Filtration

When you filter a liquid to remove solid particles, you nearly always lose a bit of liquid or a bit of solid.

1) If you want to keep the liquid, you lose the bit that remains with the solid and filter paper (as they always stay a bit wet).
2) If you want to keep the solid, some of it usually gets left behind when you scrape it off the filter paper — even if you're really careful.

4) Transferring Liquids

You always lose a bit of liquid when you transfer it from one container to another — even if you manage not to spill it.

Some of it always gets left behind on the inside surface of the old container. Think about it — it's always wet when you finish.

You can't always get what you want...

Unfortunately, no matter how careful you are, you're not going to get a 100% yield in any reaction. So you'll always get a little loss of product. In industry, people work very hard to keep wastage as low as possible — so reactants that don't react first time are collected and recycled whenever possible.

Fertilisers

There's a lot more to using fertilisers than making your garden look nice and pretty...

Fertilisers Provide Plants with the Essential Elements for Growth

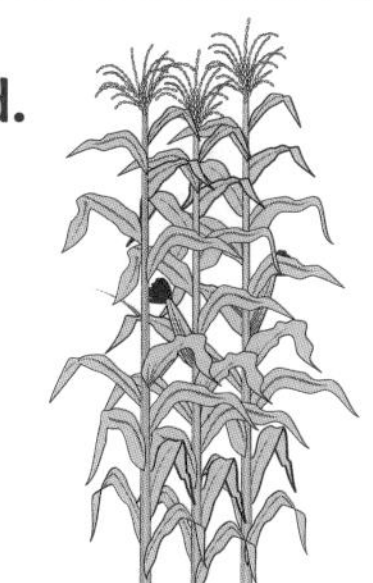

1) The three main essential elements in fertilisers are nitrogen, phosphorus and potassium. If plants don't get enough of these elements, their growth and life processes are affected. For example, nitrogen is used to make plant proteins, which are essential for growth.
2) Sometimes these elements are missing from the soil because they've been used up by a previous crop.
3) Fertilisers replace these missing elements or provide more of them. This helps to increase the crop yield.
4) The fertiliser must first dissolve in water before it can be taken in by the crop roots.

Ammonia Can be Neutralised with Acids to Produce Fertilisers

1) Ammonia is a base, and can be neutralised by acids to make ammonium salts.
2) Ammonium nitrate is an especially good fertiliser because it has nitrogen from two sources, the ammonia and the nitric acid. Kind of a double dose.

Ammonia + Nitric acid → Ammonium nitrate

3) Ammonium sulfate can also be used as a fertiliser, and is made by neutralising sulfuric acid with ammonia:

Ammonia + Sulfuric acid → Ammonium sulfate

These are neutralisation reactions, but using ammonia as the base you only get an ammonium salt — not salt + water.

4) Two other fertilisers manufactured using ammonia are ammonium phosphate and urea.
5) Potassium nitrate is also a fertiliser.

Preparing Ammonium Nitrate in the Lab

You can make most fertilisers using this titration method — just choose the right acid (nitric, sulfuric or phosphoric) and alkali (ammonia or potassium hydroxide) to get the salt you want. You'll need ammonia and nitric acid to make ammonium nitrate.

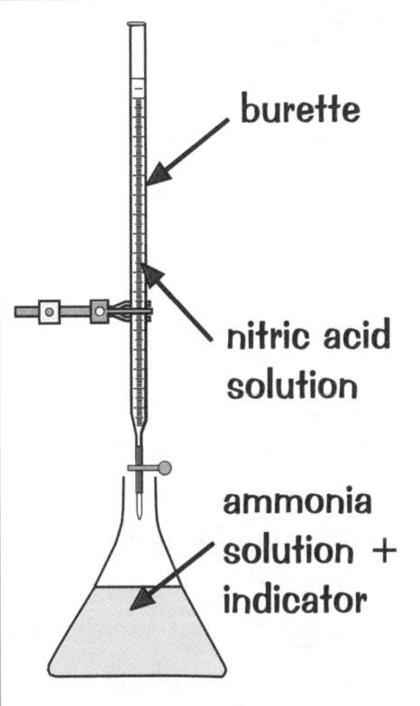

1) Set up your apparatus as in the diagram. Add a few drops of methyl orange indicator to the ammonia — it'll turn yellow.
2) Slowly add the nitric acid from the burette into the ammonia, until the yellow colour just changes to red. Gently swirl the flask as you add the acid. Go especially slowly when you think the alkali's almost neutralised. Methyl orange is yellow in alkalis, but red in acids, so this colour change means all the ammonia has been neutralised and you've got ammonium nitrate solution.
3) To get solid ammonium nitrate crystals, gently evaporate the solution until only a little bit is left. Leave it to crystallise.
4) The ammonium nitrate crystals aren't pure — they've got methyl orange in them. To get pure ammonium nitrate crystals, you need to note exactly how much nitric acid it took to neutralise the ammonia, and then repeat the titration using that volume of acid, but no indicator.

Using urea as a fertiliser — you must be taking the...

Fertilisers are really useful. With increasing population sizes we need to be able to produce bigger, better crops to feed everyone. Famine is a major problem in some places, like parts of Africa. The high temperatures and droughts decrease their crop yield, and they just can't make enough to go around.

Fertilisers

Calculating Relative Formula Mass of a Fertiliser

This is exactly the same as calculating any other relative formula mass — see page 54.
It's all the relative atomic masses added together.

Find the relative formula mass for ammonium nitrate, NH_4NO_3, using the following data:
A_r for H = 1 A_r for N = 14 A_r for O = 16

ANSWER:

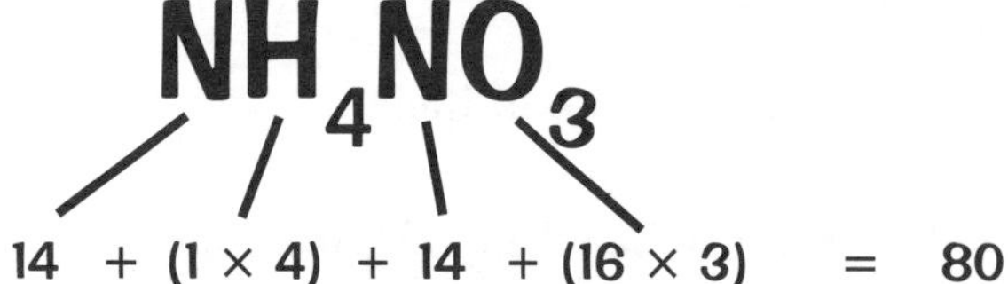

So the M_r for NH_4NO_3 is 80.

Calculating the % Mass of an Essential Element in a Fertiliser

This is actually dead easy — so long as you've learnt this formula:

$$\text{PERCENTAGE MASS OF AN ELEMENT IN A COMPOUND} = \frac{A_r \times \text{No. of atoms (of that element)}}{M_r \text{ (of whole compound)}} \times 100$$

Find the percentage mass of nitrogen in ammonium sulfate, $(NH_4)_2SO_4$, using the following data:
A_r for H = 1 A_r for N = 14 A_r for O = 16 A_r for S = 32

ANSWER: M_r of $(NH_4)_2SO_4 = 2 \times [14 + (1 \times 4)] + 32 + (16 \times 4) = 132$

Now use the formula:

$$\text{Percentage mass} = \frac{A_r \times n}{M_r} \times 100 = \frac{14 \times 2}{132} \times 100 = 21.2\%$$

So there you have it. Nitrogen represents 21.2% of the mass of ammonium sulfate.

Fertilisers Damage Lakes and Rivers — Eutrophication

1) Fertilisers which contain nitrates are essential to modern farming.
2) But you get problems if some of the rich fertiliser finds its way into rivers and streams.
3) This happens quite easily if too much fertiliser is applied, especially if it rains soon afterwards.
4) The result is EUTROPHICATION, which basically means 'too much of a good thing'.

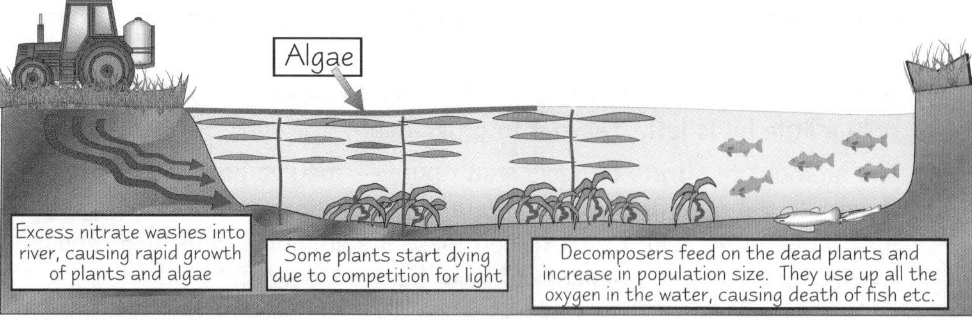

As the picture shows, too many nitrates in the water cause a sequence of 'mega-growth', 'mega-death' and 'mega-decay' involving most of the plant and animal life in the water.

5) Farmers need to take a lot more care when spreading artificial fertilisers.

There's nowt wrong wi' just spreadin' muck on it...

Unfortunately, no matter how good something is, there's always a downside. It's a good idea to learn the diagram really, really well, and make sure you understand it. Learn it mini-essay style.

The Haber Process

This is an important industrial process. It produces ammonia (NH_3), which is needed for making fertilisers.

The Haber Process is a Reversible Reaction:

$$N_2 + 3H_2 \rightleftharpoons 2NH_3 \quad (+\text{ heat})$$

1) The nitrogen is obtained easily from the air, which is 78% nitrogen (and 21% oxygen).
2) The hydrogen comes from the cracking of oil fractions or natural gas. See page 14.
3) Because the reaction is reversible (it goes in both directions), not all the nitrogen and hydrogen will convert to ammonia.
4) The N_2 and H_2 which don't react are recycled and passed through again so none is wasted.

Industrial conditions:

PRESSURE: 200 atmospheres; TEMPERATURE: 450 °C; CATALYST: Iron

Because the Reaction is Reversible, There's a Compromise to be Made:

1) Higher pressures favour the forward reaction (since there are four molecules of gas on the left-hand side, but only two molecules on the right).
2) So the pressure is set as high as possible to give the best % yield, without making the plant too expensive to build (it'd be too expensive to build a plant that'd stand pressures of over 1000 atmospheres, for example). Hence the 200 atmospheres operating pressure.
3) The forward reaction is exothermic, which means that increasing the temperature will actually move the equilibrium the wrong way — away from ammonia and towards N_2 and H_2.
   So the yield of ammonia would be greater at lower temperatures.
4) The trouble is, lower temperatures mean a slower rate of reaction. So what they do is increase the temperature anyway, to get a much faster rate of reaction.

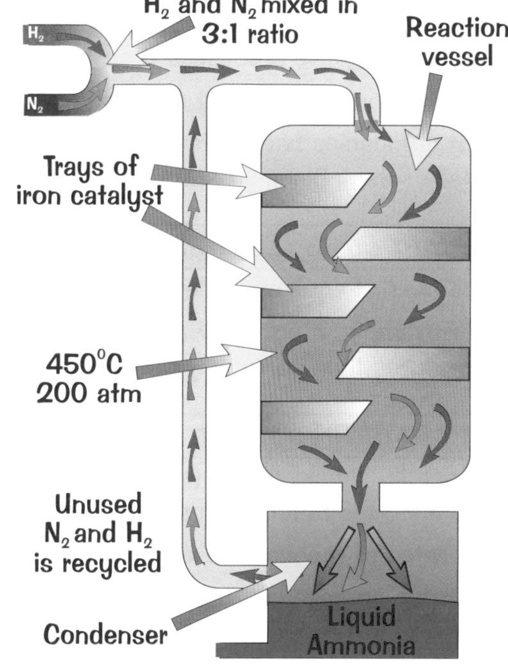

5) The 450 °C is a compromise between maximum yield and speed of reaction.
   It's better to wait just 20 seconds for a 10% yield than to have to wait 60 seconds for a 20% yield.
6) Remember, the unused hydrogen and nitrogen are recycled, so nothing is wasted.

The Iron Catalyst Speeds Up the Reaction and Keeps Costs Down

1) The iron catalyst makes the reaction go faster, which gets it to the equilibrium proportions more quickly. But remember, the catalyst doesn't affect the position of equilibrium (i.e. the % yield).
2) Without the catalyst the temperature would have to be raised even further to get a quick enough reaction, and that would reduce the % yield even further. So the catalyst is very important.

200 atmospheres? — that could give you a headache...

The Haber process makes ammonia, which is used to make fertilisers, which are great. Because it's a reversible reaction, certain factors need to be controlled to increase the percentage yield. Remember — the temperature is increased to improve speed, not the equilibrium position. Learn it mini-essay style.

Minimising the Cost of Production

Things like fast reaction rates and high % yields are nice in industry — but in the end, the important thing is keeping costs down. It all comes down to maximum efficiency...

Production Cost Depends on Several Different Factors

There are five main things that affect the cost of making a new substance. It's these five factors that companies have to consider when deciding if, and then how, to produce a chemical.

1) Price of Energy

a) Industry needs to keep its energy bills as low as possible.

b) If a reaction needs a high temperature, the running costs will be higher.

2) Cost of Raw Materials

a) This is kept to a minimum by recycling any materials that haven't reacted.

b) A good example of this is the Haber process. The % yield of the reaction is quite low (about 10%), but the unreacted N_2 and H_2 can be recycled to keep waste to a minimum.

3) Labour Costs (Wages)

a) Everyone who works for a company has got to be paid.

b) Labour-intensive processes (i.e. those that involve many people), can be very expensive.

c) Automation cuts running costs by reducing the number of people involved.

d) But companies have always got to weigh any savings they make on their wage bill against the initial cost and running costs of the machinery.

4) Plant Costs (Equipment)

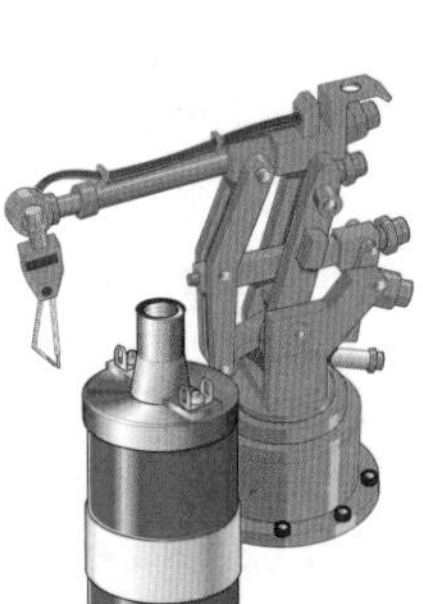

a) The cost of equipment depends on the conditions it has to cope with.

b) For example, it costs far more to make something to withstand very high pressures than something which only needs to work at atmospheric pressure.

5) Rate of Production

a) Generally speaking, the faster the reaction goes, the better it is in terms of reducing the time and costs of production.

b) So rates of reaction are often increased by using catalysts.

c) But the increase in production rate has to balance the cost of buying the catalyst in the first place and replacing any that gets lost.

Optimum Conditions are Chosen to Give the Lowest Cost

1) Optimum conditions are those that give the lowest production cost per kg of product — even if this means compromising on the speed of reaction or % yield. Learn the definition:

OPTIMUM CONDITIONS are those that give the LOWEST PRODUCTION COST.

2) However, the rate of reaction and percentage yield must both be high enough to make a sufficient amount of product each day.

3) Don't forget, a low percentage yield is okay, as long as the starting materials can be recycled.

This will make it as cheap as chips...

In industry, compromises must be made, just like in life, and the Haber process is a prime example of this. You need to learn those five different factors affecting cost, and the definition of 'optimum conditions'. Cover the page and scribble it all down — keep doing it until you get it all right.

Detergents and Dry-Cleaning

Cleanliness is next to godliness... or so they say.

Washing at Low Temperatures Saves Energy (and Your Clothes)

1) When you're washing clothes, high temperatures usually work best for getting things clean. They melt greasy dirt deposits, so your detergent can break up and remove the stain more easily.
2) But some natural fabrics (e.g. wool) shrink, and some artificial fabrics (e.g. nylon) quickly lose their shape, if they're washed at too high a temperature.
3) Also, some dyes will run in high-temperature washes. Brightly coloured clothes can quickly fade and stop looking new.
4) Nowadays you can get biological detergents, with enzymes in them. The enzymes digest protein-based and fat-based stains without the need for high temperatures, which protects your clothes. If you heat biological detergents above 40 °C, the enzymes denature and stop working.
5) Low-temperature washes also save energy, which is great for the environment and your energy bill. Less energy used means less carbon dioxide emissions, reducing the greenhouse effect and climate change.

Detergents Work by Sticking to Both Water and Grease

1) Some dirt will dissolve in water without the help of a detergent, but most won't. Anything that's oil-based won't dissolve in water at all (see next page).
2) Detergents help water and oil to mix.
3) Detergents contain molecules that have a hydrophilic (water-loving) head, and a hydrophobic (water-hating) tail.
4) The hydrophilic heads form intermolecular bonds with water.
5) And the hydrophobic tails bond to the fat molecules in greasy dirt.

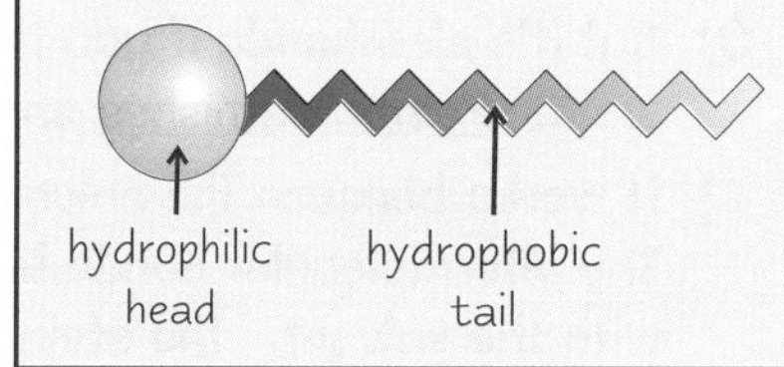

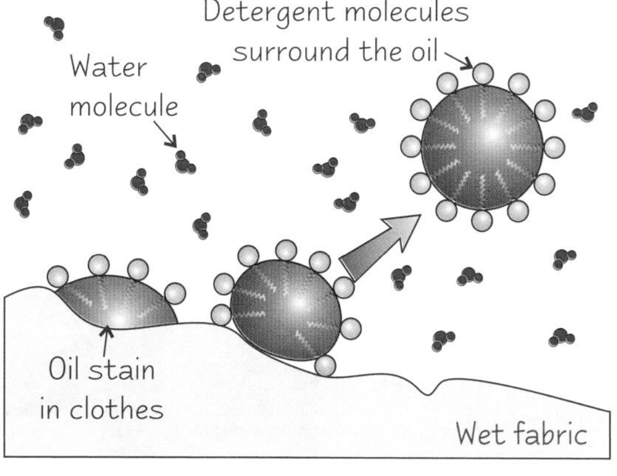

6) When you (or a washing machine) swish the fabric around, the detergent molecules find their way in between the grease and the wet fabric.
7) The detergent molecules eventually surround the grease completely, and bond to it, with their hydrophilic heads around the outside like a coat.
8) This hydrophilic coat stops the grease droplets reattaching themselves to the fabric, and they're pulled away into the wash water.
9) Then, when you rinse the fabric, the grease and dirt are rinsed away along with the water.

Most Detergents are Salts

1) The original detergents were soaps, which are made from fats. Soaps form a scum with hard water which can build up on your clothes — so they're not used so much nowadays.
2) Modern synthetic (soapless) detergents are mostly made using big organic molecules from crude oil. An acid group is added to one end of the molecule to make an organic acid. This is then neutralised with a strong alkali, usually sodium or potassium hydroxide, to form a salt:

   organic acid + strong alkali → salt (detergent) + water

   Soapless detergents don't form a scum with hard water, which is handy.
3) Both kinds of detergent work in the same way. The covalent hydrocarbon chain is the hydrophobic tail. The ionic bit on the end is the hydrophilic head.

Detergents and Dry-Cleaning

Different Solvents Dissolve Different Stains

1) When a solid dissolves in a liquid, a clear solution is formed. The liquid is called the solvent, and the solid is called the solute.
2) Here's how it works. If the solvent is water and the solute is a sugar lump:
   - the water molecules form strong intermolecular bonds with the sugar molecules,
   - as water-sugar bonds form, they pull apart the sugar-sugar bonds and the sugar lump breaks up,
   - the water molecules completely surround the sugar molecules, and you have a solution.
3) You can't dissolve every solid in every liquid — they have to be able to form the right sort of intermolecular bond. So different solids need different solvents.
4) To successfully remove a stain, you have to use the right solvent to dissolve it off the fabric.
5) A lot of stains aren't soluble in water — especially greasy stains, paints and varnishes. Sometimes using a detergent can remove the stain (see previous page), but sometimes you need to use a different, dry-cleaning solvent.

Dry-Cleaning Uses a Solvent That isn't Water

1) There are quite a few dry-cleaning solvents around, but the most common one is tetrachloroethene.
2) Dry-cleaning is usually used for clothes that would get damaged if you washed them in water — e.g. clothes with fibres that swell up and change shape when they get wet.
3) But it's also handy if you have a stain that won't dissolve in water or detergent — dry-cleaning might work. Paints, varnishes and other organic chemicals often dissolve in an organic dry-cleaning solvent.
4) It works because the solvent is strongly attracted to the oily molecules in the stain. The intermolecular bonds between the 'stain' molecules break and are replaced by bonds with the solvent. The stain dissolves.

Some Cleaners are Better than Others

All washing powders claim to clean better than their rivals. You've got to be able to compare the results of lab tests to work out which one really cleans better. You can do a test something like this:

1) Take some white cotton cloth and cut it into pieces.
2) Measure out equal amounts of some substances to test your washing powder with, e.g. egg yolk, engine oil, blackcurrant, chocolate. Stain each bit of cloth with a different substance and leave to dry.
3) Set up a 'washing machine' — a beaker of water over a Bunsen burner. Heat the water to 40 °C and dissolve some washing powder in it.
4) Add a piece of stained cloth and 'wash' (stir) for 5 minutes.
5) Remove the cloth with tongs (enzymes are irritants), rinse under a running tap, and let it dry.
6) Repeat for each washing powder, keeping the volume of water, the amount of powder, the temperature and the wash time the same.

Compare the washed cloth pieces:

Which cloth is whitest? Which detergent lived up to its claims the best? Which was best for protein stains (e.g. egg, milk, blood)? Which was best on fats (e.g. butter, engine oil, suntan lotion)?

Would your whites pass the OCR exam challenge...

Yes, I'm afraid you are going to have to do some washing at some point — you will run out of clothes eventually. And when you do, you'll have the pleasure of knowing how it all works. Isn't that nice. ☺

Chemical Production

The Type of Manufacturing Process Depends on the Product

Continuous production: large-scale industrial manufacture of popular chemicals, e.g. the Haber process for making ammonia (see p.59).

1) Production never stops, so you don't waste time emptying the reactor and setting it up again.
2) It runs automatically — you only need to interfere if something goes wrong.
3) The quality of the product is very consistent.
4) Usually the manufacturing plant only makes one product, so there's little risk of contamination.
5) Start-up costs to build the plant are huge, and it isn't cost-effective to run at less than full capacity.

Batch production: small quantities of specialist chemicals, e.g. pharmaceutical drugs, often on demand.

1) It's flexible — several different products can be made using the same equipment.
2) Start-up costs are relatively low — small-scale, multi-purpose equipment can be bought off the shelf.
3) It's labour-intensive — the equipment needs to be set up and manually controlled for each batch and then cleaned out at the end.
4) 'Downtime' between batches means there are times when you're not producing anything.
5) It's trickier to keep the same quality from batch to batch. Also, there's more chance of contamination because the same equipment is used to make more than one thing. On the other hand, any problems can be traced to a specific batch, which can be recalled.

Pharmaceutical drugs are complicated to make and there's relatively low demand for them. So, batch production is often the most cost-effective way for a company to produce small quantities of different drugs to order.

Several Factors Affect the Cost of Pharmaceutical Drugs

1) Market Research — identifying a possible new drug. Is there any competition already out there? Is there enough demand for it to make it worthwhile developing?
2) Research and Development — finding a suitable compound, testing it, modifying it, testing again, until it's ready. This involves the work of lots of highly paid scientists.
3) Trialling — no drug can be sold until it's gone through loads of time-consuming tests including animal trials and human trials to prove that it works and it's safe.
4) Marketing — advertising in medical magazines and buttering up doctors.
5) Manufacture — multi-step batch production is labour-intensive and can't be automated. Other costs include energy and raw materials. The raw materials for pharmaceuticals are often rare and sometimes need to be extracted from plants (an expensive process).

It takes about 12 years and £900 million to develop a new drug and get it onto the market. Ouch.

To extract a substance from a plant, it has to be crushed and dissolved in a suitable solvent. Then, you can extract the substance you want by chromatography.

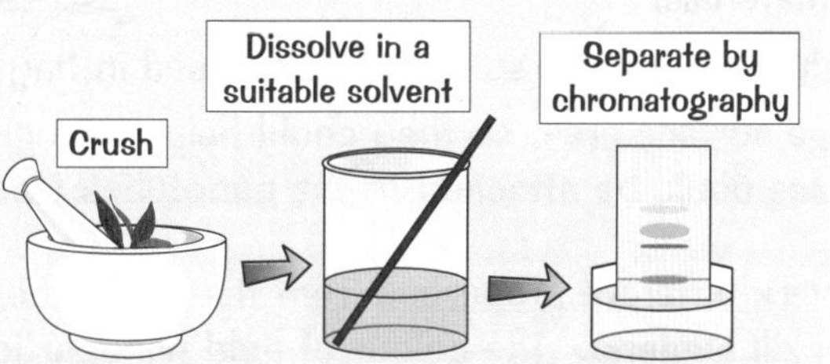

Once the active ingredient has been isolated, it can be analysed, and its chemical structure worked out.

It's often possible to make a synthetic version of the chemical.

6) The actual price per dose depends on the demand and how long the company is willing to wait to get back its initial investment. A company only holds a drug patent for 20 years — after that anyone can make it. Some drugs can cost thousands of pounds for just one dose.

I wish they'd find a drug to cure exams...

£900 million. You could buy yourself an island. And one for your mum. And a couple for your mates...

Allotropes of Carbon

Allotropes are just different structural forms of the same element — carbon has quite a few:

Diamond is Used in Jewellery and Cutting Tools

1) Diamonds are sparkly, colourless and clear. Ideal for jewellery.
2) Each carbon atom forms four covalent bonds in a very rigid giant covalent structure, which makes diamond really hard. This makes diamonds ideal as cutting tools.
3) All those strong covalent bonds give diamond a very high melting point.
4) It doesn't conduct electricity because it has no free electrons.

Graphite Makes the Lead of Your Pencil

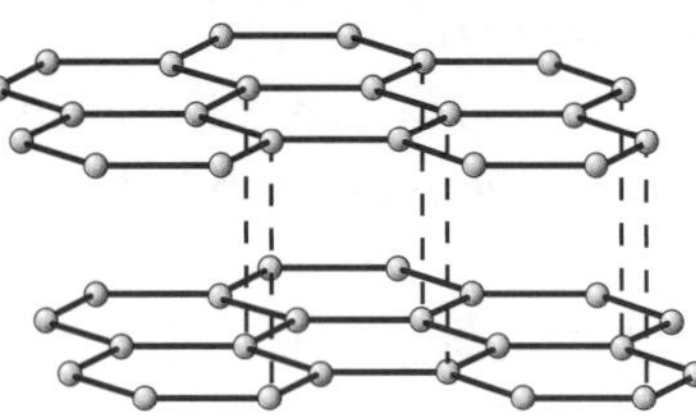

1) Graphite is black and opaque, but still kind of shiny.
2) Each carbon atom only forms three covalent bonds, creating sheets of carbon atoms which are free to slide over each other.
3) The layers are held together so loosely that they can be rubbed off onto paper to leave a black mark — that's how a pencil works. This also makes graphite slippery, so it's ideal as a lubricating material.
4) Graphite's got a high melting point — the covalent bonds need loads of energy to break.
5) Since only three out of each carbon's four outer electrons are used in bonds, there are lots of spare electrons. This means graphite conducts electricity — it's used for electrodes. See page 44.

Fullerenes are Nanoparticles

Nanoparticles are only a few nanometres (nm) across (1 nm = 0.000 000 001 m).

1) Fullerenes are molecules of carbon, shaped like hollow balls or closed tubes. Each carbon atom forms three covalent bonds with its neighbours, leaving free electrons that can conduct electricity.
2) The smallest fullerene is buckminsterfullerene, which has 60 carbon atoms joined in a ball — its molecular formula is C_{60}.
3) Fullerenes can be used to 'cage' other molecules. The fullerene structure forms around another atom or molecule, which is then trapped inside. This could be a new way of delivering a drug into the body, e.g. for slow release.

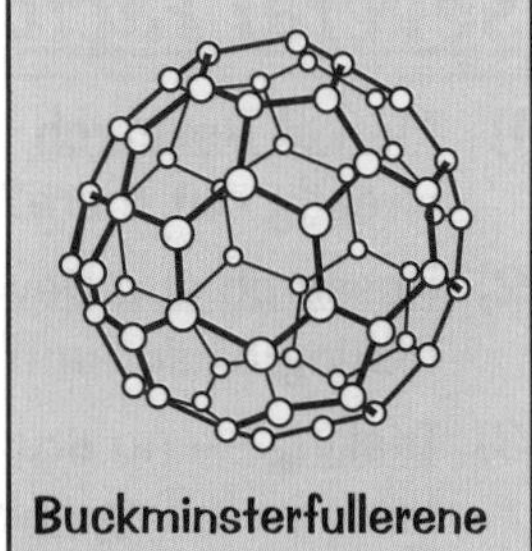
Buckminsterfullerene

Fullerenes can be joined together to form nanotubes — teeny tiny hollow carbon tubes:

a) All those covalent bonds make carbon nanotubes very strong. They can be used to reinforce graphite in tennis rackets and to make stronger, lighter building materials.

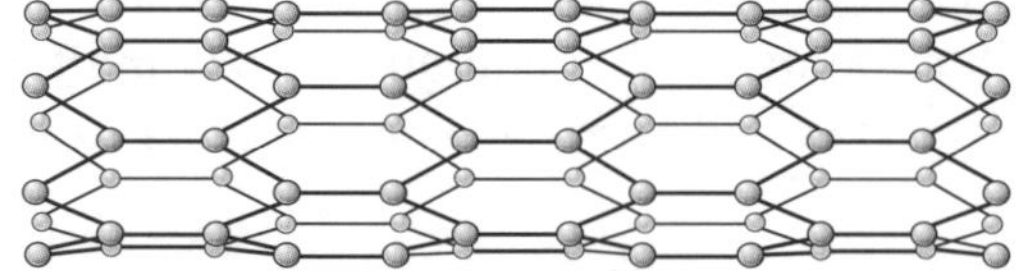

b) Nanotubes conduct electricity, so they can be used in tiny electric circuits for computer chips.
c) They have a huge surface area, so they could help make great industrial catalysts — individual catalyst molecules could be attached to the nanotubes (the bigger the surface area the better).

Nanoparticles have very different properties from the 'bulk' chemical. Nanoparticles of normally unreactive silver can kill bacteria. The colour of gold nanoparticles actually varies from red to purple.
Nanoparticles can be made by molecular engineering, but this is really hard. Molecular engineering is building a product molecule-by-molecule to a specific design — either by positioning each molecule exactly where you want it or by starting with a bigger structure and taking bits off it.

Carbon is a girl's best friend...

Nanoparticles. Confused? Just think of it as knitting teeny weeny atomic footballs, and you'll be fine...

Water Purity

Water, water, everywhere... well, there is if you live in Cumbria.

There are a Variety of Limited Water Resources in the UK

1) As well as for drinking, we need water for loads of domestic uses (mainly washing things).
2) Industrially, water is important as a cheap raw material, a coolant (especially in power stations) and a solvent. Between half and two thirds of all the fresh water used in the UK goes into industry.

> In the UK, we get our water from:
> 1) SURFACE WATER: lakes, rivers and reservoirs (artificial lakes). In much of England and Wales, these sources start to run dry during the summer months.
> 2) GROUNDWATER: aquifers (rocks that trap water underground). In parts of the south-east where surface water is very limited, as much as 70% of the domestic water supply comes from groundwater.

All these resources are limited, depending on annual rainfall, and demand for water increases every year. Experts worry that, unless we limit our water use, by 2025 we might not have enough water to supply everybody's needs. Ways to conserve water include:

1) Stopping leaks in pipes. About 20% of all the water that enters the mains is lost through leaks.
2) Not wasting water at home, e.g. not leaving taps running, using a bucket instead of a hose to wash the car, avoiding sprinklers in the garden (they use up to 1000 litres per hour), washing up by hand rather than using a dishwasher, using a water-efficient washing machine (fully loaded each time).
3) Recycling water, e.g. collecting rainwater to use in the garden.
4) Installing a water meter — you tend to waste less water if you're paying for it by the bath-full.

Water is Purified in Water Treatment Plants

How much purification the water needs depends on the source. Groundwater from aquifers is usually quite pure, but surface water needs a lot of treatment.

The processes include:

1) Filtration — a wire mesh screens out large twigs etc., and then gravel and sand beds filter out any other solid bits.
2) Sedimentation — iron sulfate or aluminium sulfate is added to the water, which makes fine particles clump together and settle at the bottom.
3) Chlorination — chlorine gas is bubbled through to kill harmful bacteria and other microbes.

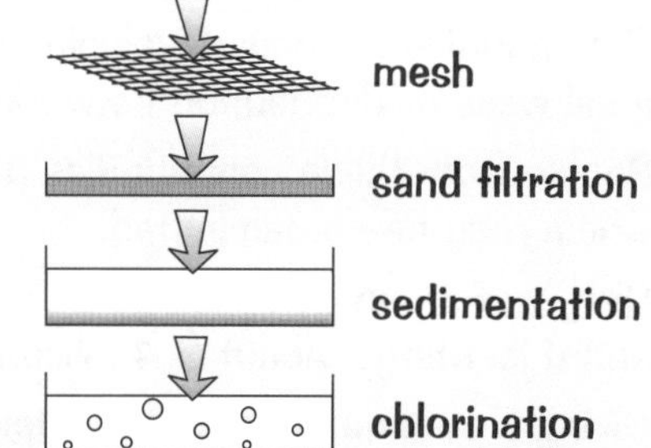

Other processes can be used to break down and remove some chemical pollutants, but it's too difficult to get rid of all the dissolved impurities, including minerals which cause water hardness and some harmful or toxic chemicals such as pesticides and fertilisers (see below).

Tap Water Can Still Contain Impurities

The water that comes out of our taps has to meet strict safety standards, but low levels of pollutants are still found. These pollutants come from various sources:

1) Nitrate residues from excess fertiliser 'run-off' into rivers and lakes. If too many nitrates get into drinking water it can cause serious health problems, especially for young babies. Nitrates prevent the blood from carrying oxygen properly.
2) Lead compounds from old lead pipes. Lead is very poisonous, particularly in children.
3) Pesticide residues from spraying too near to rivers and lakes.

Water Purity

You Can Test Water for Various Dissolved Ions

Water companies have to test their water regularly to make sure that pollutant levels don't exceed strict limits. You can test for some dissolved ions very easily using precipitation reactions (where two dissolved compounds react to form an insoluble solid — the precipitate).

1) TEST FOR SULFATE IONS: add some dilute hydrochloric acid, then 10 drops of barium chloride solution to the test sample. If you see a white precipitate, there are sulfate ions in the sample.

add $BaCl_2$ solution

white precipitate of $BaSO_4$

barium chloride + sulfate ions → barium sulfate + chloride ions

$$BaCl_2 + SO_4^{2-} \rightarrow BaSO_4 + 2Cl^-$$

e.g. if potassium sulfate (K_2SO_4) was present, you'd get $BaSO_4$ and KCl produced.

2) TEST FOR HALIDE IONS: add some dilute nitric acid, then 10 drops of silver nitrate solution to the test sample.
   Chloride ions will produce a white precipitate.
   Bromide ions will produce a cream precipitate.
   Iodide ions will produce a pale yellow precipitate.

   e.g. if sodium iodide (NaI) is present in the water, you'll get the following reaction:

$$AgNO_3 + NaI \rightarrow AgI + NaNO_3$$

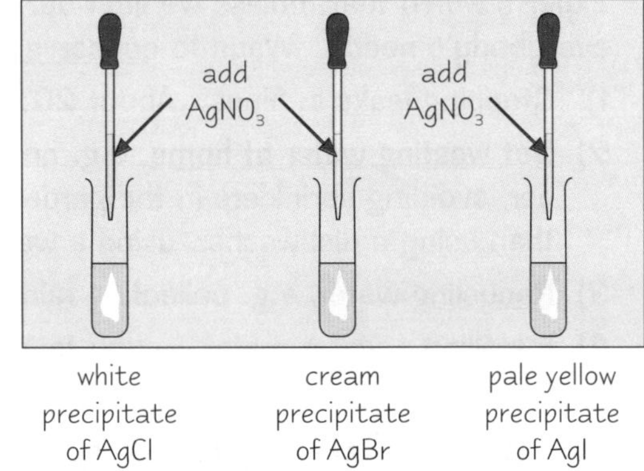

white precipitate of AgCl — cream precipitate of AgBr — pale yellow precipitate of AgI

1.4 Billion People Worldwide Can't Get Clean Water to Drink

1) Communities in some developing countries often don't have access to sources of clean water, such as local wells or distribution networks.
2) People from these communities often have to walk for miles every day to fetch water from sources which may be contaminated.
3) Dirty water can carry dangerous microbes which cause outbreaks of serious diseases such as cholera and dysentery. About 3.4 million people (mainly children) die from water-borne diseases each year.
4) Giving a community a clean water source and teaching them the skills to maintain it can save many lives. It doesn't have to be complicated — sinking a well and adding a pump is often all that's needed.

You Can Get Fresh Water by Distilling Sea Water

1) In some very dry countries, e.g. Kuwait, sea water is distilled to produce drinking water.
2) Distillation needs loads of energy, so it's really expensive and not practical for producing large quantities of fresh water.
3) Kuwait has so much oil (in other words, cheap energy) that it's the only country in the world which uses distilled water for agriculture.

Who'd have thought there'd be so much to learn about water...

In the UK we're very lucky to have clean water available at the turn of a tap — but it's not a never-ending supply. Fresh water is quite hard to come by at the end of a dry summer. Learn how water is purified and tested in the UK, and what pollutants get through the cleaning process. Cover. Scribble.

Revision Summary for Module C4

Some more tricky questions to stress you out. The thing is though, why bother doing easy questions? These meaty monsters find out what you really know, and worse, what you really don't. Yeah, I know, it's kinda scary, but if you want to get anywhere in life you've got to face up to a bit of hardship. That's just the way it is. Take a few deep breaths and then try these.

1) Describe fully the colour of universal indicator for every pH from 0 to 14.
2) Is the pH of nitric acid less than or greater than 7? What about the pH of ammonia?
3) What are acids and bases? What is an alkali?
4) What type of ions are always present when: a) acids, and b) alkalis dissolve in water?
5) Write the equation of a neutralisation reaction in terms of these ions.
6) Describe three uses of sulfuric acid in industry.
7) What type of salts do: a) hydrochloric, and b) sulfuric acid produce?
8)* Write a balanced symbol equation for the reaction between dilute nitric acid and ammonia.
9)* Find A_r or M_r for each of these (use the periodic table inside the front cover):
   a) Ca b) Ag c) CO_2 d) $MgCO_3$ e) $Al(OH)_3$
   f) ZnO g) Na_2CO_3 h) sodium chloride
10)* Write down the three steps of the method for calculating reacting masses.
   a) What mass of magnesium oxide is produced when 112.1 g of magnesium burns in air?
   b) What mass of sodium is needed to produce 108.2 g of sodium oxide?
   c) What mass of carbon will react with hydrogen to produce 24.6 g of propane (C_3H_8)?
11) What is the formula for percentage yield? How does percentage yield differ from actual yield?
12) Name four factors that prevent the percentage yield being 100%
13) Name three essential elements in fertilisers.
14) How does nitrogen increase the growth of plants?
15) Name two fertilisers which are manufactured from ammonia.
16) Describe how you could produce one of these fertilisers in the lab.
17) Describe what can happen if too much fertiliser is put onto fields. How can it be avoided?
18) What determines the choice of operating temperature for the Haber process?
19) What effect does the catalyst have on the Haber process reaction?
20) In general, how can the cost of raw materials be kept as low as possible?
21) In industry, how are the 'optimum conditions' for a process decided?
22) Explain the advantages of washing clothes at low temperatures.
23) Describe how a detergent helps remove greasy dirt from clothes.
24) Explain, in terms of intermolecular forces, how dry-cleaning works.
25) What are 'batch production' and 'continuous production'.
26) Explain the advantages of using batch production to make pharmaceutical drugs.
    What are the disadvantages?
27) It can take 12 years and about £900 million to bring a new drug to market. Explain why.
28) In terms of intermolecular bonds, explain why diamond makes a good cutting tool.
29) Why does graphite conduct electricity?
30) What properties of carbon nanotubes make them suitable for the following applications:
    a) reinforcing tennis rackets, b) computer chips, c) catalysts?
31) How might fullerenes be used to deliver drugs to the body?
32) Why is it important to preserve water. List four ways to preserve water in the home.
33) A student adds dilute hydrochloric acid and barium chloride to a water sample and a white precipitate is produced. What ions were present in the water?

* Answers on page 108.

The Mole

The mole is really confusing. I think it's the word that puts people off. It's very difficult to see the relevance of the word "mole" to anything but a small burrowing animal.

"THE MOLE" is Simply the Name Given to a Certain Number

Just like "a million" is this many: 1 000 000; or "a billion" is this many: 1 000 000 000, so "a mole" is this many: 602 300 000 000 000 000 000 000 or 6.023×10^{23}.

1) And that's all it is. Just a number. The burning question, of course, is why is it such a silly long one like that, and with a six at the front?
2) The answer is that when you get precisely that number of atoms or molecules, of any element or compound, then, conveniently, they weigh exactly the same number of grams as the relative atomic mass, A_r (or relative formula mass, M_r) of the element or compound. This is arranged on purpose of course, to make things easier.

Look back at page 54 if you've forgotten how to work out A_r and M_r.

One mole of atoms or molecules of any substance will have a mass in grams equal to the relative formula mass (A_r or M_r) for that substance.

EXAMPLES:

Carbon has an A_r of 12. So one mole of carbon weighs exactly 12 g
Iron has an A_r of 56. So one mole of iron weighs exactly 56 g
Nitrogen gas, N_2, has an M_r of 28 (2×14). So one mole of N_2 weighs exactly 28 g
Carbon dioxide, CO_2, has an M_r of 44. So one mole of CO_2 weighs exactly 44 g

This means that 12 g of carbon, or 56 g of iron, or 28 g of N_2, or 44 g of CO_2, all contain the same number of particles, namely one mole or 6.023×10^{23} atoms or molecules.

3) Molar mass of a substance is just another way of saying 'the mass of one mole'. Molar mass is measured in grams too. E.g. the molar mass of carbon is 12 g.

Nice Easy Formula for Finding the Number of Moles in a Given Mass:

$$\text{NUMBER OF MOLES} = \frac{\text{Mass in g (of element or compound)}}{M_r \text{ (of element or compound)}}$$

EXAMPLE 1: How many moles are there in 66 g of carbon dioxide?
M_r of CO_2 = 12 + (16 × 2) = 44
No. of moles = Mass (g) / M_r = 66/44 = 1.5 moles Easy Peasy

This one's a tiny bit trickier. You have to rearrange the formula above.

EXAMPLE 2: What mass of carbon is there in 4 moles of carbon dioxide?
There are 4 moles of carbon in 4 moles of CO_2.
The mass of 4 moles of carbon = number of moles × M_r = 4 × 12 = 48 g

Relative Masses are Masses of Atoms Compared to Carbon-12

Atoms and molecules are much too tiny to weigh. So their masses are compared to the mass of an atom of carbon-12. Carbon-12 is an isotope of carbon (see p.38 for more on isotopes).

Learn this definition: **The RELATIVE ATOMIC MASS of an element is the average mass of an atom of the element compared to the mass of an atom of CARBON-12.**

What do moles do for fun? Moller skate... boom boom...

Did you know that a mole can dig a tunnel at a rate of 18 feet per hour (that's really fast) and then move through an empty tunnel at 80 feet per hour. The word 'mole' can also mean a spy who infiltrates organisations and becomes a trusted member. But you need to know that it's 6.023×10^{23}. Great.

Reacting Masses and Empirical Formulas

Be prepared for loads of different calculations in this section — the title 'how much' kind of gives it away.

Things Always React in the Same Ratios

Mass is conserved during a chemical reaction. This means the mass of reactants will always equal the mass of products — it may not seem like this though, as one of the substances could be a gas.

1) In the reaction, $2Li + F_2 \rightarrow 2LiF$, 14 g of lithium will react with 38 g of fluorine.
2) The only product that's formed is lithium fluoride, so (14 + 38) 52 g will be produced.
3) The masses for this reaction will always be in the same proportions as this.
4) Multiplying or dividing these masses by the same number gives you other sets of reacting masses.

But see 'yield', on page 56.

E.g.

ELEMENT/COMPOUND IN REACTION	LITHIUM	FLUORINE	LITHIUM FLUORIDE
Original reacting masses	14 g	38 g	52 g
Reacting masses set 2	14 ÷ 2 = 7 g	38 ÷ 2 = 19 g	52 ÷ 2 = 26 g
Reacting masses set 3	14 × 1.5 = 21 g	38 × 1.5 = 57 g	52 × 1.5 = 78 g

You Need to Know How to Calculate Masses in Reactions

This was covered in Module C4 on page 55. If it's vanished from your brain, look back at it again.

Empirical Formulas are the Simplest Ratio in a Compound

The empirical formula just gives the smallest whole number ratio of atoms in a compound.

E.g. Ethane: chemical formula = C_2H_6 empirical formula = CH_3.
Glucose: chemical formula = $C_6H_{12}O_6$ empirical formula = CH_2O.

Empirical Formulas are Calculated from Masses or Percentages

You have to be able to calculate an empirical formula from the percentage composition by mass or the percentage of each element in a sample of the compound.

It doesn't matter if you're given masses or percentages — you use the same easy stepwise method:

1) List all the elements in the compound (there are usually only two or three).
2) Underneath them, write their experimental masses or percentages.
3) Divide each mass or percentage by the A_r for that particular element.
4) Turn the numbers you get into a nice simple ratio by multiplying and/or dividing them by well-chosen numbers.
5) Get the ratio in its simplest form, and that tells you the empirical formula of the compound.

EXAMPLE: Find the empirical formula of the iron oxide produced when 44.8 g of iron reacts with 19.2 g of oxygen. (A_r for iron = 56, A_r for oxygen =16)

METHOD:

	Fe	O
1) List the two elements:	Fe	O
2) Write in the experimental masses:	44.8	19.2
3) Divide by the A_r for each element:	44.8 ÷ 56 = 0.8	19.2 ÷ 16 = 1.2
4) Multiply by 10...	8	12
...then divide by 4	2	3

5) So the simplest formula is 2 atoms of Fe to 3 atoms of O, i.e. Fe_2O_3.

With this empirical formula I can rule the world! — mwa ha ha ha...

Now try these: 1) What is the empirical formula of: a) C_7H_{14}, b) $C_6H_{12}O_6$, c) $K_4S_2O_8$? Answers on page 108.
2) Find the empirical formula when 2.4 g of carbon react with 0.8 g of hydrogen.

Electrolysis

Not electrolysis again you cry. This time it's a little different. Honest. You've got to be able to predict the products of electrolysis, with both aqueous and molten electrolytes. What are you waiting for...

Electrolysis Means "Splitting Up with Electricity"

1) Electrolysis is the breaking down of a substance using electricity (see page 44).
2) An electric current is passed through a molten or dissolved ionic compound, causing it to decompose.
3) For the electrical circuit to be complete, there's got to be a flow of electrons. Electrons are taken away from ions at the positive electrode (anode) and passed by an external circuit to the negative electrode (cathode), where they're given to other ions in the electrolyte.
4) As ions gain or lose electrons they become atoms or molecules and are discharged from the solution.

Here's what you might use in your school lab:

1) Two graphite or platinum electrodes are connected to a DC power supply and placed into the electrolyte. Remember... they don't react with the electrolyte themselves.
2) The positive ions in the solution will move towards the cathode.
3) The negative ions in the solution will move towards the anode.
4) If the molecules discharged are gases, they're collected in test tubes held above the electrodes. The electrodes are partly insulated to make sure all the gas is formed beneath the test tubes.

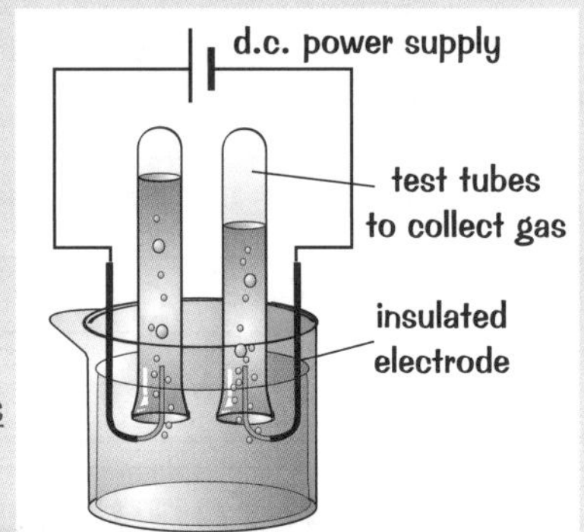

It May be Easier to Discharge Ions from Water than the Solute

1) In aqueous solutions, as well as the ions from the solute, there are hydrogen ions (H^+) and hydroxide ions (OH^-) from the water.
2) Sometimes, it's easier to discharge the ions from the water instead of the ones from the solute.
3) This means hydrogen could be produced at the cathode, and oxygen at the anode.

A solution of aqueous potassium sulfate (K_2SO_4) contains four different ions: K^+, SO_4^{2-}, H^+ and OH^-.

- Hydrogen ions (from the water) can accept the electrons easier than the potassium ions. So at the cathode, hydrogen gas is discharged.

$$2H^+ + 2e^- \rightarrow H_2$$

- Hydroxide ions (from water) can lose electrons easier than sulfate ions. So at the anode oxygen is discharged.

$$4OH^- - 4e^- \rightarrow O_2 + 2H_2O$$

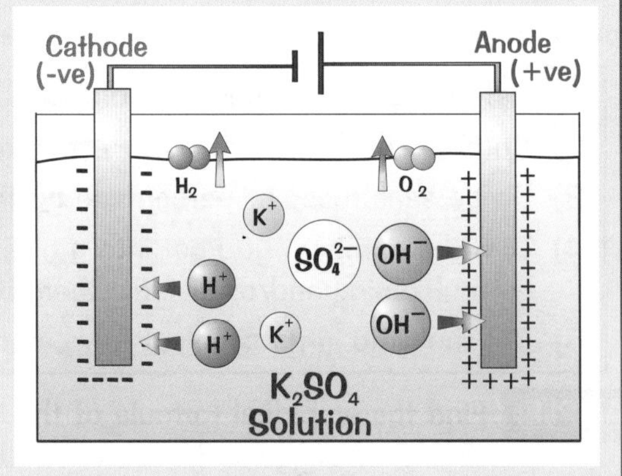

A solution of potassium nitrate (KNO_3) contains the ions K^+, NO_3^-, H^+ and OH^-.

- Hydrogen ions accept electrons easier than potassium ions — so hydrogen is produced at the cathode.
- Hydroxide ions lose electrons easier than nitrate ions — so oxygen is produced at the anode.

Cathode: $2H^+ + 2e^- \rightarrow H_2$

Anode: $4OH^- - 4e^- \rightarrow O_2 + 2H_2O$

Everyone needs good electrons...

The hardest bit's over now. Remember that with aqueous solutions, there are ions from the dissolved substance and from the water. With K_2SO_4 and KNO_3, you get hydrogen and oxygen — remember that.

Electrolysis

Moving swiftly on... molten electrolytes only contain two different kinds of ions — which makes things easier.

In Molten Salts, There's Only One Source of Ions

A salt will conduct an electric current when molten.
The salt is always broken up into elements.

Positive metal cations are reduced (i.e. they gain electrons) to atoms at the cathode (the –ve electrode):
E.g. $Pb^{2+} + 2e^- \rightarrow Pb$

Negative anions are oxidised (i.e. they lose electrons) to atoms at the anode (the +ve electrode):
$2Br^- \rightarrow Br_2 + 2e^-$

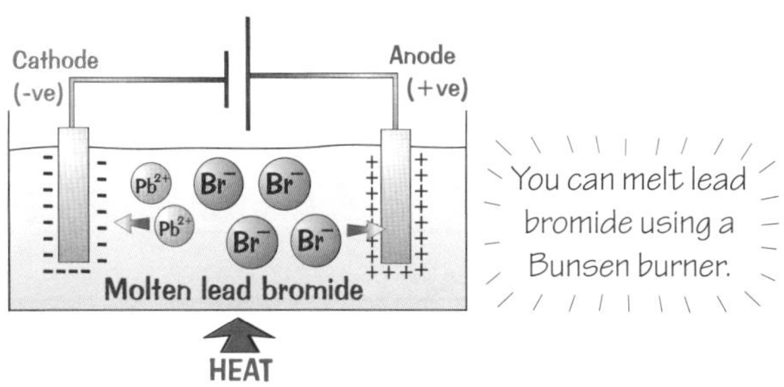

It's easy to predict what products you get when you electrolyse molten substances — it's getting the half-equations right that's difficult. Learn these to get a head start:

Molten Electolyte	Product Produced at Cathode	Half-Equation at Cathode	Product Produced at Anode	Half-Equation at Anode
Lead iodide, PbI_2	Lead	$Pb^{2+} + 2e^- \rightarrow Pb$	Iodine	$2I^- \rightarrow I_2 + 2e^-$
Potassium chloride, KCl	Potassium	$K^+ + e^- \rightarrow K$	Chlorine	$2Cl^- \rightarrow Cl_2 + 2e^-$
Aluminium oxide, Al_2O_3	Aluminium	$Al^{3+} + 3e^- \rightarrow Al$	Oxygen	$2O^{2-} \rightarrow O_2 + 4e^-$

Electrodes Can Lose or Gain Mass

Here's what happens during the electrolysis of copper(II) sulfate solution when you use copper electrodes.

The negative electrode starts as a piece of copper and more copper adds to it.

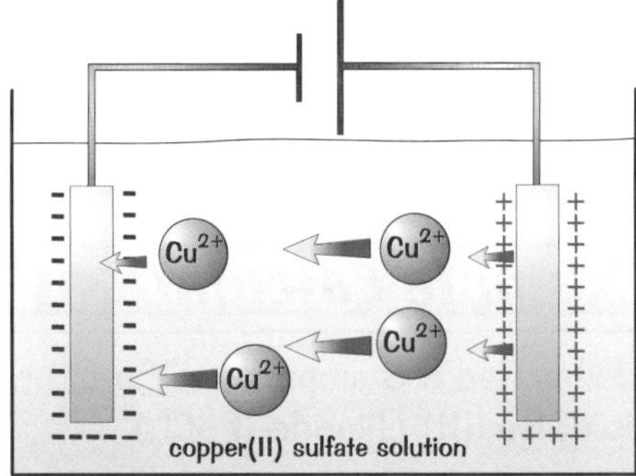

The positive copper electrode dissolves into the solution — it's easier to dissolve the copper than it is to discharge any ions from the solution.

The reaction at the negative electrode is:

$$Cu^{2+} + 2e^- \rightarrow Cu$$

The reaction at the positive electrode is:

$$Cu \rightarrow Cu^{2+} + 2e^-$$

1) When a certain number of electrons flows away from the positive electrode (along the wire), the same number of electrons must flow onto the negative electrode.
2) Looking at the negative electrode half-equation, 1 mole of copper ions picks up 2 moles of electrons. This makes 1 mole of copper atoms, which sticks to the electrode, causing an increase in mass.
3) The positive electrode half-equation shows that 1 mole of copper atoms loses 2 moles of electrons and is released as copper ions into the solution. Copper is lost from the electrode, so there's a decrease in mass.
4) So, 1 mole of copper is added to the negative electrode as 1 mole of copper is lost from the positive electrode. This means the gain in mass is equal to the loss in mass.

Which element does a robber fear most? Copper...

Remember, there's no loss of electrons through the circuit. What goes in must come out.

Electrolysis — Calculating Masses

Here come the calculations. Run... while you still can...

No. of Electrons Transferred Increases with Time and Current

1) The amount of product made during electrolysis depends on the number of electrons that are transferred.
2) If you increase the number of electrons, you increase the amount of substance produced.

This can be achieved by:
- electrolysing for a longer time,
- increasing the current.

Coulombs and Faradays are Amounts of Electricity

1) One amp flowing for one second means a charge of one coulomb has moved.
2) Generally, the amount of charge (Q, measured in coulombs) flowing through a circuit is equal to the current (I) multiplied by the time in seconds (t): $Q = It$
3) 96 000 coulombs (amps × seconds) is called one faraday.
4) One faraday (F) contains one mole of electrons.

1 A for 1 s = 1 C
$Q = I \times t$ (seconds)
96 000 C = 1 faraday
1 faraday = 1 mole of electrons

One Mole of Product Needs 'n' Moles of Electrons

A sodium ion needs one electron to make a sodium atom. So one mole of sodium ions is going to need one mole of electrons (one faraday) to make one mole of sodium atoms. But an ion with a 2^+ charge needs two moles of electrons to make one mole of atoms, and, guess what, three for a 3^+ charge...

$Na^+ + e^- \rightarrow Na$	1 mole of sodium ions + 1 mole of electrons → 1 mole of sodium atoms
$Zn^{2+} + 2e^- \rightarrow Zn$	1 mole of zinc ions + 2 moles of electrons → 1 mole of zinc atoms
$Al^{3+} + 3e^- \rightarrow Al$	1 mole of aluminium ions + 3 moles of electrons → 1 mole of aluminium atoms

Use These Steps in Example Calculations

Example: Find the mass of lead liberated if 5 amps flows for 20 minutes during the electrolysis of lead(II) chloride ($PbCl_2$).

1) Write out the BALANCED HALF-EQUATION for each electrode.
   $Pb^{2+} + 2e^- \rightarrow Pb$ and $2Cl^- \rightarrow Cl_2 + 2e^-$

Writing the half-equations is easier if you remember that the full equation is: $PbCl_2 \rightarrow Pb + Cl_2$

2) Calculate the NUMBER OF FARADAYS.
   First calculate amps × seconds = 5 × 20 × 60 = 6000 coulombs.
   Number of faradays = 6000 / 96 000 = 0.0625 F
3) Calculate the NUMBER OF MOLES OF PRODUCT.
   (divide the number of faradays by the number of electrons in the half-equation)
   0.0625 ÷ 2 = 0.03125 moles of lead atoms.
4) WRITE IN THE M_r VALUES from the periodic table to work out the mass of solid products.
   Mass of lead = M_r × No. of moles = 207 × 0.03125 = 6.5 g

The more time you spend on this page, the more you'll learn...

This stuff isn't easy. So take your time over it. Read it through once. If you don't get it, read it through again. If you still don't get it, have a cup of tea before reading it again. That should help.

Concentration

Another dull and boring page. But at least there are some more calculations on it.

Concentration is a Measure of How Crowded Things Are

The concentration of a solution can be measured in moles per dm^3 (i.e. moles per litre).
So 1 mole of stuff in 1 dm^3 of solution has a concentration of 1 mole per dm^3 (or 1 mol/dm^3).

> The more solute you dissolve in a given volume, the more crowded the solute molecules are and the more concentrated the solution.

Concentration can also be measured in grams per dm^3. So 56 grams of stuff dissolved in 1 dm^3 of solution has a concentration of 56 grams per dm^3.

There's a calculation you can do to convert moles per dm^3 to grams per dm^3 (see below). In the exam, look out for which one the question's asking for.

> 1 litre
> = 1000 cm^3
> = 1 dm^3

Concentration = No. of Moles ÷ Volume

Here's a nice formula triangle for you to learn:

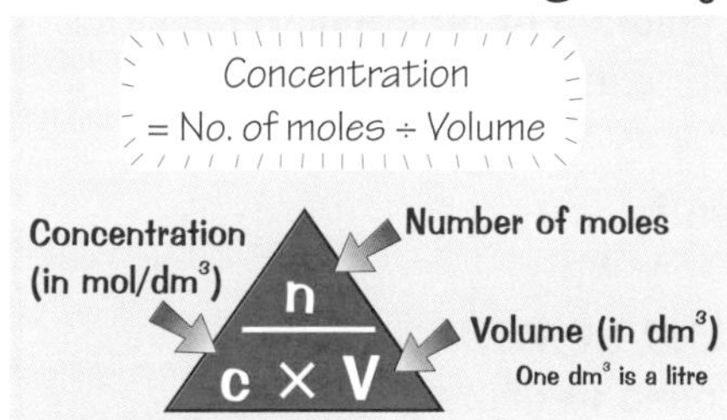

Example 1: What's the concentration of a solution with 2 moles of salt in 500 cm^3?

Answer: Easy — you've got the number of moles and the volume, so just stick it in the formula...

$$\text{Concentration} = \frac{2}{0.5} = 4 \text{ moles per dm}^3$$

Convert the volume to litres (i.e. dm^3) first by dividing by 1000.

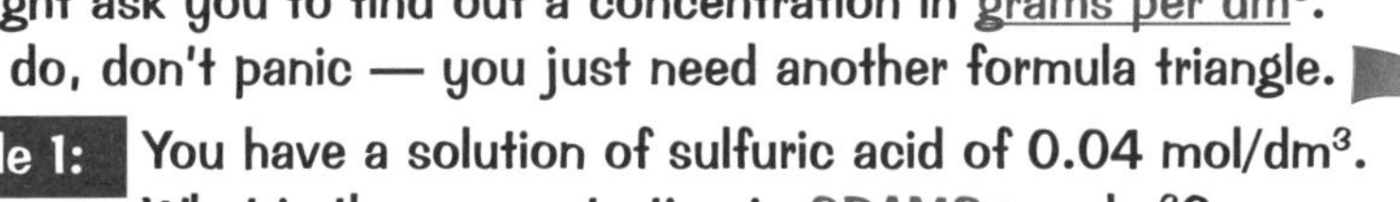

Example 2: How many moles of sodium chloride are in 250 cm^3 of a 3 molar solution of sodium chloride?

Answer: Well, 3 molar just means it's got 3 moles per dm^3. So using the formula...
Number of moles = concentration × volume = 3 × 0.25 = 0.75 moles

3 molar is sometimes written '3 M'.

Converting Grams per dm^3 to Moles per dm^3

They might ask you to find out a concentration in grams per dm^3.
If they do, don't panic — you just need another formula triangle.

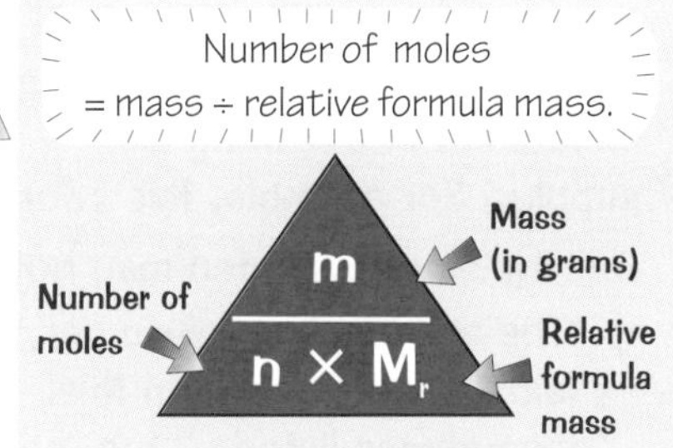

Example 1: You have a solution of sulfuric acid of 0.04 mol/dm^3. What is the concentration in GRAMS per dm^3?

Step 1: Work out the relative formula mass for the solute (you should be given the relative atomic masses, e.g. H = 1, S = 32, O = 16):
So, H_2SO_4 = (1 × 2) + 32 + (16 × 4) = 98

Step 2: Convert the concentration in moles into concentration in grams. So, in 1 dm^3:
Mass in grams = moles × relative formula mass
= 0.04 × 98 = 3.92 g
So the concentration in g/dm^3 = 3.92 g/dm^3

Example 2: The concentration of a solution of sulfuric acid is 19.6 g/dm^3. What is the concentration in MOLES per dm^3?

Step 1: The relative formula mass of H_2SO_4 = 98
Step 2: Moles = mass in grams ÷ relative formula mass
= 19.6 ÷ 98 = 0.2 g   So the concentration in mol/dm^3 = 0.2 mol/dm^3

Numbers? — and you thought you were doing chemistry...

High concentration is like the whole of a rugby team in a mini. Or everyone in Britain living on the Isle of Wight. Low concentration is like a guy stranded on a desert island, or a small fish in a big lake.

Concentration

Concentration is important. Are you listening... I said concentration is important.

It's Important to Get the Right Concentration

'Diluting' something usually means 'watering it down'.

Lots of things you can buy nowadays are in concentrated form, meaning you have to dilute it before you can use it. Here are some examples...

1) Food preparation — ingredients (e.g. gravy granules) have to be at the right concentrations so they have the right taste and consistency.
2) Medicines — these are often made pretty concentrated. If they're then diluted too much, they may not work — but not diluted enough and the patient could suffer from side-effects.

3) Baby milk — too dilute and the baby may get diarrhoea (or may not get enough nutrients), not dilute enough and they could become overweight (or dehydrated).
4) Weedkillers — you usually need to dilute them, or you'll kill your plants as well.

Calculate how much you need to dilute things using the following method:

Example: Explain how you'd produce 500 cm^3 of a 0.1 mol/dm^3 solution of hydrochloric acid if you're given a 1.0 mol/dm^3 solution of hydrochloric acid, and some water.

Step 1: Work out the RATIO of the two concentrations...
Divide the two concentrations to get a number less than 1.
$0.1 \div 1.0 = 1/10$ ← Always divide the small number by the big one.

Step 2: Multiply this ratio by the volume of stuff you want to END UP WITH.
(This tells you how much of your ORIGINAL ACID you need to dilute.)
Volume to dilute = ratio × final volume = $1/10 \times 500 = 50$ cm^3

Step 3: Work out the VOLUME OF WATER you'll need.
Volume of water = total volume – volume to dilute = 500 cm^3 – 50 cm^3 = 450 cm^3

Food Packaging Gives Recommended Daily Allowances (RDAs)

On most food packaging you'll find nutritional information tables — these tell you the amounts of nutrients in the food. Recommended Daily Allowances (RDAs) are the amounts of nutrients that an average adult should eat in a healthy diet — food labels often tell you what percentage of various RDAs a product will supply. For example, this information was found on the side of a hot oat cereal packet.

NUTRITIONAL INFORMATION	/40 g serving	RDA
Thiamin (B1)	0.5 mg	34%
Riobflavin (B2)	0.5 mg	34%
Calcium	480 mg	60%
Iron	4.8 mg	34%

But the amounts listed may not always be the amount you eat, because...

1) The amounts are given per 100 g (or 100 ml) of the food — but you may eat more or less than this. (The amount per average serving is also sometimes listed — e.g. per 40 g for this cereal.)
2) You may add other things (e.g. milk to cereals — which will increase how much calcium you get).

You Can Use Sodium Content to Estimate the Amount of Salt

You need to be careful how much salt (sodium chloride) you eat. Sometimes salt is included in the nutritional information — but if not, you can estimate it from the amount of sodium...

For example, if a slice of bread contains 0.2 g sodium — how much salt does it contain?
(M_r sodium = 23 and M_r sodium chloride = 58.5)

1) Find the ratio of sodium chloride's M_r to sodium's: $58.5 \div 23 = 2.543...$
2) Multiply this by the amount of sodium: $2.543... \times 0.2 = 0.5086... =$ 0.5 g salt

But the sodium present probably won't all come from sodium chloride — there might be other sodium compounds too, e.g. sodium nitrate (often used as a preservative). So this is probably an overestimate.

This page contains your RDA of concentration calculations...

Why is it that people only read the backs of cereal packets... one of life's little mysteries. Possibly.

Titrations

Titrations are a method of analysing the concentrations of solutions.
They're pretty important, I guess — but I wouldn't say they're the most exciting game in town.

Titrations are Used to Find Out Concentrations

You can also do titrations the other way round — adding alkali to acid.

1) Titrations allow you to find out exactly how much acid is needed to neutralise a quantity of alkali (or vice versa).
2) Using a pipette and pipette filler, add some alkali (usually about 25 cm^3) to a conical flask, along with two or three drops of indicator. (The pipette filler stops you getting a mouthful of alkali.)
3) Fill a burette with the acid. Make sure you do this BELOW EYE LEVEL — you don't want to be looking up if some acid spills over.
4) Using the burette, add the acid to the alkali a bit at a time — giving the conical flask a regular swirl. Go especially slowly when you think the end-point (colour change) is about to be reached.
5) The indicator changes colour when all the alkali has been neutralised, e.g. phenolphthalein is pink in alkalis, but colourless in acids.
6) Record the amount of acid used to neutralise the alkali.

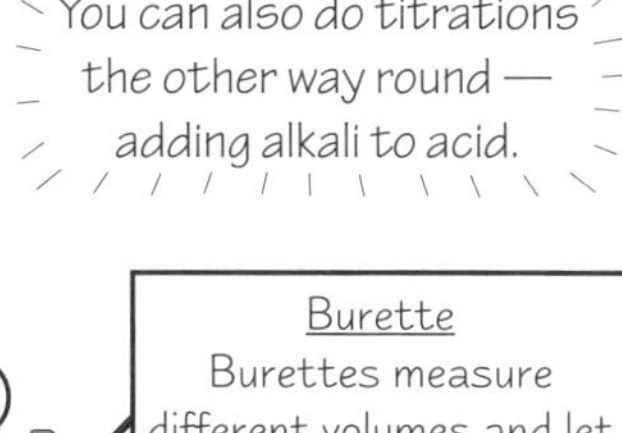

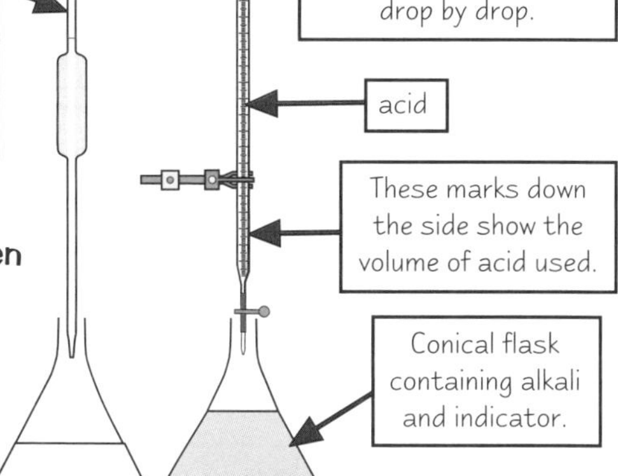

You need to get several consistent readings

To increase the accuracy of your titration and to spot any anomalous results, you need several consistent readings.

- The first titration you do should be a rough titration to get an approximate idea of where the solution changes colour (the end-point).
- You then need to repeat the whole thing a few times, making sure you get (pretty much) the same answer each time (within about 0.2 cm^3).

Use Single Indicators for Titrations

1) Universal indicator is used to estimate the pH of a solution because it can turn a variety of colours. Each colour indicates a narrow range of pH values.

pH 0 1 2 3 4 5 6 7 8 9 10 11 12 13 14
ACIDS | NEUTRAL | ALKALIS

2) It's made from a mixture of different indicators. The colour gradually changes from red in acidic solutions to violet in alkaline solutions.

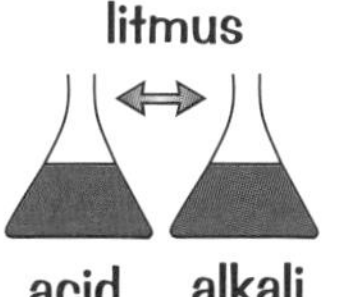

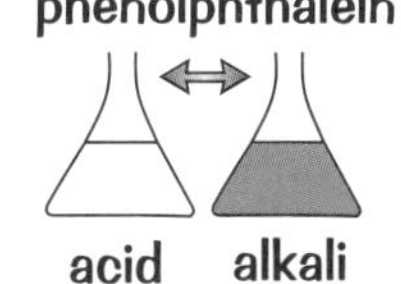

phenolphthalein
acid alkali

3) But during an acid-base titration you want to see a sudden colour change, at the end-point.
4) So you need to use a single indicator, such as litmus — this is blue in alkalis and red in acids.

How do you get lean molecules? Feed them titrations...

Before the end of this module, you'll be a dab hand at titrations — whether you want to be or not. They're not too tricky really — you just need to make as sure as you can that your results are accurate, which means going slowly near the end-point and then repeating the whole process.

More on Titration

Yes, I know — more on titrations. Complicated stuff this.

pH Curves Show pH Against Volume of Acid or Alkali Added

When an acid and an alkali react they form a salt and water. It's called a neutralisation reaction.

acid + alkali → salt + water

This pH curve shows the change in pH as an alkali is added to 25 cm^3 of acid.

1) There's a very gradual increase in pH as the alkali is added.
2) At the endpoint of the titration, there's a sudden change in pH (shown by the nearly vertical line). This happens when 25 cm^3 has been added.
3) The volume of alkali needed to neutralise the acid is 25 cm^3.

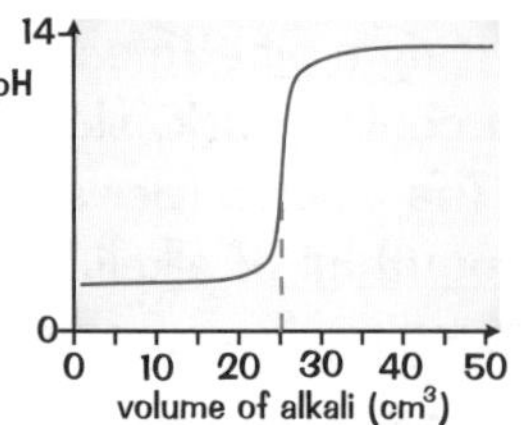

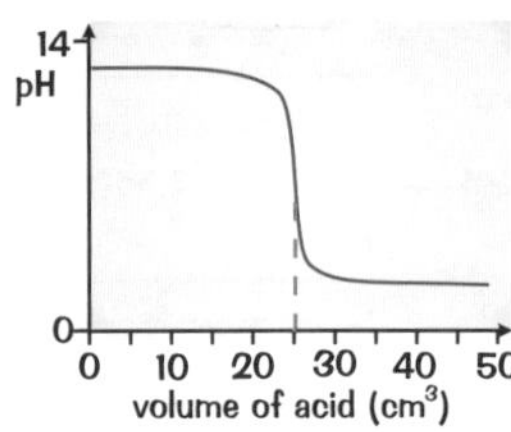

This pH curve shows the change in pH as an acid is added to 25 cm^3 of alkali.

1) There's a very gradual decrease in pH as the acid is added.
2) Again, the endpoint of this titration was after 25 cm^3 of acid had been added.

You Might be Asked to Calculate the Concentration

In the exam you might be given the results of a titration experiment, and asked to calculate the concentration of the acid when you know the concentration of the alkali (or vice versa).

Example:

Say you start off with 25 cm^3 of sodium hydroxide in your flask, and you know that its concentration is 0.1 moles per dm^3.

You then find from your titration that it takes 49 cm^3 of hydrochloric acid (whose concentration you don't know) to neutralise the sodium hydroxide.

You can work out the concentration of the acid in moles per dm^3.

Concentration = moles ÷ volume, so you can make a handy formula triangle.

Concentration (in mol/dm^3) — Number of moles — Volume (in dm^3) One dm^3 is a litre

$$\frac{n}{c \times V}$$

Cover up the thing you're trying to find — then what's left is the formula you need to use.

Step 1: Work out how many moles of the "known" substance you have:

Number of moles = concentration × volume
= 0.1 mol/dm^3 × (25 ÷ 1000) dm^3 = 0.0025 moles of sodium hydroxide

Step 2: Write down the balanced equation of the reaction...

$NaOH + HCl \longrightarrow NaCl + H_2O$

...and work out how many moles of the "unknown" stuff you must have had.

Using the equation, you can see that for every mole of sodium hydroxide you had...
...there was also one mole of hydrochloric acid.

So if you had 0.0025 moles of sodium hydroxide...
...you must have had 0.0025 moles of hydrochloric acid.

Step 3: Work out the concentration of the "unknown" stuff.

Concentration = number of moles ÷ volume
= 0.0025 mol ÷ (49 ÷ 1000) dm^3 = 0.0510 mol/dm^3

Don't forget to put the units.

You've got to concentrate whilst doing titrations...

Answer on page 108.

Time for some practice... 25 cm^3 of a 0.2 mol/dm^3 solution of sulfuric acid, H_2SO_4, was used to neutralise 40 cm^3 of calcium hydroxide, $Ca(OH)_2$. What's the concentration of calcium hydroxide?

Gas Volumes

The rate of a reaction can be measured by the amount of gas produced. But first it's got to be collected.

The Collection Method Depends on the Gas

In your experiments a conical flask is the standard apparatus to use when you're trying to collect gases. But what you connect to the flask depends on what it is you're trying to collect...

1) Gas Syringe

You can use a gas syringe to collect pretty much any gas.

Gas syringes usually give volumes accurate to the nearest cm^3, so they're pretty accurate. You have to be quite careful though — if the reaction is too vigorous, you can easily blow the plunger out the end of the syringe.

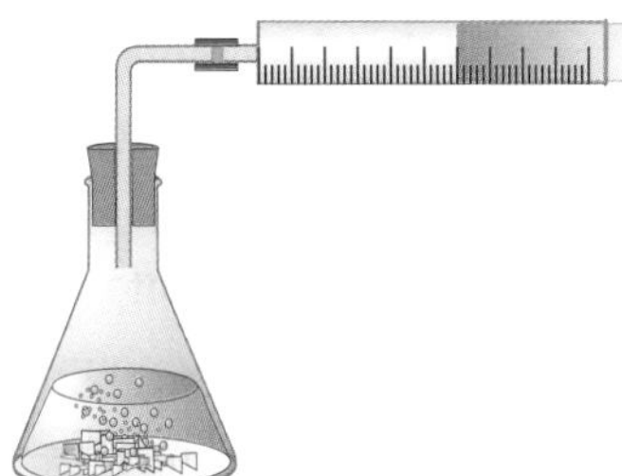

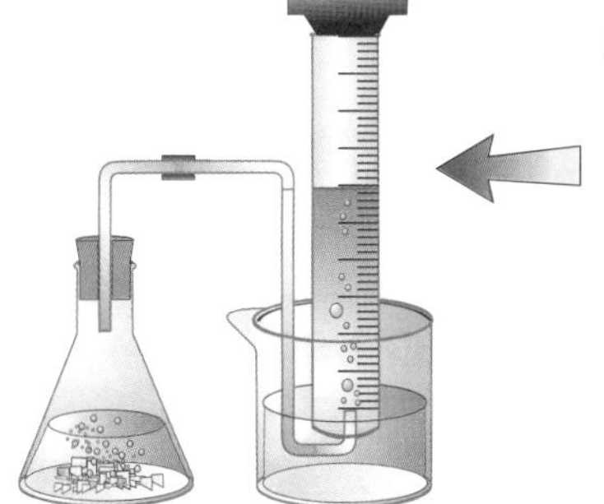

2) Upturned Measuring Cylinder or Burette

You can use a delivery tube to bubble the gas into an upside-down measuring cylinder or gas jar filled with water.

But this method's no good for collecting things like hydrogen chloride or ammonia (because they just dissolve in the water).

You can also use an upturned burette, which is a bit more accurate — you can measure to the nearest 0.1 cm^3.

You Can Measure the Mass of Gas Produced Too

1) You can measure the mass of gas that a reaction produces by carrying out the experiment on a mass balance.
2) As the gas is released, the mass disappearing is easily measured on the balance.
3) This is the most accurate of the three methods described on this page because the mass balance is very accurate. But it has the disadvantage of releasing the gas straight into the room.

One Mole of Gas Occupies a Volume of 24 dm^3

dm^3 is just a fancy way of writing 'litre', so 1 dm^3 = 1000 cm^3

Learn this fact — you're going to need it:

One mole of any gas always occupies 24 dm^3 (= 24 000 cm^3) at room temperature and pressure (RTP = 25 °C and 1 atmosphere)

Volume / Moles × 24

Example 1: What's the volume of 4.5 moles of chlorine at RTP?

Answer: 1 mole = 24 dm^3, so 4.5 moles = 4.5 × 24 dm^3 = 108 dm^3

Example 2: How many moles are there in 8280 cm^3 of hydrogen gas at RTP?

Answer: Number of moles = $\frac{\text{Volume of gas}}{\text{Volume of 1 mole}} = \frac{8.28}{24}$ = 0.345 moles

Don't forget to convert from cm^3 to dm^3.

Pity there's no laughing gas around...

Measuring the mass of gas is more accurate than measuring the volume. Some gas will always escape between starting the reaction and managing to get the bung into the conical flask. There's no way you can do it fast enough. I doubt even Superman could... well, maybe he could.

Following Reactions

Easy but ever so slightly dull — that's how I'd sum this page up. You need to learn it though.

Reactions Stop When One Reactant is Used Up

When some marble chips ($CaCO_3$) are dropped into a beaker of hydrochloric acid, you can tell a reaction is taking place because you see lots of bubbles of gas being given off.

After a while, the amount of fizzing slows down and the reaction eventually stops...

1) The reaction stops when one of the reactants is used up.
2) The reactant that's used up first in a reaction is called the limiting reactant. (If the limiting reactant was the acid, you'd see unreacted marble chips in the bottom of the flask.)
3) If you halve the amount of limiting reactant, the volume of gas produced will also halve (the amount of gas is directly proportional to the amount of limiting reactant). Careful though... if you double the amount of limiting reactant (but not the other reactant), it might not be the limiting reactant any more.

You've Got to be Able to Read Graphs and Tables...

In this experiment, some marble chips were added to a solution of hydrochloric acid. Any gases released were collected using a gas syringe (see p77) — the volume was recorded every 10 s.

Time (s)	0	10	20	30	40	50	60	70	80	90
Volume of gas (cm^3)	0	34	58	76	84	90	94	96	96	96

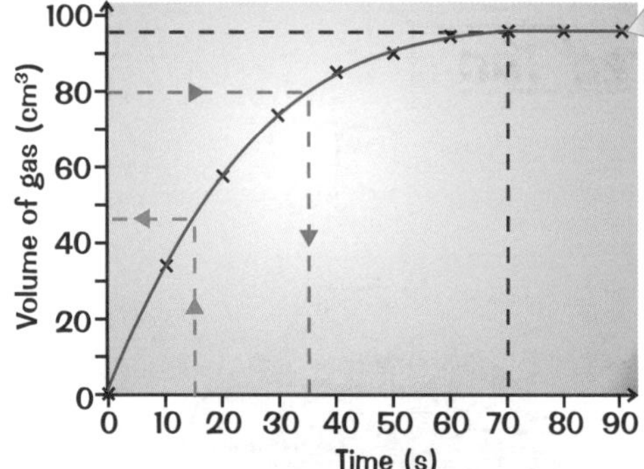

The results are on this graph.

1) The total volume of gas produced is 96 cm^3.
2) The reaction had stopped after about 70 s — no more gas was produced (so the line on the graph went horizontal).

Examples: How much gas was produced after 15 s? 47 cm^3
How long did it take to produce 80 cm^3 of gas? 35 s

Easy.

Faster Rates of Reaction are Shown by Steeper Curves

If the above reaction had been quicker, the graph would have been steeper. (The rate of reaction depends on the conditions it's carried out in — see p33.)

1) Reaction 1 on the right represents a fairly slow reaction. It's not too steep.
2) Reactions 1, 2 and 3 all produce the same amount of product (the lines go horizontal at the same height) — this shows they all have the same amount of limiting reactant.
   But lines 2 and 3 are steeper, which shows that the reactions are happening more quickly.
3) Reaction 4 produces more product as well as going faster. This can only happen if there's more of the limiting reactant.

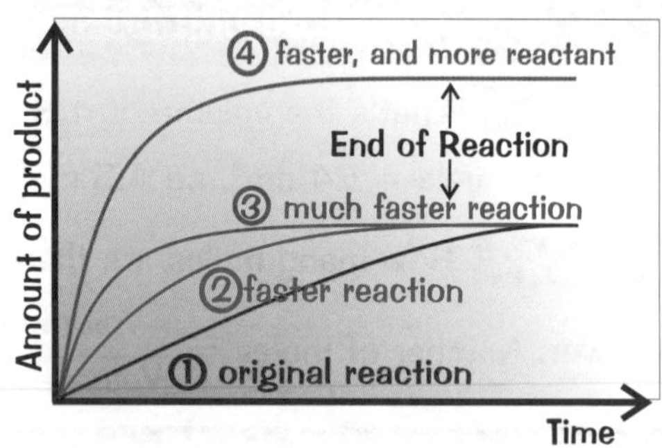

Reactions always slow down — no stamina, you see...

Reactions always go fastest right at the beginning — it's when there are the highest concentrations of reactants. The reactants eventually run out, or at least one of them does. Nothing ever lasts. Sigh...

Equilibrium

A reversible reaction is one where the products can react with each other and convert back to the original chemicals. In other words, it can go both ways.

A REVERSIBLE REACTION is one where the PRODUCTS of the reaction can THEMSELVES REACT to produce the ORIGINAL REACTANTS

$$A + B \rightleftharpoons C + D$$

The '⇌' shows the reaction goes both ways.

Reversible Reactions Will Reach Equilibrium

1) As the reactants (A and B) react, their concentrations fall — so the forward reaction will slow down. But as more and more products (C and D) are made and their concentrations rise, the backward reaction will speed up.
2) After a while the forward reaction will be going at exactly the same rate as the backward one — this is equilibrium.
3) At equilibrium both reactions are still happening, but there's no overall effect (it's a dynamic equilibrium). This means the concentrations of reactants and products have reached a balance and won't change.
4) Equilibrium is only reached if the reversible reaction takes place in a 'closed system'. A closed system just means that none of the reactants or products can escape.

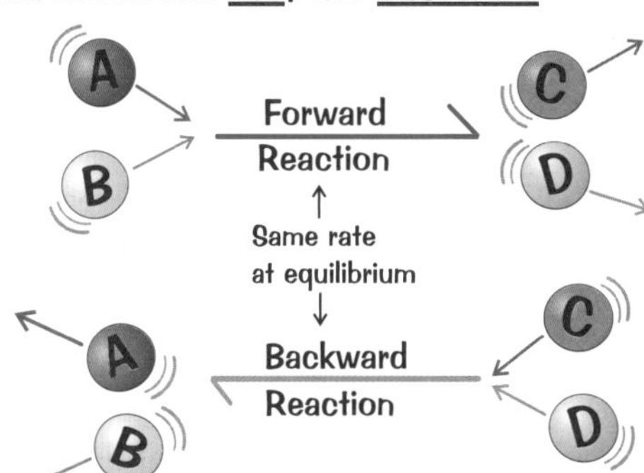

The Position of Equilibrium Can be on the Right or the Left

When a reaction's at equilibrium it doesn't mean the amounts of reactants and products are equal.

1) Sometimes the equilibrium will lie to the right — this basically means "lots of the products and not much of the reactants" (i.e. the concentration of product is greater than the concentration of reactant).
2) Sometimes the equilibrium will lie to the left — this basically means "lots of the reactants but not much of the products" (the concentration of reactant is greater than the concentration of product).
3) The exact position of equilibrium depends on the conditions (as well as the reaction itself).

Three Things Can Change the Position of Equilibrium:

1) TEMPERATURE
2) PRESSURE (only affects equilibria involving gases)
3) CONCENTRATION

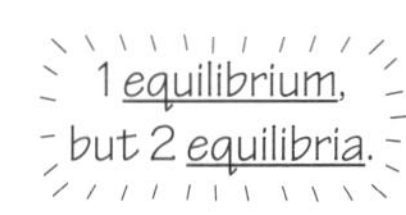

The next page tells you why these things affect the equilibrium position — for now just learn that they do. But now's a good time to make a mental note of this potential elephant trap...

Adding a CATALYST doesn't change the equilibrium position:

1) Catalysts speed up both the forward and backward reactions by the same amount.
2) So, adding a catalyst means the reaction reaches equilibrium quicker, but you end up with the same amount of product as you would without the catalyst.

Dynamic equilibrium — lots of activity, but not to any great effect...*

Many important industrial reactions (e.g. the Haber process — see p59) are reversible. But chances are, just sticking the reactants together into a sealed box won't give a very good yield (i.e. not much products). So what you do is change the conditions — if you do it right, you get more products, and so more money. And that keeps the accountants happy, which, after all, is the main thing in life.

* Much like the England football team.

Changing Equilibrium

Now here's an interesting thing — if you change the conditions, the equilibrium will try to counteract that change. So if you decrease the temperature, the equilibrium will move to produce more heat. Sneaky.

The Equilibrium Tries to Minimise Any Changes You Make

TEMPERATURE All reactions are exothermic in one direction and endothermic in the other (see p17).

1) If you decrease the temperature, the equilibrium will move to try and increase it — the equilibrium moves in the exothermic direction to produce more heat.
2) If you raise the temperature, the equilibrium will move to try and decrease it — the equilibrium moves in the endothermic direction.

$N_2 + 3H_2 \rightleftharpoons 2NH_3$

The forward reaction is exothermic — a decrease in temperature moves the equilibrium to the right (more products).

PRESSURE Changing this only affects an equilibrium involving gases.

1) If you increase the pressure, the equilibrium tries to reduce it — the equilibrium moves in the direction where there are fewer moles of gas.
2) If you decrease the pressure, the equilibrium tries to increase it — it moves in the direction where there are more moles of gas.

$N_2 + 3H_2 \rightleftharpoons 2NH_3$

There are 4 moles on the left, but only 2 on the right. So, if you increase the pressure, the equilibrium shifts to the right.

CONCENTRATION Same reaction again... $N_2 + 3H_2 \rightleftharpoons 2NH_3$

1) If you increase the concentration of N_2 or H_2, the equilibrium tries to decrease it by shifting to the right (making more NH_3).
2) If you increase the concentration of NH_3, the equilibrium tries to reduce it again by shifting to the left (making more N_2 and H_2).

If you decrease the concentration of N_2, H_2 or NH_3, the equilibrium moves to try and increase the concentration again.

Make Sure You Can Read Equilibrium Tables and Graphs

You might be asked to interpret data about equilibrium, so you'd better know what you're doing. The Haber process (see page 59) is a great example of all this...

$$N_2 + 3H_2 \rightleftharpoons 2NH_3$$

The forward reaction is exothermic.

First off, a table...

Pressure (atmospheres)	100	200	300	400	500
% of ammonia at 450 °C	14	26	34	39	42

1) As the pressure increases, the proportion of ammonia increases (exactly what you'd expect — since increasing the pressure shifts the equilibrium to the side with fewer moles of gas — here, the right).

And now a graph...

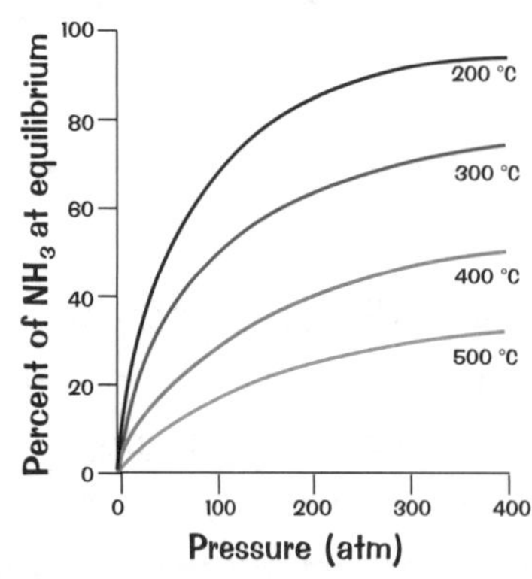

2) This time, each different line represents a different temperature.
3) As the temperature increases, the proportion of ammonia decreases (the backward reaction is endothermic, so this speeds up to try and reduce the temperature again).
4) The conditions that will give you most ammonia are high pressure and low temperature.

An equilibrium is like a particularly stubborn mule...

It's good science this stuff. You do one thing, and the reaction does the other. On the face of it, that sounds like it'd be pretty annoying, but in reality it's what gives you control of what happens. And in industry, control is what makes the whole shebang profitable. Accountants love it.

The Contact Process

And here's another example where getting the conditions right makes for a better yield.

The Contact Process is Used to Make Sulfuric Acid

1) The first stage is to make sulfur dioxide (SO_2) — usually by burning sulfur in air.

sulfur + oxygen → sulfur dioxide
$S + O_2 \rightarrow SO_2$

2) The sulfur dioxide is then oxidised (with the help of a catalyst) to make sulfur trioxide (SO_3).

sulfur dioxide + oxygen ⇌ sulfur trioxide
$2SO_2 + O_2 \rightleftharpoons 2SO_3$

3) Next, the sulfur trioxide is used to make sulfuric acid.

sulfur trioxide + water → sulfuric acid
$SO_3 + H_2O \rightarrow H_2SO_4$

In reality, dissolving SO_3 like this doesn't work — the reaction is dangerous as a lot of heat's produced — but this is the reaction you need to know, so learn it. (In practice, you dissolve SO_3 in sulfuric acid first.)

The Conditions Used to Make SO_3 are Carefully Chosen

The reaction in step 2 is reversible. So, the conditions used can be controlled, to get more product.

$2SO_2 + O_2 \rightleftharpoons 2SO_3$

The forward reaction is exothermic.

TEMPERATURE

1) Oxidising sulfur dioxide to form sulfur trioxide is exothermic (it gives out heat).
2) So to get more product you'd think the temperature should be reduced (so the equilibrium will shift to the right to replace the heat).
3) Unfortunately, reducing the temperature slows the reaction right down — not much good.
4) So an optimum temperature of 450 °C is used, as a compromise.

PRESSURE

1) There are two moles of product, compared to three moles of reactants.
2) So to get more product, you'd think the pressure should be increased (so that the equilibrium will shift to the right to reduce the pressure).
3) But increasing the pressure is expensive, and as the equilibrium is already on the right, it's not really necessary. (And increasing the pressure liquefies the SO_2, so it's no use anyway.)
4) In fact, atmospheric pressure is used.

CATALYST

1) To increase the rate of reaction a vanadium pentoxide catalyst (V_2O_5) is used.
2) It DOESN'T change the position of the equilibrium.

With a fairly high temperature, a low pressure and a vanadium pentoxide catalyst, the reaction goes pretty quickly and you get a good yield of SO_3 (about 99%).

And that's how chemistry works in real life.

The lonely hearts column — go on, start the contact process...

It's a tough one... do you raise the temperature to get a faster rate of reaction, or reduce it to get a better yield... In the end you compromise (as is so often the case in life... sigh). And that's before you even start to worry about the cost of raising the temperature. Decisions, decisions...

Strong and Weak Acids

Right then. Acids. Brace yourself.

Acids Release Protons in Water

An H^+ ion is just a proton.

The thing about acids is that they ionise — they release hydrogen ions, H^+.
For example,

$$HCl \rightarrow H^+ + Cl^-$$
$$H_2SO_4 \rightarrow 2H^+ + SO_4^{2-}$$

But HCl doesn't release hydrogen ions until it meets water — so hydrogen chloride gas isn't an acid.

Acids Can be Strong or Weak

1) Strong acids (e.g. sulfuric, hydrochloric and nitric) ionise almost completely in water. This means almost every hydrogen atom is released — so there are loads of H^+ ions.
2) Weak acids (e.g. ethanoic, citric, carbonic) ionise only very slightly. Only some of the hydrogen atoms in the compound are released — so only small numbers of H^+ ions are formed.

   For example,

   Strong acid: $HCl \longrightarrow H^+ + Cl^-$

   Weak acid: $CH_3COOH \rightleftharpoons H^+ + CH_3COO^-$

   Use a 'reversible reaction' arrow for a weak acid.

3) The ionisation of a weak acid is a reversible reaction. Since only a few H^+ ions are released, the equilibrium lies well to the left.
4) The pH of an acid or alkali is a measure of the concentration of H^+ ions in the solution. Strong acids typically have a pH of about 1 or 2, while the pH of a weak acid might be 4, 5 or 6.
5) The pH of an acid or alkali can be measured with a pH meter or with universal indicator paper (or can be estimated by seeing how fast a sample reacts with, say, magnesium).

Don't Confuse Strong Acids with Concentrated Acids

1) Acid strength (i.e. strong or weak) tells you what proportion of the acid molecules ionise in water.
2) The concentration of an acid is different. Concentration measures how many moles of acid molecules there are in a litre (1 dm^3) of water. Concentration is basically how watered down your acid is.
3) Note that concentration describes the total number of acid molecules — not the number of molecules that release hydrogen ions.
4) The more moles of acid molecules per dm^3, the more concentrated the acid is.
5) So you can have a dilute but strong acid, or a concentrated but weak acid.

Strong Acids are Better Electrical Conductors than Weak Acids

1) Hydrochloric acid has a much higher electrical conductivity than the same concentration of ethanoic acid. It's all to do with the concentration of the ions.
2) It's the ions that carry the charge through the acid solutions. So the greater concentration of ions in the strong acid means more charge can be carried. Simple.

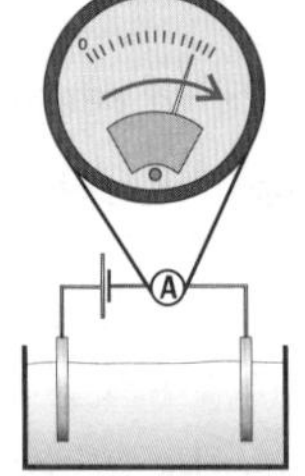

Hydrochloric acid (1 mol/dm^3)

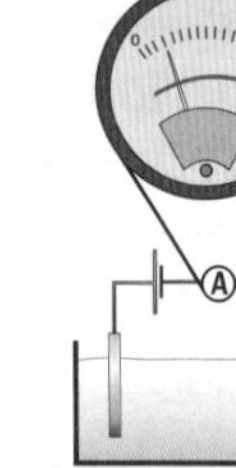

Ethanoic acid (1 mol/dm^3)

Concentration — oh so important when revising chemistry...

Acids are acidic because of H^+ ions. And strong acids are strong because they let go of all their H^+ ions at the drop of a hat... well, at the drop of a drop of water. This is tricky — no doubt about it, but if you can get your head round this, then you can probably cope with just about anything.

Strong and Weak Acids

Here's a nice bit of science... not the easiest thing in the book, but I like it.

Strong Acids React Faster Than Weak Acids

Strong and weak acids react with reactive metals and with carbonates in the same way.

1) Both hydrochloric acid (strong) and ethanoic acid (weak) will react with magnesium to give hydrogen. And both hydrochloric acid and ethanoic acid will react with calcium carbonate to give carbon dioxide.

$$2HCl + Mg \rightarrow MgCl_2 + H_2$$
$$2CH_3COOH + Mg \rightarrow Mg(CH_3COO)_2 + H_2$$

$$2HCl + CaCO_3 \rightarrow CaCl_2 + H_2O + CO_2$$
$$2CH_3COOH + CaCO_3 \rightarrow Ca(CH_3COO)_2 + H_2O + CO_2$$

2) The difference between the reactions of the two acids will be the rate of reaction. Ethanoic acid will react more slowly than hydrochloric acid of the same concentration.
3) It's all to do with the equilibrium in the weak acid reaction ($CH_3COOH \rightleftharpoons H^+ + CH_3COO^-$)...
4) When you put a weak acid into water, it releases a few H^+ ions (but not that many compared to what you'd get with a strong acid). When you add magnesium (or calcium carbonate), these H^+ ions react.
5) This means the concentration of H^+ ions decreases, so the equilibrium shifts to compensate — meaning more H+ ions are released. These ions then react, so the equilibrium shifts... and so on. As more ions are removed, more are supplied — kind of a drip-feed arrangement.
6) This is completely different to what you get with a strong acid, where all the acid molecules will react pretty gosh-darn quickly — since all the H^+ ions are just sitting there ready and waiting to go.

The Amount of Gas Produced Depends Upon the Amount of Acid

1) Hydrochloric acid (strong) will react faster than ethanoic acid (weak), but the amount of product you get will be the same (if you start with the same amount and they're the same concentration, etc.).

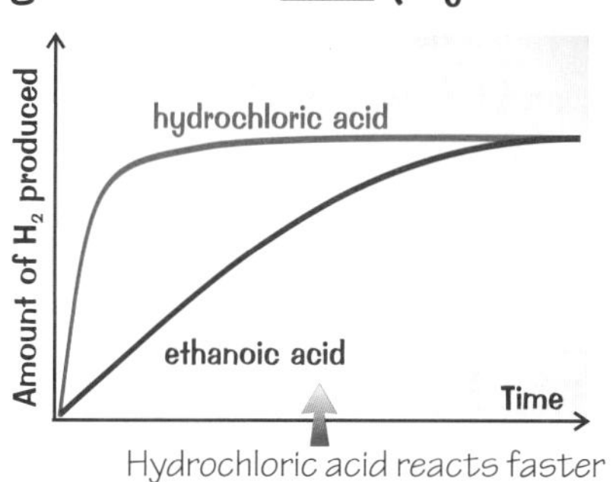

Hydrochloric acid reacts faster (steeper curve), but both reactions give the same amount of hydrogen.

2) This is because if the concentrations are the same, the number of molecules in a litre (say) of water will be the same.
3) And each of these molecules can let go of one H^+ ion.

   $HCl \longrightarrow H^+ + Cl^-$, and $CH_3COOH \rightleftharpoons H^+ + CH_3COO^-$

   It's just that hydrochloric acid will let go of them all at once, whereas ethanoic acid lets them go gradually.
4) But since the total number of H^+ ions available is the same, the amount of product will be the same (it's the H^+ ions that are the important bits in acid reactions).

Weak Acids Can be Really Useful

Weak acids can be more useful than dilute strong acids.

1) A strong acid reacts very fast — all its H^+ ions are released straight away and ready for action. But this might not always be as useful as it sounds — for example, if you want a slightly more controllable reaction, like with kettle descalers.
2) A strong acid would react very quickly with the scale — but before you know it, it may also react with the metal of the kettle. A weak acid still removes the scale, but the lower concentration of H^+ ions means the reaction will be slower and easier to control. And you can just tip the solution away when the scale's gone.

There's a hole in my kettle, dear Liza, dear Liza...

Hydrochloric acid is really nasty stuff. It's corrosive and irritating, difficult to store, damages almost everything it touches and will severely burn skin. Yet we have it in our stomachs. Surprising... But luckily we have a thick layer of mucus to protect our stomach walls. Neat, eh...

Precipitation Reactions

Precipitates don't dissolve, remember...

Precipitation Reactions Make an Insoluble Substance

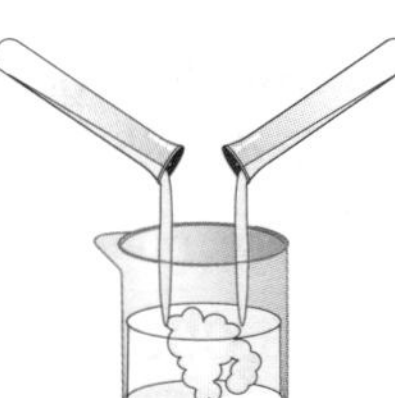

1) Precipitation reactions normally involve two solutions reacting together to make an insoluble substance.
2) The insoluble substance is called the precipitate, and it makes the solution turn murky or cloudy (and this usually happens extremely quickly).
3) Most precipitation reactions involve ions. To react with each other, these ions need to collide, so they have to be able to move.
4) This means the ionic substances have to be in solution or molten (see p44).

Ionic Equations Show Just the Useful Bits of Reactions

Look at this precipitation reaction...

Barium chloride + sodium sulfate → barium sulfate + sodium chloride

$$BaCl_2\,(aq) + Na_2SO_4\,(aq) \rightarrow BaSO_4\,(s) + 2NaCl\,(aq)$$

The (aq) and the (s) are state symbols — make sure you know them.
(s) = solid,
(l) = liquid,
(g) = gas,
(aq) = aqueous (dissolved in water)

1) You can tell it's a precipitation reaction because you start off with two solutions (look at the state symbols — they're both 'aq'), but you end up with a solid. This solid is the precipitate — it'll turn the water cloudy.
2) The 'interesting' bit of this reaction is the bit involving the barium and the sulfate ions — it's these that form the precipitate.
3) The sodium and chloride ions were dissolved in solution before the reaction, and they're still dissolved afterwards. They're called spectator ions — they're not really of any interest.
4) An ionic equation concentrates on the interesting bits of a reaction, and ignores the dull stuff. So the ionic equation for this equation would be:

$$Ba^{2+}(aq) + SO_4^{2-}\,(aq) \rightarrow BaSO_4\,(s)$$

Test for Sulfates (SO_4^{2-}) and Halides (Cl^-, Br^-, I^-)

You can use precipitation reactions to try and identify mystery substances. The colour of any precipitate can help you decide what ions are present.

Test for Sulfate ions, (SO_4^{2-})

1) To test for a sulfate ion, SO_4^{2-}, add dilute HCl, followed by barium nitrate, $Ba(NO_3)_2$.
2) A white precipitate of barium sulfate means the original compound was a sulfate.

$$Ba^{2+}(aq) + SO_4^{2-}(aq) \longrightarrow BaSO_4(s)$$

Test for Chloride (Cl^-), Bromide (Br^-) or Iodide (I^-) ions

To test for chloride, bromide or iodide ions, add dilute nitric acid, HNO_3, followed by lead nitrate, $Pb(NO_3)_2$.

A chloride gives a **white** precipitate of lead chloride.
A bromide gives a **cream** precipitate of lead bromide.
An iodide gives a **yellow** precipitate of lead iodide.

$$Pb^{2+}(aq) + 2Cl^-(aq) \longrightarrow PbCl_2(s)$$
$$Pb^{2+}(aq) + 2Br^-(aq) \longrightarrow PbBr_2(s)$$
$$Pb^{2+}(aq) + 2I^-(aq) \longrightarrow PbI_2(s)$$

If you aren't part of the solution, you're part of the precipitate...

Think of an ionic equation as a bit like Match of the Day — just an edited highlights package.

Preparing Insoluble Salts

You can use precipitation reactions to make insoluble salts.
You just need to pick the right reactants, then mix them together.

Pick the Right Reactants...

1) To make an insoluble salt you need some ions — e.g. to make lead iodide (PbI_2), you need some lead ions and some iodide ions. And these ions need to be in solution, so they can move about.
2) Fortunately, most nitrates are soluble — so if you use a solution of lead nitrate ($Pb(NO_3)_2$), you have your supply of lead ions. You can get your iodide ions from, say, sodium iodide (NaI).
3) Mix your ingredients together, and voilà — you have yourself an insoluble salt. Here's the reaction.

lead nitrate + sodium iodide → lead iodide + sodium nitrate

$$Pb(NO_3)_2\,(aq) + 2NaI\,(aq) \rightarrow PbI_2\,(s) + 2NaNO_3\,(aq)$$

Or even...

$$Pb^{2+}\,(aq) + 2I^-\,(aq) \rightarrow PbI_2\,(s)$$

4) If this is all you do, your salt will be wet, and mixed in with other stuff.
The method below will help you avoid that...

...Then Precipitate, Filter and Dry

Stage 1

First thing's first — check each reactant and product for any hazardous information, and make sure you take any necessary precautions.

1) Add 1 spatula of lead nitrate to a test tube, and fill it with distilled water. Shake it thoroughly to ensure that all the lead nitrate has dissolved. Then do the same with 1 spatula of sodium iodide. (Use distilled water to make sure there are no other ions about.)
2) Tip the two solutions into a small beaker, and give it a good stir to make sure it's all mixed together. The salt should precipitate out.

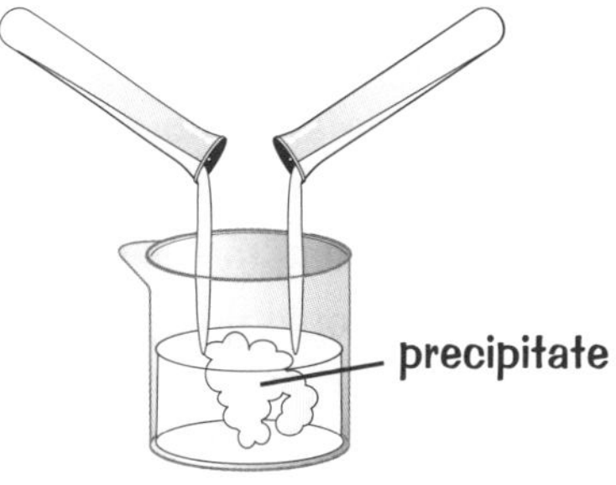

Stage 2

1) Put a folded piece of filter paper into a filter funnel, and stick the funnel into a conical flask.
2) Pour the contents of the beaker into the middle of the filter paper. (Make sure that the solution doesn't go above the filter paper — otherwise some of the solid could dribble down the side.)
3) Swill out the beaker with more distilled water, and tip this into the filter paper — to make sure you get all the product from the beaker.

Stage 3

1) Rinse the contents of the filter paper with distilled water to make sure that all the soluble salts have been washed away.
2) Then just scrape the lead iodide on to some fresh filter paper and leave it to dry.

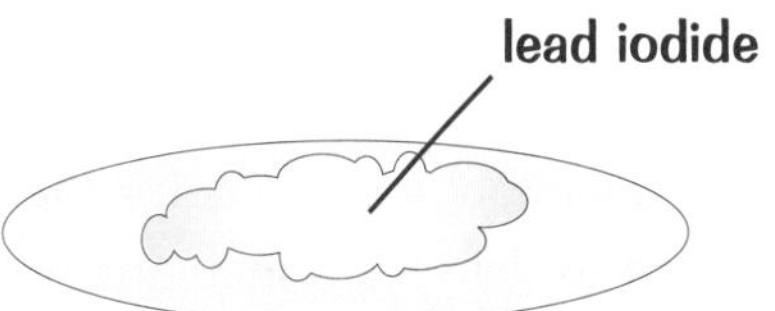

Get two solutions, mix 'em together — job's a good 'un...

Well, wouldn't you know — precipitation reactions can be used for all sorts of things. Testing for ions in solutions, making insoluble salts, and urmm... demonstrating the absolute wonderness of ionic equations. Ah-hem. Never mind. You've gotta learn about them anyway...

Revision Summary for Module C5

Ah, revision summaries... my favourite part of the section. And yours no doubt, since they're always at the end. There's a lot of calculations in this section, but that's good (honest), because you can expect a fair few in the exam as well. And as a wise man once said... it's best to practise before the exam, because once you're in there, it's a bit late really. So get your calculator fired up, and away you go...

1) What is a mole? Why is it that precise number?
2)* How many moles are there in 284 g of sodium sulfate, Na_2SO_4?
3)* What mass of chlorine is there in 2 moles of magnesium chloride, $MgCl_2$?
4) Give the definition of the relative atomic mass of an element.
5)* What mass of sodium is needed to produce 108.2 g of sodium oxide (Na_2O)?
6)* What is an empirical formula? Find the empirical formula of the compound formed when 21.9 g of magnesium, 29.3 g of sulfur and 58.4 g of oxygen react.
7) Why is hydrogen released during the electrolytic decomposition of $K_2SO_4(aq)$?
8) Write the half-equations at each electrode for the electrolytic decomposition of $PbI_2(l)$.
9) Describe two ways in which you could increase the amount of product made during electrolysis.
10)* If 2 amps of current flows for 3 seconds, how much charge is that, in coulombs?
11) What's the name for the amount of charge equal to 1 mole of electrons? How many coulombs is this?
12)* If 3 amps flows for 30 minutes in the electrolysis of copper(II) chloride solution, find:
a) the mass of copper formed, b) the volume of chlorine formed (at RTP).
13)* Calculate the concentration of the solution in g/dm³ formed when 7.5 g of calcium hydroxide, $Ca(OH)_2$, is dissolved in: a) 1 dm³ of water, b) 2 dm³ of water.
14)* How many moles of barium chloride are in 500 cm³ of a 0.2 molar solution of barium chloride?
15)* How would you produce 250 cm³ of a 0.2 mol/dm³ solution of sulfuric acid if you were given a 1.0 mol/dm³ solution of sulfuric acid, and water?
16) This nutritional information table was found on an orange juice carton: Angela says that one glass will give her 42% of the recommended daily amount of vitamin C. Why might she be wrong?

NUTRITIONAL INFORMATION Typical values for 100 ml	
Energy	197 kJ 46 kcal
Carbohydrate	10.4 g
Vitamin C	25 mg (42% RDA)

17) Why do you need to get several consistent readings in titrations?
18) Why is a single indicator like phenolphthalein used in titrations?
19) Sketch a pH curve for the titration where hydrochloric acid is added to sodium hydroxide.
20)* In a titration, 22.5 cm³ of nitric acid was required to neutralise 25 cm³ of potassium hydroxide with a concentration of 0.15 moles per dm³.
Calculate the concentration of the nitric acid in: a) mol/dm³, b) g/dm³.
21) Name 3 methods used for measuring the amount of gas produced in a reaction. Give their advantages.
22) What is the limiting reactant in a reaction?
23)* The graph shows the amount of hydrogen produced when magnesium metal was placed into a hydrochloric acid solution.
a) How much hydrogen had evolved at the end of the reaction?
b) How long did it take to produce 35 cm³ of hydrogen?
24) What is a reversible reaction? Explain why it could reach an equilibrium.
25) Describe how three different factors affect the position of equilibrium.
26) Write the symbol equations for the three reactions in the contact process.
27) State and explain the conditions used in the contact process.
28) What is the difference between the strength of an acid and its concentration?
29) Explain why weak acids react slower than strong acids.
30)* What is the ionic equation for the reaction between silver nitrate and sodium bromide?
31) How would you test for: a) a sulfate, b) a halide?
32) Describe how you would obtain a dry sample of lead chloride from lead nitrate and calcium chloride.

* Answers on page 108.

Redox and Displacement Reactions

In chemistry, things get oxidised and reduced all the time. And you need to learn about it.

If Electrons are Transferred, It's a Redox Reaction

"OXIDATION" DOESN'T HAVE TO INVOLVE OXYGEN

1) A loss of electrons is called oxidation. A gain in electrons is called reduction.
2) REDuction and OXidation happen at the same time — hence the term "REDOX".
3) An oxidising agent accepts electrons and gets reduced.
4) A reducing agent donates electrons and gets oxidised.

Oxidation Is Loss	Reduction Is Gain

Remember it as OIL RIG.

Some Examples of Redox Reactions:

1) Chlorine gas is passed into a solution of an iron(II) salt. The solution turns from green to yellow as the iron(II) ion is oxidised to iron(III). The Fe^{2+} ion loses an electron to form Fe^{3+}.
2) The chlorine causes this to happen — it's the oxidising agent.
3) The chlorine must've gained the electrons that the Fe^{2+} lost. The chlorine's been reduced. The iron(II) ion must be the reducing agent.

$$Fe^{2+} - e^- \rightarrow Fe^{3+}$$

$$Cl_2 + 2e^- \rightarrow 2Cl^-$$

1) Iron atoms are oxidised to iron(II) ions when they react with dilute acid.
2) The iron atoms lose electrons. They're oxidised by the hydrogen ions.
3) The hydrogen ions gain electrons. They're reduced by the iron atoms.

$$Fe - 2e^- \rightarrow Fe^{2+}$$

$$2H^+ + 2e^- \rightarrow H_2$$

A More Reactive Metal Displaces a Less Reactive Metal

1) Displacement reactions involve one metal kicking another one out of a compound. Learn this rule:

A MORE REACTIVE metal will displace a LESS REACTIVE metal from its compound.

2) If you put a reactive metal into the solution of a dissolved metal compound, the reactive metal will replace the less reactive metal in the compound.
3) E.g. put magnesium in a solution of iron sulfate and the more reactive magnesium will "kick out" the less reactive iron from the solution. You end up with magnesium sulfate solution and iron metal. The "kicked out" metal coats itself on the reactive metal — you'd see a coating of iron on the magnesium.

An Investigation into the Reactivity of Metals

Method: Add equal amounts of magnesium powder to test tubes containing equal strength solutions of zinc sulfate, iron sulfate and tin chloride. Measure the temperature before and after. Magnesium is more reactive than zinc, iron and tin, so it'll displace these metals from their solutions (an exothermic reaction).

1) Magnesium and zinc sulfate gave a temperature rise of 6 °C.
2) Magnesium and iron sulfate gave a temperature rise of 10 °C.
3) Magnesium and tin chloride gave a temperature rise of 17 °C.

The further apart the metals are in the reactivity series, the higher the temperature change in the displacement reaction.

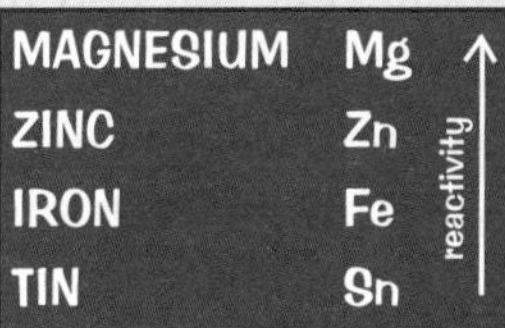

Examiners can ask you to write word or symbol equations for displacement reactions. Here's an example:

Magnesium + zinc sulfate → magnesium sulfate + zinc

$$Mg(s) + ZnSO_4(aq) \rightarrow MgSO_4(aq) + Zn(s)$$

REDOX — great for bubblebaths. Oh no, wait...

Try writing some displacement reaction equations now — write a symbol equation for the reaction between zinc and iron chloride ($FeCl_2$). What's being oxidised? What's being reduced? These are the kind of questions you'll get — so practise till you can do it in your sleep.

Rusting of Iron

Rusting is a favourite topic of examiners everywhere...

Rusting of Iron is a Redox Reaction

1) Iron and some steels will rust if they come into contact with air and water. Rusting only happens when the iron's in contact with both oxygen (from the air) and water.
2) Rust is a form of hydrated iron(III) oxide.
3) Learn the equation for rust: **iron + oxygen + water → hydrated iron(III) oxide**
4) Rusting of iron is a redox reaction.
5) This is why. Iron loses electrons when it reacts with oxygen. Each Fe atom loses three electrons to become Fe^{3+}. Iron's oxidised.
6) Oxygen gains electrons when it reacts with iron. Each O atom gains two electrons to become O^{2-}. Oxygen's reduced.

Metals are Combined with Other Things to Prevent Rust

1) Iron can be prevented from rusting by mixing it with other metals to make alloys.
2) Steels are alloys of iron with carbon and small quantities of other metals.
3) One of the most common steels is stainless steel — a rustproof alloy of iron, carbon and chromium.

Oil, Grease and Paint Prevent Rusting

You can prevent rusting by coating the iron with a barrier. This keeps out the water, oxygen or both.

1) Painting is ideal for large and small structures. It can also be nice and colourful.
2) Oiling or greasing has to be used when moving parts are involved, like on bike chains.

A Coat of Tin Can Protect Steel from Rust

1) Tinning is where a coat of tin is applied to the object, e.g. food cans.
2) This only works as long as the tin remains intact. If the tin is scratched to reveal some iron, the iron will lose electrons in preference to the tin. Iron is more reactive than tin, remember.
3) That's why it's not always a good idea to buy the reduced bashed tins of food at the supermarket. They could be starting to rust.

More Reactive Metals Can Also be Used to Prevent Iron Rusting

You can also prevent rusting using the sacrificial method. You place a more reactive metal with the iron. The water and oxygen then react with this "sacrificial" metal instead of with the iron.

1) Galvanising is where a coat of zinc is put onto the object. The zinc acts as sacrificial protection — it's more reactive than iron so it'll lose electrons in preference to iron. The zinc also acts as a barrier. Steel buckets and corrugated iron roofing are often galvanised.
2) Blocks of metal, e.g. magnesium, can be bolted to the iron. Magnesium will lose electrons in preference to iron. It's used on the hulls of ships, or on underground iron pipes.

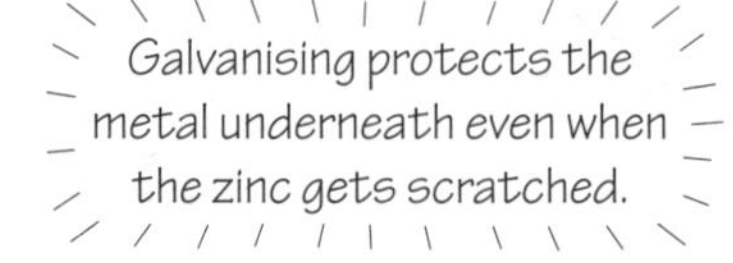

Don't get confused about sacrificial protection — it's not a displacement reaction. There isn't a metal reacting with a metal salt — oxygen's reacting with a more reactive metal instead of a less reactive one.

Alloy there Jim Lad...

Rust is one of those really annoying things. It eats your bike, your car, your ship... but then doesn't touch that lovely woolly cardigan that your gran gave you. But, you can use it to dye your clothes, just place a rusty object on the fabric, add a splash of vinegar, and voilá — a beautiful orange stain.

Fuel Cells

Fuel cells are great — they use hydrogen and oxygen to make electricity.

Hydrogen and Oxygen Give Out Energy When They React

Remember the lab tests for hydrogen and oxygen. Hydrogen plus a lighted splint gives that good old squeaky pop. Oxygen relights a glowing splint.

1) Hydrogen and oxygen react to produce water — which isn't a pollutant.
2) The reaction between hydrogen and oxygen is exothermic — it releases energy.
3) Put these two facts together, and you get something useful: you can get energy by reacting hydrogen and oxygen — and it doesn't produce any nasty pollutants, only nice clean water...

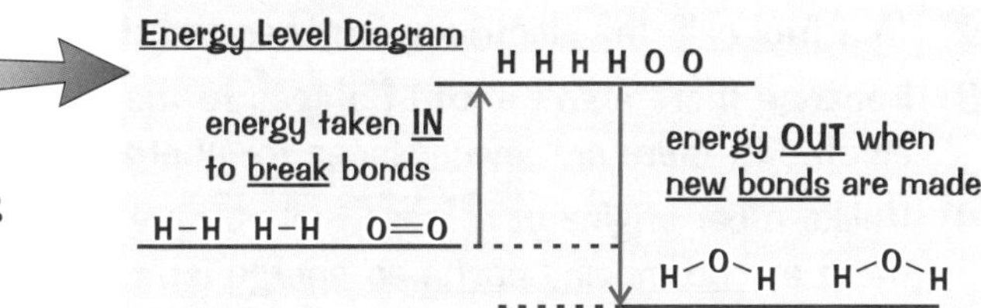

Fuel Cells Use Fuel and Oxygen to Produce Electrical Energy

A fuel cell is an electrical cell that's supplied with a fuel and oxygen and uses energy from the reaction between them to generate an electrical voltage.

I'd learn that if I were you.

1) Fuel cells were developed in the 1960s as part of the space programme, to provide electrical power on spacecraft — they were more practical than solar cells and safer than nuclear power. (They're still used on the Space Shuttle missions.)
2) Unlike a battery, a fuel cell doesn't run down or need recharging from the mains. It'll produce energy in the form of electricity and heat as long as fuel is supplied.
3) There are a few different types of fuel cells, using different fuels and different electrolytes. The one they want you to know about is the hydrogen-oxygen fuel cell.

Hydrogen-Oxygen Fuel Cells Involve a Redox Reaction

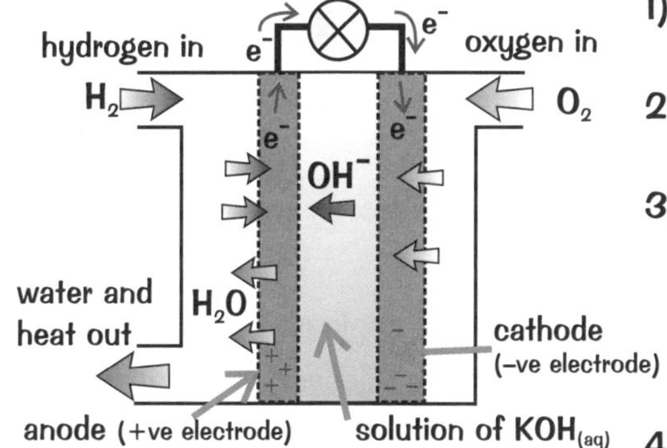

1) The electrolyte is often a solution of potassium hydroxide. The electrodes are often porous carbon with a catalyst.
2) Hydrogen goes into the anode compartment and oxygen goes into the cathode compartment.
3) At the –ve cathode, oxygen gains electrons (from the cathode) and reacts with water (from the electrolyte) to make OH^- ions.

$$O_2 + 4e^- + 2H_2O \rightarrow 4OH^-$$

The oxygen gas is gaining electrons — this is reduction.

4) OH^- ions in the electrolyte move to the anode (+ve).
5) At the +ve anode, hydrogen combines with the hydroxide ions to produce water and electrons. The hydrogen gas loses electrons. This is oxidation.

$$2H_2 + 4OH^- \rightarrow 4H_2O + 4e^-$$

6) The electrons flow through an external circuit from the anode to the cathode — this is the electric current.
7) The overall reaction is hydrogen plus oxygen, which gives water.

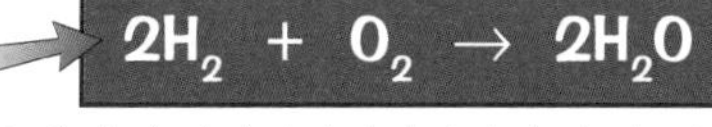

$$2H_2 + O_2 \rightarrow 2H_2O$$

They can ask you for this equation in the exam — luckily it's a nice simple one.

There's reduction at the cathode and oxidation at the anode, so the whole thing is a REDOX reaction.

Fuel cells — they're simply electrifying...

This page is tough stuff. If you want the marks, you'll have to learn it — yes, even the nasty fuel cell diagram and equations. They can ask what happens at each electrode, including oxidation and reduction.

Fuel Cells

They can ask you about the real-world applications of fuel cells. Spacecraft and (one day soon maybe) cars are the main ones. You'll probably need to describe a few advantages of fuel cells while you're at it.

Hydrogen-Oxygen Fuel Cells Have Lots of Advantages

1) Hydrogen fuel cells are great — they're much more efficient than power stations or batteries at producing electricity. If you use the heat produced as well, their efficiency can be greater than 80%.
2) In a fuel cell, the electricity is generated directly from the reaction (so no turbines, generators, etc.).
3) Because there aren't a lot of stages to the process of generating electricity there are fewer places for energy to be lost as heat.
4) Unlike a car engine or a fossil fuel burning power station, there are no moving parts, so energy isn't lost through friction.
5) With hydrogen as the fuel, the only product is water. There's no pollution.

This could mean no more smelly petrol and diesel cars, lorries and buses.

It could also replace batteries — which are incredibly polluting to dispose of because they're usually made of highly toxic metal compounds.

However, it's not likely to mean the end of either conventional power stations or our dependence on fossil fuels. That's because the hydrogen fuel is often made either from hydrocarbons (from fossil fuels), or by electrolysis of water, which uses electricity (and that electricity's got to be generated somehow — usually this involves fossil fuels).

Hydrogen-Oxygen Fuel Cells are Used in Spacecraft

1) Hydrogen fuel cells are used to provide electrical power in spacecraft such as the Space Shuttle.
2) Hydrogen and oxygen are readily available from the spacecraft rocket fuel tanks (the reaction between hydrogen and oxygen is used to fuel the spacecraft's rockets).
3) Some of the product of the reaction (water) is used as drinking water — which saves the astronauts having to take gallons of drinking water with them.
4) There are no other waste products or pollutants to get rid of.

The Car Industry is Developing Fuel Cells

1) The car industry is developing fuel cells to replace conventional petrol/diesel engines.
2) Fuel cell vehicles don't produce any conventional pollutants — no greenhouse gases, no nitrogen oxides, no sulfur dioxide, no carbon monoxide. The only by-products are water and heat. This would be a major advantage in cities, where air pollution from traffic is a big problem.
3) Fuel cells could eventually help countries to become less dependent on crude oil.

There are fuel cell powered road signs actually in use (in New Jersey, USA).

There are prototypes of fuel cell powered vacuum cleaners and vending machines.

Fuel cells are used to provide back-up power for hospitals, airports etc.

Mini fuel cells for mobile phones, laptops and PDAs are in development. (There are already mini fuel cells for PDAs and the like but they use zinc as the fuel, not hydrogen.)

PDAs (personal digital assistants) are handheld electronic organisers.

Could we all be filling up our cars with hydrogen one day...

These fuel cells sound great — but you have to think. Once you've got the hydrogen, yeah, fuel cells are ace. But producing that hydrogen takes a lot of either fossil fuels or energy. That doesn't mean fuel cells won't be more important in the future, only that you need to look at the whole picture.

Alcohols

There's a whole group of compounds called alcohols, and they're rather useful to industrial chemists.

Alcohols Have an '-OH' Functional Group and End in '-ol'

1) The general formula of an alcohol is $C_nH_{2n+1}OH$.
2) So if an alcohol has 2 carbons (n = 2), its formula will be $C_2H_{(2\times2)+1}OH$, which is C_2H_5OH.
3) The basic naming system is the same as for alkanes (see p.11) — but replace the final '-e' with '-ol'.

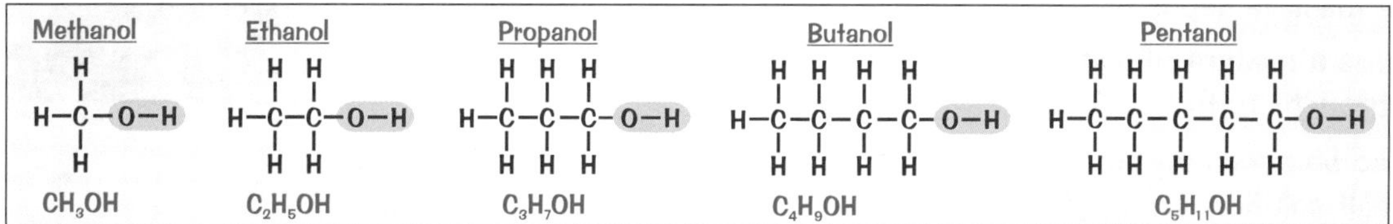

Don't write CH_4O instead of CH_3OH, or C_2H_6O instead of C_2H_5OH, etc. — it doesn't show the functional -OH group.

Fermentation Produces Ethanol

glucose → ethanol + carbon dioxide

$$C_6H_{12}O_6 \rightarrow 2C_2H_5OH + 2CO_2$$

1) Fermentation converts sugars (usually glucose) into ethanol.
2) The reaction is brought about by enzymes (biological catalysts) found in yeasts.
3) The temperature needs to be carefully controlled. If it's too cold the yeast is inactive, so the reaction's really slow — but if it's too hot the enzymes in the yeast are destroyed. The reaction's carried out at an optimum (ideal) temperature between 25 °C and 50 °C.
4) It's also important to prevent oxygen getting at the alcohol. This is because oxygen converts ethanol to ethanoic acid (which is what you get in vinegar).
5) When the concentration of alcohol reaches about 10-20%, the reaction stops — the yeast is killed by the alcohol. The mixture can be distilled to give pure alcohol.
6) Fermentation uses a renewable resource (e.g. sugar cane or sugar beets), so we'll never run out.
7) But it's expensive to concentrate and purify the ethanol. And the whole process is slow and inefficient.

Ethene Can be Reacted with Steam to Produce Ethanol

ethene + steam → ethanol

$$C_2H_4 + H_2O \longrightarrow C_2H_5OH$$

1) This is how ethanol is usually made industrially.
2) Ethene (C_2H_4) will react with steam (H_2O) to make ethanol.
3) The reaction needs a temperature of 300 °C and a pressure of 70 atmospheres. Phosphoric acid is used as a catalyst.
4) At the moment this is a cheap process, because ethene's fairly cheap and not much of it is wasted.
5) The trouble is that ethene's produced from crude oil, which is a non-renewable resource and which will start running out fairly soon. This means using ethene to make ethanol will become very expensive.
6) It's made in a large chemical plant, so it's made continuously and quickly. The product is high quality.

Ethanol Can be Dehydrated Back to Ethene

1) The plastics and polymers industry uses lots of ethene.
2) Countries which have no oil but plenty of land for growing crops for fermentation can make ethene through the dehydration of ethanol.
3) Ethanol vapour is passed over a hot aluminium oxide catalyst.

ethanol → ethene + water

$$C_2H_5OH \rightarrow C_2H_4 + H_2O$$

300 °C, 70 atm, acid — why don't home brewers hydrate ethene...

Learn the equations for the hydration of ethene and the dehydration of ethanol. Hydration of ethene's useful if you've got crude oil and need ethanol, dehydration's useful if you have ethanol but no crude oil.

Salt

In hot countries they get salt by pouring sea water into big flat open tanks and letting the Sun evaporate the water, leaving the salt behind. This is no good in Britain though — there isn't enough sunshine.

Salt is Mined from Underneath Cheshire

1) In Britain (a cold country — as if you need reminding), salt is extracted from underground deposits left millions of years ago when ancient seas evaporated.
2) There are massive deposits of this rock salt under Cheshire and Teeside.
3) Rock salt is a mixture of salt and impurities. It's drilled, blasted and dug out and brought to the surface using machinery.
4) It can also be mined by pumping hot water underground. The salt dissolves and the salt solution is forced to the surface by the pressure of the water.
5) When the mining is finished, it's important to fill in the holes in the ground. If not, the land could collapse and slide into the holes — this is called subsidence.
6) Rock salt can be used in its raw state on roads to stop ice forming, or the salt can be filtered out and used to enhance the flavour in food or for making chemicals. If salt's going to be used to make chemicals, usually the first thing they do is electrolyse it, like this:

Salt for the roads is blasted and dug out. White salt for food and chemicals is extracted with hot water.

Electrolysis of Brine Gives Hydrogen, Chlorine and NaOH

Concentrated brine (sodium chloride solution) is electrolysed industrially using a set-up a bit like this one.

There are three useful products:

a) Hydrogen gas is given off at the (–ve) cathode.
b) Chlorine gas is given off at the (+ve) anode.
c) Sodium hydroxide (NaOH) is left in solution.

These are collected, and then used in all sorts of industries to make various products, detailed on the following page.

The electrodes are made of an inert material — they shouldn't react with either the electrolyte or the products of the electrolysis.

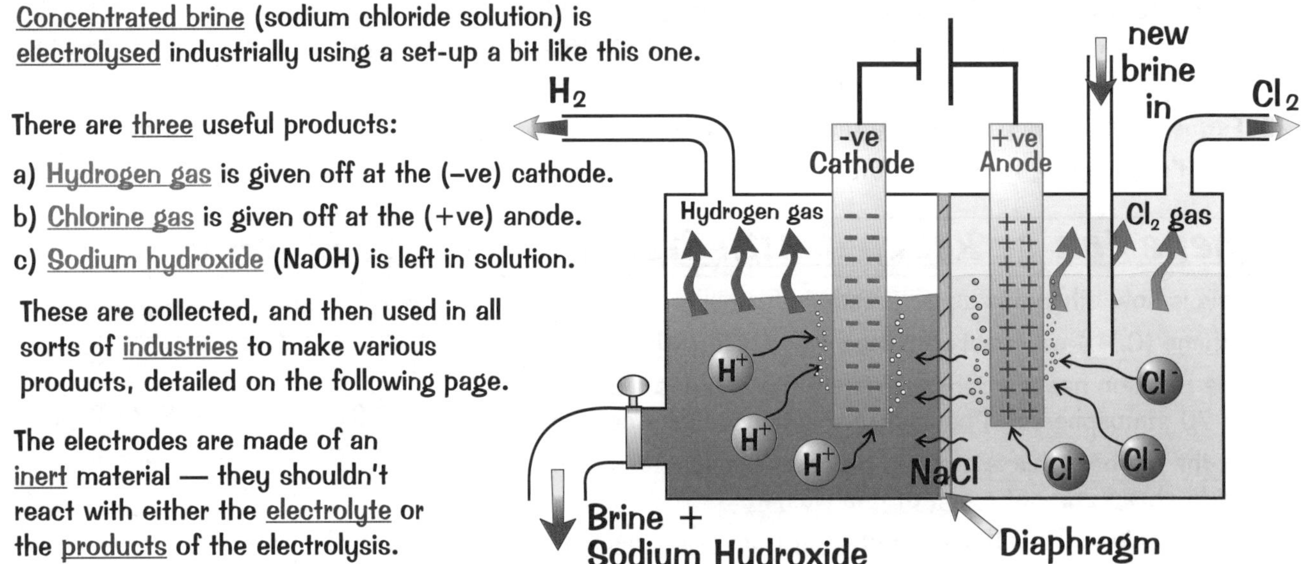

The Half-Equations — Make Sure the Electrons Balance

1) At the cathode, two hydrogen ions accept one electron each to become one hydrogen molecule.
2) At the anode, two chloride (Cl^-) ions lose one electron each to become one chlorine molecule.

Cathode: $2H^+ + 2e^- \rightarrow H_2$

Anode: $2Cl^- - 2e^- \rightarrow Cl_2$

Salt — it's not just for chips any more...

Salt's used for a lot of chemical products as well as for food and gritting the roads. Learn the diagram and equations for the industrial electrolysis of brine — you need to know what's produced and where.

Salt

Electrolysis of brine is really useful for the chemical industry — all sorts of things are made from chlorine, hydrogen and sodium hydroxide. But first, something slightly tricky...

Dilute Brine Produces Oxygen — not Chlorine

1) A solution of sodium chloride contains sodium ions and chloride ions, but it also contains a few hydrogen ions (H^+) and hydroxide ions (OH^-) from the water.
2) As it happens, the OH^- is the most easily discharged anion. In other words, it'll come out of solution first, before other negative ions (see page 70 for a bit more info).
3) So in a dilute solution of brine, the OH^- ions are discharged before the chloride ions, and so oxygen is produced at the anode.

$$4OH^- - 4e^- \rightarrow O_2 + 2H_2O$$

4) In a concentrated solution of brine, there are a huge number of chloride ions and very few hydroxide ions. The chloride ions win by sheer numbers — chlorine is formed at the anode.

$$2Cl^- - 2e^- \rightarrow Cl_2$$

Note that if you electrolyse molten sodium chloride, you get sodium at the cathode and chlorine at the anode. Learn the equations for the reactions at the electrodes:

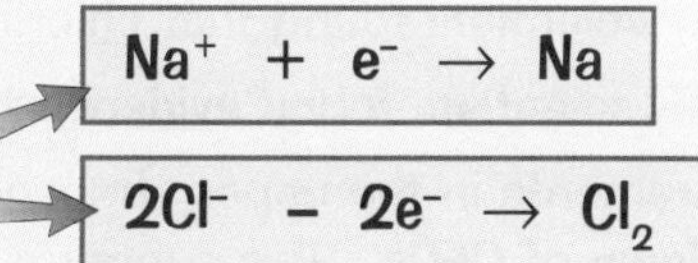

$$Na^+ + e^- \rightarrow Na$$

$$2Cl^- - 2e^- \rightarrow Cl_2$$

Useful Products from the Electrolysis of Brine

With all that effort and expense going into the electrolysis of brine, there'd better be some pretty useful stuff coming out of it — and so there is... and you have to learn it all too. Ace.

1) Chlorine

Used in: 1) disinfectants 2) killing bacteria (e.g. in swimming pools) 3) household bleach 4) plastics (e.g. PVC) 5) HCl 6) insecticides.

(Don't forget the simple lab test for chlorine — it bleaches damp litmus paper.)

Cl_2 gas

Damp Litmus Paper

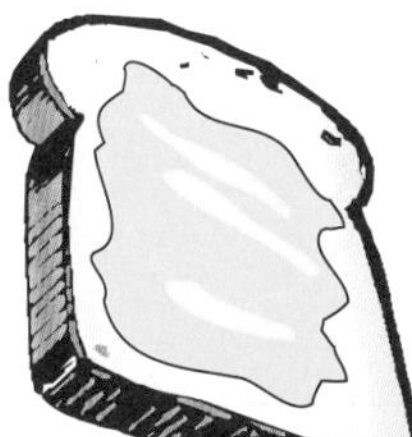

2) Hydrogen

1) Used in the Haber process to make ammonia (remember?).
2) Used to change oils into fats for making margarine ("hydrogenated vegetable oil"). Think about that when you spread it on your toast in the morning. Yum.

3) Sodium Hydroxide

Sodium hydroxide is a very strong alkali and is used widely in the chemical industry. For example, it's used in the manufacture of:

1) soap 2) ceramics 3) organic chemicals 4) paper pulp 5) oven cleaner 6) household bleach

About Bleach...

Household bleach is made by reacting chlorine with sodium hydroxide.

Salt — it's a tasty little resource for industrial chemists...

It's not much trouble to learn a few products made from chlorine, hydrogen and sodium hydroxide. And make double sure you know how bleach is made. One last thing... get the differences between electrolysis of weak NaCl solution and electrolysis of strong NaCl solution sorted (the OH^- ions stuff).

CFCs and the Ozone Layer

Scientists changed their minds about CFCs as they found out more evidence about them.

At First Scientists Thought CFCs were Great...

1) Chlorofluorocarbons (CFCs for short) are organic molecules containing carbon, chlorine and fluorine, e.g. dichlorodifluoromethane CCl_2F_2 — this is like methane but with two chlorine and two fluorine atoms (and an extremely long name) instead of the four hydrogen atoms.
2) CFCs are non-toxic, non-flammable and non-reactive with other chemicals. They're insoluble in water and have low boiling points. Scientists were very happy that they'd found some non-toxic and unreactive chemicals which were ideal for many uses.
3) Chlorofluorocarbons were used as coolants in refrigerators and air-conditioning systems.
4) CFCs were also used as propellants in aerosol spray cans.

...But Then They Discovered the Shocking Truth

This is called the "hole in the ozone layer".

1) In 1974 scientists found that chlorine could help to destroy ozone. (See equations on p95.)
2) In 1985 scientists found evidence of decreasing ozone levels in the atmosphere over Antarctica.
3) Measurements in the upper atmosphere show high levels of compounds produced by the breakdown of CFCs. This supports the hypothesis that CFCs break down and destroy ozone.
4) Scientists are now sure that CFCs are linked to the depletion (thinning) of the ozone layer.

Ozone is a form of oxygen with the formula O_3 — it has three oxygen atoms per molecule, unlike ordinary oxygen which has two atoms per molecule.
It hangs about in the ozone layer, way up in the stratosphere (part of the upper atmosphere), doing the very important job of absorbing ultraviolet (UV) light from the Sun. Ozone absorbs UV light and breaks down into an oxygen molecule and an oxygen atom: $O_3 + \text{UV light} \rightarrow O + O_2$
The oxygen molecule and oxygen atom join together to make ozone again: $O + O_2 \rightarrow O_3$
Reducing the amount of ozone in the stratosphere results in more UV light passing through the atmosphere. Increased levels of UV light hitting the surface of the Earth can cause medical problems...

1) There's an increased risk of sunburn.
2) More ultraviolet light causes skin to age faster.
3) There are more cases of skin cancer. Ultraviolet light mucks about with the DNA in skin cells.
4) There's an increased risk of cataracts. A cataract is cloudiness in the lens of the eye — as cataracts get worse, they lead to blindness.

Some Countries Have Banned the Use of CFCs

1) The hypothesis that CFCs could damage the ozone layer caused a lot of concern, and in 1978 the USA, Canada, Sweden and Norway banned CFCs as aerosol propellants.
2) After the ozone hole was discovered many countries got together and decided to reduce CFC production and eventually ban CFCs completely (the agreement's called the Montreal Protocol). The UK has banned CFCs.
3) Some poorer countries haven't banned CFCs because of the cost of replacing them with alternatives.
4) Depletion of the ozone layer is a global problem. CFCs are easily blown by the wind all over the Earth — they affect everybody, not just the countries which allow them.
5) Poorer countries who sign up to the Montreal Protocol can get help with the cost of replacing CFCs.

That's "chlorofluorocarbon" not "Chelsea Football Club"...

Ozone's amazing stuff — it absorbs UV light and stops us from having to bear the full force of the Sun's UV output. Too much UV causes sunburn and skin cancer, so anything that damages the ozone and lets more UV through is a bad thing in the long run. So no more CFCs in fridges and spray cans.

CFCs and the Ozone Layer

CFCs damage ozone by forming free radicals. Learn what they are first, then how they attack ozone.

Free Radicals are Made by Breaking Covalent Bonds

1) A covalent bond, remember, is one where two atoms share electrons between them, like in H_2.
2) A covalent bond can break unevenly to form two ions, e.g. $H\text{–}H \rightarrow H^+ + H^-$.
   The H^- has both of the shared electrons, and the poor old H^+ has neither of them.
3) But a covalent bond can also break evenly — and then each atom gets one of the shared electrons, e.g. $H\text{–}H \rightarrow H\cdot + H\cdot$ — the $H\cdot$ is called a free radical. (The unpaired electron is shown by a dot.)
4) The unpaired electron makes the free radical very, very reactive.

Chlorine Free Radicals from CFCs Damage the Ozone Layer

1) Ultraviolet light makes CFCs break up to form free radicals:

$$CCl_2F_2 \rightarrow CClF_2\cdot + Cl\cdot$$

2) This happens high up in the atmosphere (in the stratosphere), where the ultraviolet light from the Sun is stronger.
3) Chlorine free radicals from this reaction react with ozone (O_3), turning it into ordinary oxygen molecules (O_2):

$$O_3 + Cl\cdot \rightarrow ClO\cdot + O_2$$

4) The chlorine oxide molecule ClO is very reactive, and reacts with ozone to make two oxygen molecules and another Cl· free radical:

$$ClO\cdot + O_3 \rightarrow 2O_2 + Cl\cdot$$

5) This Cl· free radical now goes and reacts with another ozone molecule. This is a chain reaction, so just one chlorine free radical from one CFC molecule can go around breaking up a lot of ozone molecules.

Learn these equations.

CFCs don't attack ozone directly. They break up and form chlorine atoms (free radicals) which attack ozone. The chlorine atoms aren't used up, so they can carry on breaking down ozone.

CFCs Stay in the Stratosphere for Ages

1) CFCs are not very reactive and will only react with one or two chemicals that are present in the atmosphere. And they'll only break up to form chlorine atoms in the stratosphere, where there's plenty of high-energy ultraviolet light around. They won't do it in the lower atmosphere.
2) This means that the CFCs in the atmosphere now will take a long time to be removed.
3) Remember, each CFC molecule produces one chlorine atom which can react with an awful lot of ozone molecules. Thousands of them, in fact.
4) So the millions of CFC molecules that are present in the stratosphere will continue to destroy ozone for a long time — even after all CFCs have been banned. Each molecule will stay around for a long time, and each molecule will destroy a lot of ozone molecules.

Alkanes and HFCs are Safe Alternatives to CFCs

1) Alkanes don't react with ozone, so they can provide a safe alternative to CFCs.
2) Hydrofluorocarbons (HFCs) are compounds very similar to CFCs — but they contain no chlorine. It's the chlorine in CFCs that attacks ozone, remember.
3) Scientists have investigated the compounds that could be produced by breakdown of HFCs in the upper atmosphere, and none of them seem to be able to attack ozone. Evidence suggests HFCs are safe.

Oooh, here comes the tricky science bit...

Here's the deal — yes, you do need to know what a free radical is, and yes you do need to learn the equations for the reaction between chlorine atoms and ozone. You can't just glide your eyes over the equations and hope for the best. Cover the page and scribble them down, then check what you wrote.

Hardness of Water

Water where you live might be hard or soft. It depends on the rocks your water meets on its way to you.

Hard Water Makes Scum and Scale

1) Hard water won't easily form a lather with soap. It makes a nasty scum instead. So to get a decent lather you need to use more soap.
2) Hard water also forms limescale (calcium carbonate) on the insides of pipes, boilers and kettles. Limescale is a thermal insulator. This means that a kettle with limescale on the heating element takes longer to boil than a clean non-scaled-up kettle. Scale can even eventually block pipes.
3) Worst of all, hard water also causes a horrible scum to form on the surface of tea.

Hardness is Caused by Ca^{2+} and Mg^{2+} ions

Hard water contains calcium ions (Ca^{2+}), magnesium ions (Mg^{2+}), or both. As water flows over rocks and through soils containing calcium and magnesium compounds, these ions dissolve in it.

1) Magnesium sulfate $MgSO_4$ dissolves in water — and so does calcium sulfate $CaSO_4$ (though only a little bit).
2) Calcium carbonate commonly exists as chalk, limestone or marble. It doesn't dissolve in water, but it will react with acids. And since CO_2 from the air dissolves in rainwater (forming carbonic acid, $CO_2 + H_2O \rightarrow H_2CO_3$), rainwater is slightly acidic. This means that calcium carbonate can react with rainwater to form calcium hydrogencarbonate ($H_2CO_3 + CaCO_3 \rightarrow Ca(HCO_3)_2$), which is soluble.

   Overall the equation for the reaction is:

   carbon dioxide + water + calcium carbonate → calcium hydrogencarbonate

   $$CO_2(g) + H_2O(l) + CaCO_3(s) \rightarrow Ca(HCO_3)_2(aq)$$

Temporary Hardness Can be Removed by Boiling

There are two kinds of hardness — temporary and permanent.
Temporary hardness is caused by the hydrogencarbonate ion, HCO_3^-, in $Ca(HCO_3)_2$.
Hardness caused by dissolved calcium sulfate (among other things) is permanent hardness.

1) Temporary hardness is removed by boiling. The calcium hydrogencarbonate decomposes to form insoluble $CaCO_3$. This won't work for permanent hardness, though. Heating a sulfate ion does nowt. (This calcium carbonate precipitate is the 'limescale' on your kettle — it's insoluble.)

   calcium hydrogencarbonate → calcium carbonate + water + carbon dioxide

   $$Ca(HCO_3)_2(aq) \rightarrow CaCO_3(s) + H_2O(l) + CO_2(g)$$

2) Both types of hardness are removed by adding washing soda — sodium carbonate, Na_2CO_3. The carbonate ions join onto the calcium ions and make an insoluble precipitate of calcium carbonate. This works whether the hardness is due to calcium sulfate or calcium hydrogencarbonate.

   $$Ca^{2+}(aq) + CO_3^{2-}(aq) \rightarrow CaCO_3(s)$$

3) Both types of hardness can also be removed by 'ion exchange columns'. These clever bits of chemistry have lots of sodium ions (or hydrogen ions) and 'exchange' them for calcium or magnesium ions.

Ice is fairly hard, come to think of it...

One thing that I've never understood is that they sell water softeners in areas that already have soft water. Hmm... For the exam, you're supposed to know how the salts that cause hard water get into the water in the first place, and how they can be removed. So make sure you know it.

Hardness of Water

Limescale is horrible stuff, as you'll know if you're unlucky enough to live where there's really hard water.

Limescale Can be Removed Using a Weak Acid

Limescale is just calcium carbonate. This means it can be dissolved by an acid, which is what commercial limescale removers (descalers) are.

1) Carbonates react with many acids to produce a soluble salt, water and carbon dioxide.
2) Limescale should be removed from a kettle by using a weak acid. A strong acid could react with the metal of the kettle's electric element — not what you need. Weak acids give a nice slow reaction.
3) It's the H^+ ion from the acid that reacts with calcium carbonate. Here's an equation to learn:

Calcium carbonate + hydrogen ions → calcium ions + water + carbon dioxide

$$CaCO_3 + 2H^+ \rightarrow Ca^{2+} + H_2O + CO_2$$

4) Here's the equation for the reaction of limescale with ethanoic acid (the acid in vinegar). You can use vinegar to descale a kettle, but it needs rinsing out well unless you like vinegar flavoured tea.

Calcium carbonate + ethanoic acid → calcium ethanoate + water + carbon dioxide

$$CaCO_3 + 2CH_3COOH \rightarrow Ca(CH_3COO)_2 + H_2O + CO_2$$

An Experiment to Compare the Hardness of Water Samples

Method:

1) Add 100 cm³ of water to a conical flask.
2) Add 1 cm³ soap solution to the water. Put a bung in and shake.
3) Repeat this until a good lasting lather is formed. (A lasting lather is one where the bubbles cover the surface for at least 30 seconds.)
4) Record how much soap was needed.

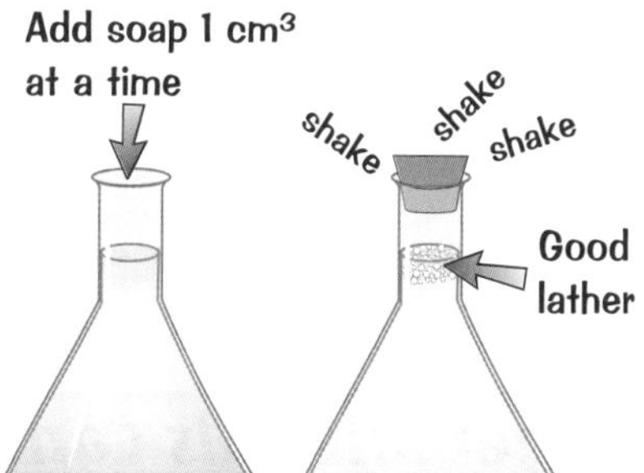

This method was carried out on 3 different samples of water — distilled water, local tap water and imported tap water.

Fresh samples of each type of water were then boiled, and the experiment was repeated.

Here's the table of results:

Sample	Volume of soap solution needed to give a good lather	
	using unboiled water in cm³	using boiled water in cm³
Distilled	1	1
Local water	7	1
Imported water	14	8

The results tell you the following things about the water:

1) Distilled water contains little or no hardness — only the minimum amount of soap was needed.
2) Imported water contains more hardness than local water — more soap was needed to produce a lather.
3) The local water contains only temporary hardness — all the hardness is removed by boiling. You can tell because the same amount of soap was needed for boiled local water as for distilled water.
4) The imported water contains both temporary and permanent hardness. 8 cm³ of soap is still needed to produce lather after boiling.
5) If your brain's really switched on, you'll see that the local water and the imported water contain the same amount of temporary hardness. In both cases, the amount of soap needed in the boiled sample is 6 cm³ less than in the unboiled sample.

Limescale — nothing to do with weighing fruit...

To add further insult, they sell limescale removers in soft water areas as well. Y'know, where there isn't any limescale. Sigh. Anyhow, the usual message here. There is an exam coming up, and any of this hard water stuff could be on it. Read through experimental data carefully — don't drop the easy marks.

Fats and Oils

Lard, glorious lard! Hot butter and blubber...

Fats and Oils Come from Animals or Plants

1) Animal fats and oils include lard (pork fat), blubber (whale fat), ghee (butter oil) and cod liver oil.
2) Plant fats and oils include walnut oil, coconut oil, olive oil and soya oil.
3) Fats are solid and oils are liquid at room temperature. For example, lard is solid at room temperature, olive oil is liquid at room temperature.
4) Fats and oils are esters. Remember, an ester is what you get when you react an acid with an alcohol. Fats and oils are produced when an alcohol called glycerol reacts with some acids called fatty acids.
5) These natural fats and oils are important raw materials for the chemical industry — e.g. in paints, machine lubricants, detergents and cosmetics. They can be used as alternatives to chemicals made from crude oil.

Emulsions Can be Made from Oil and Water

1) Oils don't mix in water — they're immiscible.
2) However, you can mix an oil with water to make an emulsion. You have to shake the two liquids vigorously. This'll break up the oil into very small droplets which disperse through the water.

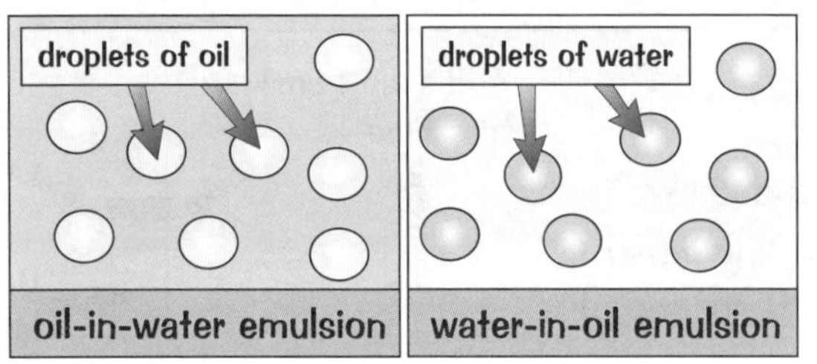

3) Milk is an oil-in-water emulsion (oil droplets suspended in water). There's less oil than water.
4) Butter is a water-in-oil emulsion (water droplets suspended in oil). There's more oil than water.

Vegetable Oils Can be Used to Produce Biodiesel

1) Vegetable oils such as rapeseed oil and soybean oil can be processed and turned into fuels.
2) Vegetable oil provides a lot of energy — that's why it's suitable for use as a fuel.
3) A particularly useful fuel made from vegetable oils is called biodiesel. Biodiesel has similar properties to ordinary diesel fuel — it burns in the same way, so you can use it as an alternative to diesel fuel.

Fats and Oils are Used to Make Soaps

1) Vegetable oils react with alkali to make soap.
2) Natural fats and oils are boiled up with sodium hydroxide. The hot sodium hydroxide splits up the fats and oils to produce a soap and glycerol.
3) This process is called saponification. Yes, yet another long chemistry word.
4) The chemical reaction first breaks up the fat or oil to release glycerol and fatty acids. This is called hydrolysis (it means "breaking apart with water"). Then the fatty acids react with the sodium hydroxide to make soap.

Learn the word equation: **fat + sodium hydroxide → soap + glycerol**

Oil not be pleased if you don't bother learning this...

Hundreds of years ago they used to make soap mainly from animal fat. Today vegetable fats and oils are used as well — e.g. palm oil and olive oil, as in Palmolive.

Using Plant Oils

Oils are usually quite runny at room temperature. That's fine for salad dressing, say, but not so good for spreading in your sandwiches. For that, you could hydrogenate the oil to make margarine...

Unsaturated Oils Contain C=C Double Bonds

1) Oils and fats contain long-chain molecules with lots of carbon atoms.
2) Oils and fats are either saturated or unsaturated.
3) Unsaturated oils contain double bonds between some of the carbon atoms in their carbon chains.

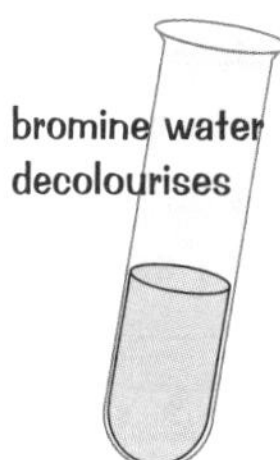

4) C=C double bonds can be detected by reacting with bromine. An unsaturated oil will decolourise bromine water (the bromine opens up the double bond and joins on).
5) Monounsaturated fats contain one C=C double bond somewhere in their carbon chains. Polyunsaturated fats contain more than one C=C double bond.

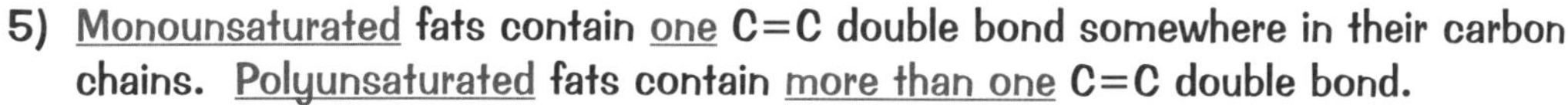

Unsaturated Oils Can be Hydrogenated

1) Unsaturated vegetable oils are liquid at room temperature.
2) They can be hardened by reacting them with hydrogen in the presence of a nickel catalyst at about 60 °C. This is called hydrogenation. The hydrogen reacts with the double-bonded carbons and opens out the double bonds.

Carbon chain(H)C=CH₂ + H_2 —(nickel catalyst)→ Carbon chain—CH₂—CH₃

$$\text{Carbon chain}(H)C{=}CH_2 + H_2 \xrightarrow{\text{nickel catalyst}} \text{Carbon chain}{-}CH_2{-}CH_3$$

3) Hydrogenated oils have higher melting points than unsaturated oils, so they're more solid at room temperature. This makes them useful as spreads and for baking cakes.
4) Margarine is usually made from partially hydrogenated vegetable oil — turning all the double bonds in vegetable oil to single bonds would make the margarine too hard and difficult to spread. Hydrogenating most of them gives margarine a nice, buttery, spreadable consistency.
5) Partially hydrogenated vegetable oils are often used instead of butter in processed foods, e.g. biscuits. These oils are a lot cheaper than butter and they keep longer. This makes biscuits cheaper and gives them a long shelf-life.

Vegetable Oils in Foods Can Affect Health

1) Vegetable fats and oils tend to be unsaturated, while animal fats and oils tend to be saturated.
2) In general, saturated fats are less healthy than unsaturated fats (as saturated fats increase the amount of cholesterol in the blood, which can block up the arteries and increase the risk of heart disease).
3) Natural unsaturated fats such as olive oil and sunflower oil reduce the amount of blood cholesterol.
4) Partially hydrogenated vegetable oil increases the amount of "bad" cholesterol in the blood, and decreases the amount of "good" cholesterol, which is particularly bad news. Eating foods made with partially hydrogenated vegetable oils can increase the risk of heart disease.

Cholesterol in the blood can be either high density lipoproteins (HDLs) or low density lipoproteins (LDLs). HDLs are called 'good cholesterol' and LDLs are 'bad cholesterol' — so ideally you want more HDLs than LDLs in your blood.

Double bonds — licensed to saturate...

This is tricky stuff. In a nutshell... there's saturated and unsaturated fat, which are generally bad and good for you (in that order) — easy enough. But... partially hydrogenated vegetable oil (which is unsaturated) is bad for you. Too much of the wrong types of fats can lead to heart disease. Got that...

Drugs

Drugs aren't just things you're told to say no to — they're anything which alters your body's chemistry.

Drugs Affect Chemical Reactions in the Body

1) Medicines contain drugs that are used to treat disease or injury.
2) Drugs are taken into the body and change some of the chemical reactions inside the body. These changes should reduce or stop the effects of the disease or injury.
3) Most medicines are sold in shops where there's a trained pharmacist. Pharmacists can advise a patient which drugs to take for common non-serious medical conditions. They know how different drugs can interfere with each other, and how much of the drug it's safe to take at once.

Analgesics are Painkillers

1) Analgesics are drugs used to reduce pain, e.g. aspirin, paracetamol and ibuprofen.
2) The chemicals used in making the analgesics (or any drug) must be very pure. Any impurity could produce chemicals which cause unwanted or dangerous side effects.

Here are the displayed formulas of aspirin, paracetamol and ibuprofen:

Aspirin

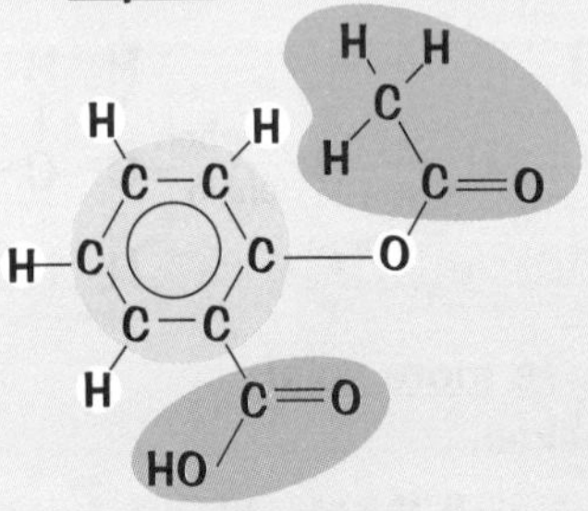

9 carbon atoms, 8 hydrogen atoms and 4 oxygen atoms, so the molecular formula's $C_9H_8O_4$.

Paracetamol

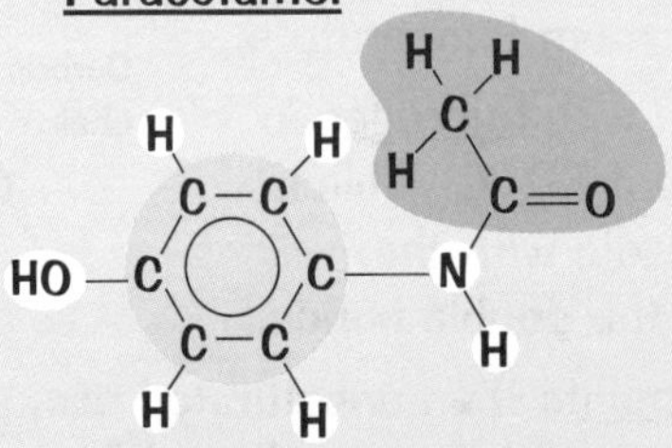

8 carbon atoms, 9 hydrogen atoms, 2 oxygen atoms and 1 nitrogen atom, so the molecular formula's $C_8H_9O_2N$.

Ibuprofen

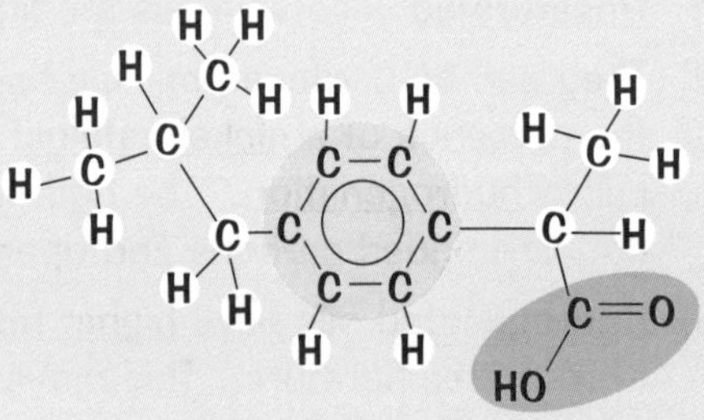

13 carbon atoms, 18 hydrogen atoms and 2 oxygen atoms, so the molecular formula's $C_{13}H_{18}O_2$.

1) There are similarities between them — they all have a benzene ring (highlighted in blue).
2) Aspirin and paracetamol have a $-COCH_3$ group (highlighted in green).
3) Aspirin and ibuprofen have a -COOH group (highlighted in pink).
4) Paracetamol's different from the other two because it contains a nitrogen atom and the OH group is attached directly to the benzene ring.

They can ask you for similarities and differences based on the displayed formulas — but you don't need to learn the formulas themselves.

Painkillers Have Their Dangers

1) An overdose of aspirin can lower blood pressure and raise heart rate, and it can cause breathing problems. Aspirin can irritate the stomach, causing nausea and vomiting and even internal bleeding.
2) Aspirin overdose can be fatal, but if it's caught in time there's a fairly good chance of recovery.
3) Paracetamol overdose causes horrendous liver damage. If it isn't treated quickly (and I mean really quickly) it's very, very dangerous. As little as 10-15 g (20-30 tablets) taken in one go can be fatal. And paracetamol's especially dangerous after alcohol, so it's not a good idea for hangovers.
4) A paracetamol overdose is particularly dangerous because the damage sometimes isn't apparent for 4-6 days after the drug's been taken. By that time, it's too late — there's nothing doctors can do to repair the damage. Dying from liver failure takes several days, and involves heavy-duty pain.
5) Paracetamol taken in normal doses won't damage the liver — only an overdose can do that (though accidental overdoses are pretty common).

What about something to relieve the pain of revision...

The danger of painkiller overdose is why painkillers are only sold in small amounts, even in places where there's a qualified pharmacist. They really don't want people taking overdoses.

Aspirin

Aspirin was originally made from trees. Honest, it was.

Aspirin is Made from Salicylic Acid

1) About 2500 years ago the Ancient Greeks used the leaves and bark of willow trees to ease pain.
2) About 250 years ago, the Royal Society (the highest ranking scientific society) discussed the pain relieving effects of chewing willow bark.
3) The search was on for the active ingredient. It was eventually isolated in 1828 and named salicylic acid.
4) Unfortunately, it caused mouth ulcers and reacted with the stomach lining.
5) In 1897, aspirin (acetylsalicylic acid) was first synthesised. It didn't irritate the stomach like plain salicylic acid.
6) Aspirin is manufactured from salicylic acid.

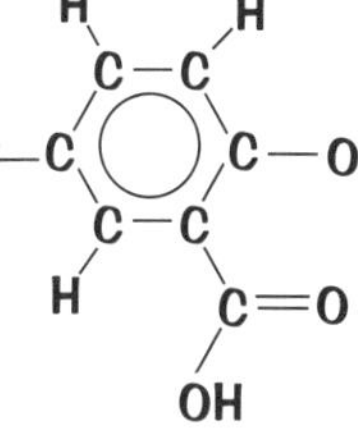

Method: Mix salicylic acid with a substance called ethanoic anhydride, and add a few drops of concentrated sulfuric acid. Heat the mixture to 50 °C for a few minutes. Acetylsalicylic acid is formed and precipitates out as a solid on cooling. You can filter it out, and crystallise it.

The industrial method is similar, but more hardcore. Salicylic acid is mixed with ethanoic anhydride and an organic solvent. The mixture is heated to 90 °C for 24 hours and then cooled for 3-4 days.

Soluble Aspirin Works Faster than Normal Aspirin

1) Aspirin works at the site of an injury by stopping prostaglandins being made. Prostaglandins are chemicals which cause swelling and are involved in the feeling of pain.
2) Aspirin molecules are not very soluble, so they get to the injury slowly.
3) Soluble aspirin allows quick absorption into the blood and speedier relief of symptoms.
4) Soluble aspirin is produced by reacting ordinary aspirin with sodium hydroxide or sodium carbonate.
5) Acetylsalicylic acid reacts with the alkali to produce a salt and water. This salt is the soluble form of aspirin and gets into the blood more quickly. Hurrah.

Aspirin + $NaOH$ ⟶ Soluble Aspirin + H_2O + Na^+

6) Ordinary aspirin is completely covalent — there are no ions available for water to latch on to and dissolve it. Soluble aspirin is a negatively charged ion which water can latch on to and dissolve.

Aspirin Has Some Non-Analgesic Effects

1) Aspirin can reduce the temperature of the body quickly — useful for reducing a fever.
2) Aspirin can thin the blood. This can help prevent strokes and heart attacks because the thinner the blood is, the less likely it is to form clots. Some people take aspirin every day to thin their blood.
3) People with stomach ulcers often find it aggravates their ulcers and causes stomach bleeding. Nasty.
4) Headaches, dizziness and ringing in the ears are potential side effects of aspirin.
5) Children and teenagers who take aspirin for viral illnesses (e.g. cold, flu, chickenpox) can get Reye's syndrome, which is a nasty illness affecting the liver and brain. Reye's syndrome can be fatal.
6) Aspirin's blood thinning ability can lead to increased bleeding in women during menstruation.

Soluble aspirin — better than chewing a twig...

The things they expect you to know at GCSE nowadays... how to make your own pain relief, for example. It's not easy. And probably not useful... even if you do make your own aspirin, you shouldn't take it — it could easily be contaminated. Or it could give you Reye's syndrome. Not cool.

Revision Summary for Module C6

Time to test yourself. If you can't answer these now, you won't be able to answer them in the exam. But this is the end of the book. So when you've done these you can just sit back and wait for your exam. Well, you could... but that would be silly. You need to keep your brain in the chemistry mood all the way through to the exam — don't let any of that hard-earned knowledge just dribble away.
Go back and try the questions on the earlier modules again. Just to check you've still got what it takes.

1) Fill in the gaps: A loss of electrons is __________. A gain in electrons is __________.
2) Give a symbol half-equation for the oxidation of Fe^{2+} to Fe^{3+}.
3) Iron reacts with dilute HCl. What's the reducing agent in this reaction? What's the oxidising agent?
4) What is a displacement reaction?
5) Iron is added to a solution of $ZnSO_4$. Nothing happens. Is iron more or less reactive than zinc?
6)* Magnesium powder is added to a test tube of tin chloride. The temperature rises by 8 °C. Magnesium powder is then added to a test tube of iron chloride. Describe the temperature change (assuming all the quantities are kept the same, etc.).
7) Give the word equation for the rusting of iron.
8) Explain how the following protect against rust: greasing, painting, galvanising.
9) Why isn't it always a good plan to buy dented cans of beans?
10) An oil drilling platform uses sacrificial protection. What's "sacrificial protection"?
11) Sketch an energy level diagram for the reaction between hydrogen and oxygen.
12) Give the definition of a fuel cell.
13) In an hydrogen-oxygen fuel cell, what happens to oxygen at the negative electrode?
14) Write down the overall reaction in an hydrogen-oxygen fuel cell.
15) Give two advantages of hydrogen fuel cells over conventional ways of generating electricity
16) Give an advantage of hydrogen fuel cells as a power source in a spacecraft.
17) Why is the car industry researching fuel cells?
18) What's the general formula for alcohols?
19) What's the optimum temperature for fermentation?
20) What is the best method of preparing ethanol from the point of view of efficiency, yield and quality?
21) Briefly describe two methods of salt mining.
22) What are the products of the industrial electrolysis of brine?
23) What are the products when a weak sodium chloride solution is electrolysed?
24) What is bleach made from?
25) Why were CFCs initially popular?
26) Give three possible health consequences of ozone depletion.
27) Most countries have banned CFCs. Explain why it's a problem that some countries haven't.
28) How are free radicals formed?
29) Write an equation for the reaction between ozone and chlorine atoms.
30) One CFC molecule can destroy thousands of ozone molecules. Why is this?
31) Is water hardness caused by calcium sulfate permanent or temporary?
32) Washing soda (sodium carbonate) can remove hardness. Explain how.
33) Give a balanced symbol equation for the action of ethanoic acid on limescale.
34) Are fats and oils: a) alkanes, b) alcohols, c) esters?
35) Write down a word equation for saponification.
36) How would you test margarine to see if it's saturated or unsaturated?
37) Which are healthier, saturated or unsaturated fats?
38) What is an analgesic?
39) Why is a paracetamol overdose particularly dangerous?
40) Describe the lab method for the preparation of aspirin.
41) What's the difference in structure between aspirin and soluble aspirin?
42) Give three side effects of aspirin, and explain why children shouldn't be given aspirin for the flu.

* Answers on page 108.

Thinking in Exams

The examiners reckon that it's not enough to just know stuff. They reckon if you can't apply what you know to real life then it's no use knowing it. Fair point, I suppose. So chances are, they'll throw something like this into the exam — just to check you're keeping all these facts in some kind of context.

Remember — You Might Have to Think During the Exam

1) Nowadays, the examiners want you to be able to apply your scientific knowledge to newspaper articles you're reading or to situations you've not met before. Eeek.
2) The trick is not to panic. They're not expecting you to show Einstein-like levels of scientific insight (not usually, anyway).
3) They're just expecting you to use the science you know in an unfamiliar setting — and usually they'll give you some extra info too that you should use in your answer.

So to give you an idea of what to expect come exam-time, use the new CGP Exam Simulator (below). Read the article, and have a go at the questions. It's guaranteed to be just as much fun as the real thing.

Underlining or making notes of the main bits as you read is a good idea.

1. Nanoparticles called fullerenes can be used in medicine.

2. The structure of fullerenes is important — can trap other molecules.

3. Fullerenes could behave differently from ordinary molecules.
→ tiny size
→ huge surface area

Professor Julie Wakeling, a leading nanotechnologist, warned that more research is needed into the behaviour of nanoparticles before their use in medicine and technology becomes commonplace.

The warning followed last week's news from a research centre in Australia. Researchers claimed that early trials targeting drugs specifically to cancerous human cells had been successful. The research involved using a particular fullerene, whose molecular structure allows it to 'trap' the toxic chemical, to carry the drug into the cancerous cells.

Professor Wakeling feels that there could be unforeseen dangers with fullerenes — they themselves could be toxic to living cells in a way we haven't tested for. She believes they may behave very differently from conventional chemicals due to their relatively small size and huge surface area, and that proper safe-handling guidelines need to be set down.

Questions:

1. How does the structure of fullerenes make them well suited to uses like administering drugs?
2. Why does Professor Wakeling feel that fullerenes should be tested differently from conventional chemicals?
3. Dr Gerald Newman, a nanoparticle researcher, has created a new nanoparticle. Describe how and suggest why he might want to tell other scientists.

Clues — don't read unless you need a bit of a hand...

1. How are fullerenes structured? What sort of shape would trap another molecule?
2. How are fullerenes different from ordinary particles?
3. This isn't a trick question — think about how you would expect to read or hear about scientific discoveries, and think about Professor Wakeling's views on safety, Dr Newman's personal interests, etc.

Answers

1) Fullerenes form round ball-shaped molecules that could trap other molecules inside the ball.
2) The fact that they're so small and have a relatively large surface area means that they could behave differently from conventional chemicals.
3) Any two sensible means of communication, e.g. conference, scientific paper, internet, journal, phone, meeting. Any sensible answer, e.g. to get recognition, so that the new nanoparticle can be tested for safety, so they could be tested for other useful properties, etc.

Thinking in an exam — it's not like the old days...

See, it's not as bad as you'd think. Just takes a little practice, that's all. Most of the information you need is in the passage — a little bit of background knowledge about fullerenes and you're there.

Answering Experiment Questions

Science is all (well... a lot) about doing experiments carefully, and interpreting results.
And so that's what they're going to test you on when you do your exam. Among other things.

Read the Question Carefully

Expect at least some questions to describe experiments — a bit like the one below.

Q1 Ellen has three different bottles of citric acid: A, B and C.
The citric acid in each bottle has a different concentration.

Ellen also has another quantity of citric acid, in the form of kitchen descaler.

Ellen wants to know if any of her three acids have the same concentration as the kitchen descaler. She plans to titrate each of the four citric acid solutions against a solution of sodium hydroxide of a known concentration, as shown.

She repeats the titration 3 times for each acid.

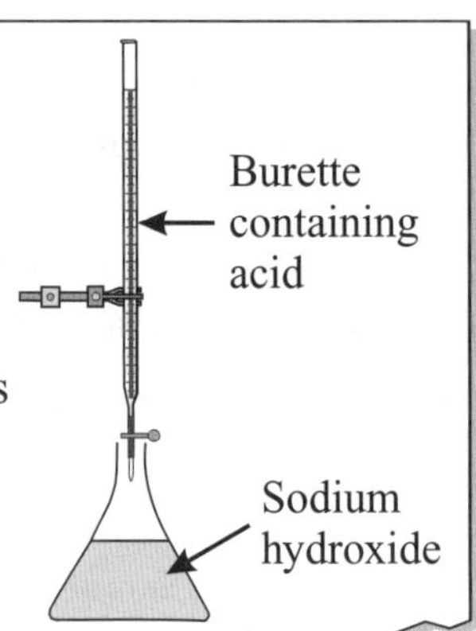

a) Give two variables that must be kept the same to make it a fair test.

1. The amount of NaOH.

2. The amount of indicator used.

b) The table below shows the amount of acid required in each titration.

	1st result (cm^3)	2nd result (cm^3)	3rd result (cm^3)	Mean (cm^3)
Kitchen descaler	24.1	23.9	23.7	23.9
Acid A	23.9	23.5	24.0	23.8
Acid B	33.3	33.7	38.6	33.5
Acid C	23.7	23.9	24.1	23.9

c) One of the results on the table is anomalous. Circle the result and suggest why it may have occurred.

It may be that the reading wasn't taken correctly or the wrong quantity of NaOH was used.

d) From these results, which acid can you say is not the same concentration as the kitchen descaler?

Acid B

To make it a fair test, you've got to keep all the other variables the same so you're only changing one thing. That way you know that there's only one thing that can be affecting the result.

If one result doesn't seem to fit in — it's wildly out compared to all the others — then it's called an anomalous result. You should usually ignore an anomalous result (or even better — investigate it and try to work out what happened).

You have to be careful here — both Acids A and C could be the same concentration, since all experiments have a 'margin of error' — meaning results are never absolutely spot on. So you can say that Acid B has a different concentration — but you can't say that about Acids A and C as they're so close that they could be the same.

Don't go testing things on your brother — that's not fair...

The point of this page is NOT to remember the details of this particular experiment — they could ask this kind of question about any random chemistry experiment. The point is you need to know how to make it a fair test and how to interpret your results when you've got them.

Index

Index

Index

Index and Answers

Answers

Revision Summary for Module C1 (page 19)

1) 14 H and 6 C

2)
```
   H H H
   | | |
H-C-C-C-H
   | | |
   H H H
```

4) $2Na + 2H_2O \rightarrow 2NaOH + H_2$

33) Your equation should have ethane and oxygen on one side, and water, carbon dioxide, carbon and carbon monoxide on the other. There are loads of ways to make it balanced. Here's one way:
$2C_2H_6 + 5O_2 \rightarrow 2CO + C + 6H_2O + CO_2$

Revision Summary for Module C2 (page 36)

40) When using the concentrated acid it will take less time to produce the same amount of gas than when using the dilute acid — the rate of reaction is faster. The slope of the graph (time vs volume of gas) will be steeper for the acid which produces the faster rate of reaction.

Revision Summary for Module C3 (page 51)

1) a) $CaCO_3 + 2HCl \rightarrow CaCl_2 + H_2O + CO_2$
b) $Ca + 2H_2O \rightarrow Ca(OH)_2 + H_2$
c) $H_2SO_4 + 2KOH \rightarrow K_2SO_4 + 2H_2O$
d) $Fe_2O_3 + 3H_2 \rightarrow 2Fe + 3H_2O$

21) a) bromine + lithium → lithium bromide
$Br_2 + 2Li \rightarrow 2LiBr$
b) chlorine + potassium → potassium chloride
$Cl_2 + 2K \rightarrow 2KCl$
c) iodine + sodium → sodium iodide
$I_2 + 2Na \rightarrow 2NaI$

Bottom of page 54

1) Cu : 64, K : 39, Kr : 84, Cl : 35.5
2) NaOH : 40, Fe_2O_3 : 160, C_6H_{14} : 86, $Mg(NO_3)_2$: 148

Revision Summary for Module C4 (page 67)

8) $HNO_3 + NH_3 \rightarrow NH_4NO_3$

9) a) 40
b) 108
c) $12 + (16 \times 2) = 44$
d) $24 + 12 + (16 \times 3) = 84$
e) $27 + 3 \times (16 + 1) = 78$
f) $65 + 16 = 81$
g) $(23 \times 2) + 12 + (16 \times 3) = 106$
h) $23 + 35.5 = 58.5$

10) a) 186.8 g
b) 80.3 g
c) 20.1 g

Bottom of page 69

1) a) CH_2
b) CH_2O
c) K_2SO_4
2) CH_4

Bottom of page 76

1) 0.125 mol/dm³

Revision Summary for Module C5 (page 86)

2) 2 moles

3) 142 g

5) 80.3 g

6) $MgSO_4$

10) 6 C

12) a) 1.8 g
b) 0.675 dm³

13) a) 7.5 g/dm³
b) 3.75 g/dm³

14) 0.1 moles

15) Take 50 cm³ of the 1 mol/dm³ sulfuric acid solution, and dilute it with 200 cm³ of water.

20) a) 0.167 mol/dm³
b) 10.5 g/dm³

23) a) 50 cm³ b) about 13 s

30) $Ag^+(aq) + Br^-(aq) \rightarrow AgBr(s)$

Revision Summary for Module C6 (page 102)

6) There will be a temperature change, but it'll be less than 8 °C (since the difference in reactivities is smaller).